The Semiotic Engineering of Human-Computer Interaction

Acting with Technology
Bonnie Nardi, Victor Kaptelinin, and Kirsten Foot, editors

Tracing Genres through Organizations: A Sociocultural Approach to Information Design
Clay Spinuzzi, 2003

Activity-Centered Design: An Ecological Approach to Designing Smart Tools and Usable Systems
Geri Gay and Helene Hembrooke, 2004

The Semiotic Engineering of Human-Computer Interaction
Clarisse Sieckenius de Souza, 2004

The Semiotic Engineering of Human-Computer Interaction

Clarisse Sieckenius de Souza

The MIT Press
Cambridge, Massachusetts
London, England

MIT Press books may be purchased at special quantity discounts for business or sales promotional use. For information, please email special_sales@mitpress.mit.edu or write to Special Sales Department, The MIT Press, 5 Cambridge Center, Cambridge, MA 02142.

This book was set in Sabon by SNP Best-set Typesetter Ltd., Hong Kong
Printed and bound in the United States of America.

Library of Congress Cataloging-in-Publication Data

De Souza, Clarisse Sieckenius.
The semiotic engineering of human-computer interaction / Clarisse Sieckenius de Souza.
p. cm. — (Acting with technology)
Includes bibliographical references and index.
ISBN 0-262-04220-7 (alk. paper)
1. Human-computer interaction. 2. Semiotics. I. Title. II. Series.

QA76.9.H85D465 2005
004′.01′9—dc22

2004055937

10 9 8 7 6 5 4 3 2 1

For Lucas, Karina, Magnus, and Biba

Contents

Series Foreword

The MIT Press Acting with Technology series is concerned with the study of meaningful human activity as it is mediated by tools and technologies. The goal of the series is to publish the best new books—both research monographs and textbooks—that contribute to an understanding of technology as a crucial facet of human activity enacted in rich social and physical contexts.

The focus of the series is on tool-mediated processes of working, playing, and learning in and across a wide variety of social settings. The series explores developments in post-cognitivist theory and practice from the fields of sociology, communication, education, and organizational studies, as well as from science and technology studies, human-computer interaction, and computer-supported collaborative work. It aims to encompass theoretical frameworks, including cultural-historical activity theory, actor network theory, distributed cognition, and those developed through ethnomethodological and grounded theory approaches.

This book deals with communication, signs, and sense making in human-computer interaction. Its main focus is on a basic aspect of design and use of information technologies, which is often underestimated or altogether ignored. De Souza takes the perspective that interactive technologies are *metacommunication artifacts*. Not only do they enable and support interaction, they also convey to users designers' visions of communication with and through artifacts.

Designers, de Souza claims, are in a very real sense present in the interaction between users and technologies. Their visions direct, constrain, and in other ways determine users' understanding of the system in general and user interface features in particular. Metacommunication messages sent by designers are gradually, and not necessarily accurately, discovered and interpreted by users. The book proposes an approach intended to help address specific problems of designing information technologies as metacommunication artifacts. The approach, semiotic engineering, draws upon a rich corpus of semiotic theories. By applying these theories to human-computer interaction, de Souza identifies a range of design concepts and strategies, which are illustrated with concrete examples.

The book integrates a wealth of novel, exciting, and useful ideas, which are both theoretically sound and practically useful. We believe it is valuable reading for anyone interested in technology studies or semiotics, as well as human-computer interaction.

Bonnie Nardi, Victor Kaptelinin, and Kirsten Foot

Illustrations

Tables

List of Abbreviations

AI	artificial intelligence
CMC	computer-mediated communication
CSCW	computer-supported collaborative work
DCM	direct concept manipulation
DOM	direct object manipulation
EUD	end-user development
EUP	end-user programming
GUI	graphical user interface
HCI	human-computer interaction
LAP	language-action perspective
NLP	natural language processing
RDCM	reflective direct concept manipulation
TSP	theory of sign production
UCD	user-centered design
WYSIWYG	what you see is what you get

Preface

Back in the late eighties when I finished my Ph.D. in linguistics, I began to teach graduate courses in natural language processing (NLP) in a computer science department. As a visiting professor without any formal training in computing, I used the tools I had learned from formal linguistics to build my own understanding of computers and computing. I was then struggling to learn enough about my students' backgrounds, so that I could share my vision of NLP with them before I started to talk about scientific and technical issues. Because my students and I came from very different academic traditions, we explored all possible connections in what we knew. There was a lot of intellectual excitement in finding analogies and contrasts, and this is how this book started. Of course I was not aware of what was really happening then, just as I may probably not be aware of what is really happening now.

After some years teaching NLP and other topics in artificial intelligence, I learned to cross-examine theories springing from different disciplines and started to find my way in computer science. I realized that I had been using a kind of intuitive semiotic analysis to interpret a field that was new to me and to teach concepts from a new field to students trained in computer science. So I decided to explore semiotics methodically. I thought that this way of teaching and learning could be used to build not only scholarly accounts of theories and relations among them, but also very naïve accounts of how complicated things work. And this led me into human-computer interaction (HCI), and into applying semiotics to try to tell users what computer programs mean and how they can be used.

This book is about sense making and how HCI can be designed not only to help users understand computers, but in fact to help them come closer to understanding *computing*. Computing is playing with signs. Every program or system is like a game. You can only play if you can make sense of the rules. And once you learn the rules, you immediately begin to see how rules can be changed and how the game can be adapted to many different play situations.

At the heart of every game is *communication* and how the players agree to represent and interpret their moves. This is the essence of semiotic engineering—a theory of HCI, where communication between designers and users at interaction time is the focus of investigation. Designers must somehow be *there* to tell users how to play with the signs they have invented, so that the game can start. The theory makes many connections among concepts borrowed from semiotics and computer science and produces a different account of HCI if compared to existing theories of cognitive breed. Hopefully it will help designers communicate their vision to users in much easier ways. And maybe then users will begin to understand *designs*, and not just struggle to learn which controls to activate.

I have many people to thank for having come this far. In particular, I am thankful to Terry Winograd for having invited me to be a visiting researcher at the Center for the Study of Language and Information (CSLI), where I learned the foundations of HCI and started to shape the thoughts presented in this book. I am also very thankful to Tom Carey, who patiently listened to the ongoing semiotic engineering story in its early years and showed me where I could go with it. Don Norman asked me many difficult questions on different occasions and helped me to see what makes theories differ from one another. Ben Shneiderman pushed me into thinking about why and how semiotic engineering is expected to affect the quality of HCI products and, ultimately, the user's experience. Ben has also been incredibly supportive in helping me find my way in book writing. Jenny Preece generously commented on many of my papers and on the complete manuscript. She often called my attention to where and how I should try to make my work more readable. More than a helpful colleague, Jenny has been a dear friend, encouraging me to keep on trying when promising roads occasionally turned out to be dead ends.

I have had the privilege of having wonderful students and colleagues at PUC-Rio, without whom I would have never been able to achieve this project. My doctoral students, in particular, have made capital contributions to the theory. I am deeply grateful to my colleagues and friends Raquel Prates and Simone Barbosa, whose intellectual and emotional support is encoded in many lines of this book.

I would not have come this far without my loving family. Altair, Ingrid, Ibá, Cid, Tania, Mônica, and Cristina have been my guardian angels throughout this project. Our teamwork for this project in Pittsburgh and Rio de Janeiro is an unforgettable "sign" of love, and I am lucky that I can just go on interpreting this sign forever, in truly "unlimited semiosis."

I would finally like to thank CNPq—the Brazilian Council for Scientific and Technological Development—for the financial support that I have received to do a large portion of this research. And also Kathy Caruso and the other editors and staff at The MIT Press, for helping me improve my nonnative writing and make this book much more readable.

C. S. S.
Rio de Janeiro
December 2003

I

Foundation

There is interaction if there is a call for it,
no interaction if there is no call for it.
—Zen master Yangshan

1

Introduction

"Semiotic" or "semiotics" are terms not frequently found in the HCI literature. Search results can be taken as a rough indication of the relative scarcity of semiotic approaches to HCI. In December 2003 a search for *semiotic* in the HCI Bibliography (see HCI Bibliography) returned 22 records, whereas a search for *ethnographic* returned 104, one for *ergonomic* returned 344, and finally one for *cognitive* returned 1,729. Although these numbers cannot be taken as a precise measure, the difference in scale speaks for itself. Semiotics is the study of signs, signification processes, and how signs and signification take part in communication. It is neither a new discipline, nor one whose object of investigation is foreign to HCI. In its modern guise, it has been established for approximately one century. But the debate about its central themes of investigation—meaning assignment, meaning codification, and the forms, ways, and effects of meaning in communication—dates back to the Greek classics.

Most of the relatively rare allusions to semiotic principles or theories in HCI concentrate on aspects of graphical user interfaces and visual languages. However, the World Wide Web and the multicultural issues of Internet applications have raised another wave of interest in semiotics. Since sign systems are produced and perpetuated by cultures, some contemporary semioticians define semiotics as a theory of culture (Eco 1976; Danesi and Perron 1999). Their views are naturally an attractive foundation for those interested in understanding the nature and enhancing the design of computer-mediated communication in various social contexts, such as computer-supported collaborative work, online communities, computer-supported learning, and distance education.

1.1 Semiotic Theories of HCI

To date only a few authors have taken a broader and more radically committed semiotic perspective on the whole field of HCI (see, e.g., Nadin 1988; Andersen, Holmqvist, and Jensen 1993; de Souza 1993; Andersen 1997). This is mainly because, in spite of its being a resourceful discipline for HCI researchers, teachers, and practitioners, semiotics covers a vast territory of concepts and uses a wide variety of analytic methods that are neither familiar nor necessarily useful to them. Semiotic engineering is one of the few attempts to bring together semiotics and HCI in a concise and consistent way, so as to support new knowledge organization and discovery, the establishment of useful research methods for analysis and synthesis, and also the derivation of theoretically sound tools for professional training and practice.

First presented as a semiotic approach to user interface design (de Souza 1993), semiotic engineering has evolved into a theory of HCI. As its name implies, it draws on semiotics and on engineering to build a comprehensive theoretical account of HCI. Semiotics is important because HCI involves signification and meaning-related processes that take place in both computer systems and human minds. And engineering is important because the theory is expected to support the design and construction of artifacts. Moreover, semiotics and engineering become tightly coupled when we think that HCI artifacts are intellectual constructs, namely, the result of choices and decisions guided by reasoning, sense making, and technical skills, rather than predictable natural laws. Like all other intellectual products, HCI artifacts are communicated as signs, in a particular kind of discourse that we must be able to interpret, learn, use, and adapt to various contexts of need and opportunity. Thus, the semiotic engineering of HCI artifacts is about the principles, the materials, the processes, the effects, and the possibilities for producing meaningful interactive computer system discourse.

The semiotic engineering account of HCI makes explicit references to the theory's object of investigation, the interests and values involved in establishing this object as such, the epistemological conditions and methodological commitments that affect the results of investigation, and the prospect of scientific knowledge advancement in relation to its perceived conditions of use and validity. It also aims to provide the basis for useful technical knowledge for HCI professions—that is, knowledge that can be translated into professional tools (abstract or concrete), knowledge that can improve the quality of professional products or services, knowledge that can be taught to young professionals and refined by practice, and knowledge that can be consistently compared to other practical knowledge, and be complemented, supplemented, or replaced by it.

The importance of dealing explicitly with epistemological issues in a theory of HCI, namely, with issues related to how knowledge is gained, analyzed, tested, and used or rejected lies in our need to discriminate the validity, the reach, and the applicability of HCI knowledge coming from such widely different areas as computer science, psychology, sociology, anthropology, linguistics, semiotics, design, and engineering, among others. We aim to help semiotic engineering adopters identify the need and the opportunity to use the knowledge this theory proposes, as well as the limitations and gaps that call for further investigation and other types of theories.

One of the prime advantages of a semiotic perspective on HCI is to center a researcher's attention on signs. Signs have a concrete objective stance that is produced and interpreted by individuals and groups in a variety of psychological, social, and cultural contexts. They are encoded in natural or artificial signification systems of widely diverse kinds, and they are typically used to communicate attitudes, intents, and contents in a multiplicity of media. Most semiotic approaches to HCI view computer programs as (sources of) artificial signification systems, and computer-based devices as media. For example, in figure 1.1 we see various signs in SmartFTP© v.1.0.979's interface: English words and technical terms on the main menu bar; drawings and sketches of various objects on toolbars; pull-down menus, text boxes, grids, and other widgets. Each one means something, to users and designers. Other signs appear as a result of interaction, such as the ability to drag items from a SmartFTP window into another application's window or workspace, and vice versa. These signs also mean things, such as the user's convenience or a system's requirement. SmartFTP incorporates a complex signification system that users must understand in order to take full advantage of the system's features.

The attitudes, intents, and contents communicated through interactive systems in computer media are those of the various stakeholders involved in the development of HCI artifacts—clients, owners, users, developers, designers, technical support professionals. Two of them have a distinguished status in HCI: designers and users. Designers, because they must be able to embed in the artifact they are about to produce the whole range of messages that are expected by and useful to all stakeholders (including themselves). And users, because they are the ultimate judges of whether the artifact is good or not.

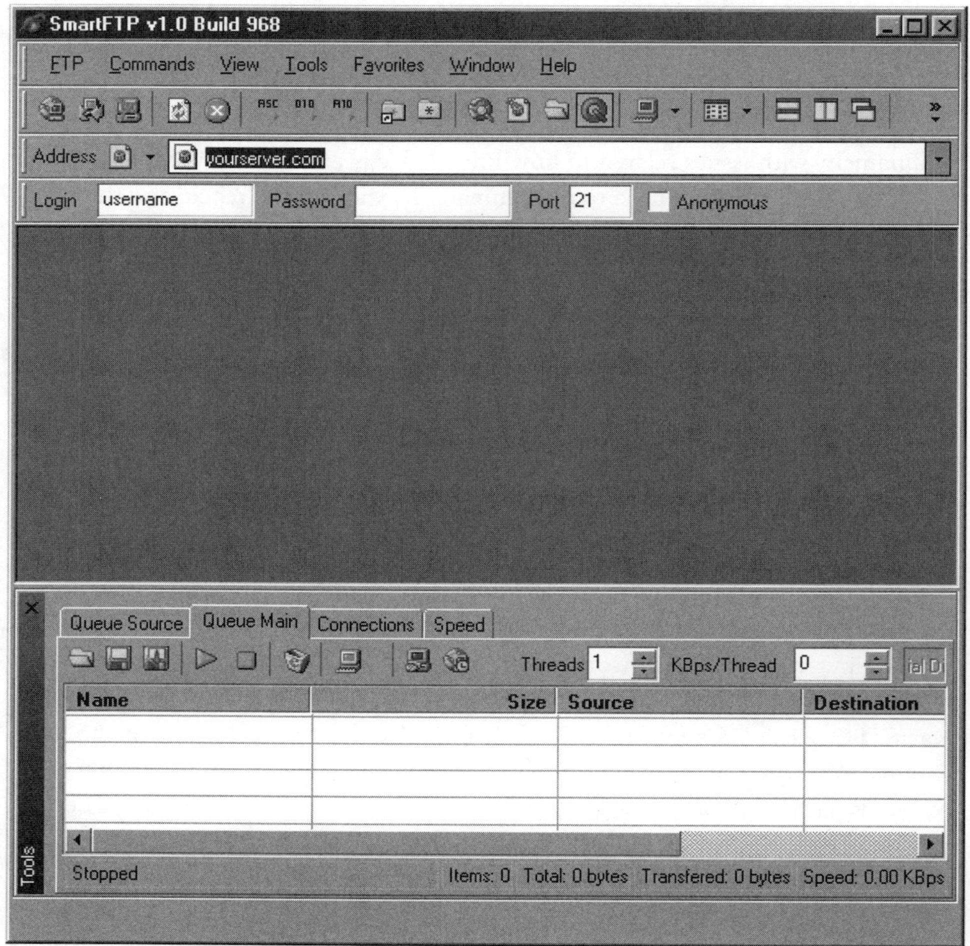

Figure 1.1
SmartFTP© v.1.0.979's interface. Screen shot reprinted by courtesy of SmartFTP© (http://www.smartftp.com).

1.2 The Semiotic Engineering Framework

Semiotic engineering starts from this general semiotic perspective and assigns to both designers and users the same role in HCI, namely, that of interlocutors in an overall communicative process. Designers must tell users what they mean by the artifact they have created, and users are expected to understand and respond to what they are being told. This kind of communication is achieved through the artifact's interface, by means of numerous messages encoded in words, graphics, behavior, online help, and explanations. Thus, by using this theory to study, analyze, and make decisions about users and their expected reactions, designers are simultaneously studying, analyzing, and making decisions about their own communicative behavior and strategies. Semiotic engineering is therefore an eminently reflective theory, which explicitly brings designers onto the stage of HCI processes and assigns them an ontological position as important as that of the users'.

This perspective is considerably different from and complementary to the user-centered perspective that has shaped our field in the last two decades following Norman and Draper's seminal publication (1986). In user-centered design (UCD), designers try to identify as precisely as possible what the users want and need. User studies and task analysis allow designers to form a design model that matches such wants and needs. The design model is projected by the system image, which users must understand and interact with to achieve their goals. Thus the system image is the ultimate key to success. If the design model is conveyed through the appropriate system image, which rests on familiar concepts and intuitive relations, users can easily grasp and remember how the system works. In semiotic engineering, however, although designers also start by trying to understand users and what they need or want to do, they are not just trying to build the system image. They are trying to communicate their design vision to users. Their design vision amounts to how users may or must interact with a particular computer system in order to achieve their goal through many communicative codes integrated in the system's interface. In figure 1.2 we see a schematic comparison of UCD and semiotic engineering. On the UCD side, the system image is the only trace of all the intellectual work that has taken place during design, and it is what the user is required to learn. On the semiotic engineering side, the designer herself is present at interaction time, telling the user about her design vision, to which the user will respond in various ways (including unexpected and creative ways). The ideal of UCD is that the user model captures the essence of the design model, projected in the system image. The ideal of

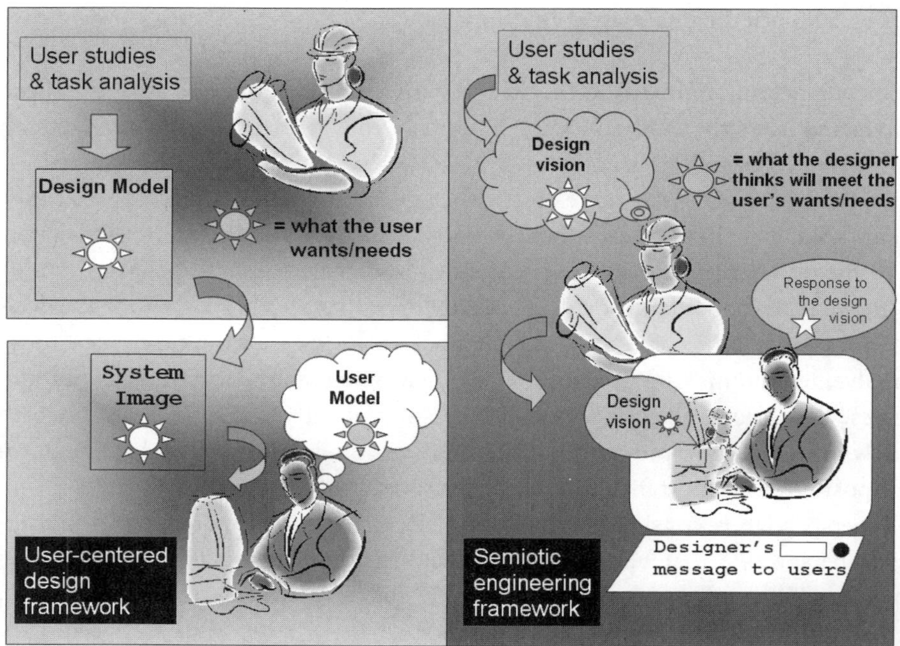

Figure 1.2
User-centered design compared to semiotic engineering.

semiotic engineering is that designer and user understand each other, and that users find the designer's vision useful and enjoyable.

The gist of user-centeredness is a radical commitment to understanding the users and asking them what they want and need. Their answers set the goals that professional HCI design practices must meet for interactive computer-based artifacts to be usable, useful, and widely adopted. Most of the technical knowledge required for successful UCD has resulted from empirical studies that attempted to associate certain features of interactive software to certain kinds of user behavior and reaction. Design features and patterns that have demonstrably met user-centeredness targets in a statistically significant quantity of situations have been compiled into legitimate technical knowledge in the form of principles, heuristic rules, and guidelines. The greatest difficulty with this kind of research practice in our field, however, has been the cost of sound predictive theories, especially in view of the speed of technological progress. The statistic validity of empirical studies requires that numerous experiments be run with hundreds, if not thousands, of subjects before any piece of knowledge is legitimately added to an existing theory.

But two familiar obstacles have been always in the way of such extensive studies—the pressure exercised by industrial stakeholders, who can't afford the time and money involved in extensive latitudinal and/or longitudinal user studies, and the pace of technological change, which often precipitates the obsolescence of systems and techniques employed in long-term research projects. As a result, sound predictive theories of HCI have typically concentrated on specific phenomena that cut across technologies (e.g., Fitt's Law [Fitt 1954]), but are of little use when it comes to making other types design decisions (e.g., choosing between adaptive or customizable interfaces). Moreover, we have witnessed a certain glorification of guidelines and heuristic rules. In some cases, practitioners have focused on conforming to guidelines and heuristic rules instead of using them appropriately as decision-support tools. Others have overemphasized the value of checklists and forgone much of their own intellectual ability to analyze and critique the artifact they are about to build. Those who exercise this power have often been misled into thinking that because guidelines don't take them all the way to a final and unique design solution, research work from which guidelines are derived is really of little use (Bellotti et al. 1995; Rogers, Bannon, and Button 1994).

Adding other types of theories to HCI, such as explanatory theories and intervention-oriented theories (Braa and Vidgen 1997), helps us gain sound knowledge that supports decision making in design, although not on the basis of empirical data. Conceptual schemas and interpretive models can enrich our analysis of problem situations and candidate solutions. They can also help us frame problems in different ways and find opportunities for exploring design paths that would possibly not emerge in causal reasoning processes that are typical of predictive theories.

1.3 Theorizing about Software as an Intellectual Artifact

In order to illustrate the need and opportunity for such other types of theories and research practices (i.e., nonpredictive), let us explore the intellectual nature of software artifacts. What is an intellectual artifact? What is not an intellectual artifact?

All artifacts are by definition nonnatural objects created by human beings. Some of them are concrete, like forks and knives—material artifacts that were made to facilitate certain eating practices in our culture. Others are more abstract, like safety measures—procedural artifacts that are meant to prevent accidents. Some are meant for physical purposes, like chairs. Others are meant for mental purposes, like logic truth tables. Thus, strictly speaking, all artifacts result from human ingenuity and intellectual exercise. But what we call an intellectual artifact is one that has the following features:

- it encodes a particular understanding or interpretation of a problem situation;
- it also encodes a particular set of solutions for the perceived problem situation;
- the encoding of both the problem situation and the corresponding solutions is fundamentally linguistic (i.e., based on a system of symbols—verbal, visual, aural, or other—that can be interpreted by consistent semantic rules); and
- the artifact's ultimate purpose can only be completely achieved by its users if they can formulate it within the linguistic system in which the artifact is encoded (i.e., users must be able to understand and use a particular *linguistic encoding system* in order to explore and effect the solutions enabled through the artifact).

According to this definition, knives and forks are not intellectual artifacts, nor are safety measures and chairs. But logic truth tables are intellectual artifacts, and so are books (if we think of their content), although books can also be viewed as physical artifacts (if we think of the physical media where ideas and information are stored). All intellectual artifacts require that producer and consumer use the same language. And language is not a metaphor in this case; it is a genuine system of symbols with a defined vocabulary, grammar, and set of semantic rules. Natural language descriptions have an additional set of pragmatic rules, which refine the way in which semantic rules are applied in communicative contexts. But artificial languages usually don't include such pragmatic rules in their description.

The advent of graphical user interfaces (GUIs) popularized the idea that software was some kind of tool. Almost every interface began to include tools, toolboxes, and toolbars, with explicit reference to concrete physical artifacts. Gibson's theorizing on affordances (Gibson 1979) inspired HCI researchers (Norman 1988), and the idea of direct manipulation (Shneiderman 1983) turned the tool metaphor into one of the pillars of HCI design. But soon the metaphor started to show some of its limitations. For example, the Gibsonian notion of affordance could not be directly applied to the HCI. Designers intuitively began to speak of "putting affordances" in the interfaces (Norman 1999); evaluation methods spoke of users "missing and declining affordances" (de Souza, Prates, and Carey 2000), a sign that affordances were themselves being used as a metaphor and not as a technical concept. The invariant feature of all metaphorical uses of the term was the presence

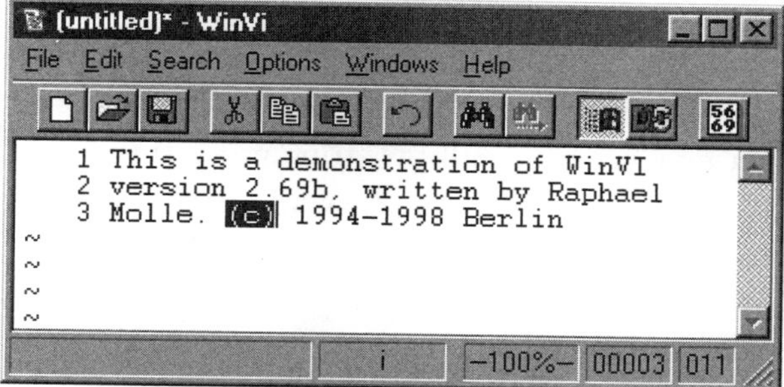

Figure 1.3
WinVi©, a graphical user interface for VI®. Screen shot reprinted by courtesy of Raphael Molle.

of an intended meaning, of what designers meant to do, or what they meant to say with specific interface elements. And discussions turned around the occasional mismatches between what was meant by designers and users when they referred to certain signs in the interface. Relevant issues having to do with how the designers' intent was encoded in the interface, how users decoded (interpreted) them, and how they used them to express their own intent during interaction could not fit into the category of typical concrete artifacts. They referred essentially to linguistic processes (though not necessarily involving only natural language signs). And the kinds of tools needed to support these processes are not material (like hammers, screwdrivers, paintbrushes, which all apply to concrete artifacts that we can manipulate), but rather immaterial (like illustrations, demonstrations, explanatory conversations, clarification dialogs, which all refer to intellectual artifacts that we can learn). They are epistemic tools, or tools that can leverage our use of intellectual artifacts.

Epistemic tools can benefit both designers and users, since they are both involved in communication with or about the same intellectual artifacts. It may be difficult to see why we need epistemic tools to use a basic text editor like WinVi©, shown in figure 1.3. The concrete tools in this GUI must all be familiar to computer-literate users, except perhaps for the last three that mean, respectively, ANSI character set, DOS® character set, and hexadecimal mode. So one might expect any computer-literate user to be able to write the text seen in figure 1.3, to edit it with the familiar cut, copy, and paste tools, and to open and save files, just as easily as he or she would use pencils, pens, paper, classifiers, and folders. However, unless the user is introduced to the idea behind WinVi, there is a chance that the power of this intellectual artifact will never be understood. Unless the user knows the Vi

Editor and its command language, the string operations that can be performed with WinVi, and the situations in which such operations are desirable and needed, he or she may end up complaining about the barrenness of this piece of software (e.g., compared to user-friendly ones that may not have half the string processing power of WinVi). Epistemic tools, like a useful online help system, with clever examples, explanations, and suggestions for how to use WinVi, should be provided with the artifact in order to enable users to take full advantage of this product.

Treemap© 3.2 (a visualization tool for hierarchical structures in which color and size may be used to highlight the attributes of leaf nodes) is another example of why epistemic tools are needed, just as theories that can help us build them. Visualizations allow for comparisons among substructures and facilitate the discovery of patterns. All interactions are based on direct manipulation of interface elements, either pertaining to the visualization itself or to specific controls applicable to it. In figure 1.4 we see data referring to the 2000 presidential elections in the United States. Lighter-colored rectangles correspond to states with population ranging from over 10 million to nearly 30 million people. The size of rectangles is proportionate to Gore's votes, whereas the brightness of the color is proportionate to Bush's votes. The pop-up rectangle provides details about the number of electoral votes and each of the candidates' votes in each state (or rectangle). In the "slice and dice" visualization mode shown in figure 1.4, the layout represents the states grouped in a fashion that mimics the geographical layout. The user may choose which label to see on the rectangles. On the upper right part of the screen is more information about Florida, the selected state on the left side. On the lower part, in the Filters tab, are various sliders that can help the user narrow in on specific ranges of values for the various attributes of the data.

As was the case with WinVi, Treemap may go underestimated and underutilized if users are not introduced to the power of this data visualization tool. Although the interactive patterns are not difficult to learn and support manipulations that can help the user find aspects of information that might be lost in tabular presentations, they are not obvious for average users. The intellectual value added to the tool by its designers is not clear from the signs in the interface. There is no reference to patterns of data, and no hint of when or why one kind of visualization is better than the other. But of course the designers included alternative visualizations because some are better than others in certain situations. However, unless the users are told about the relative advantages of each or get at least some sort of cue, they may miss the whole idea of the tool.

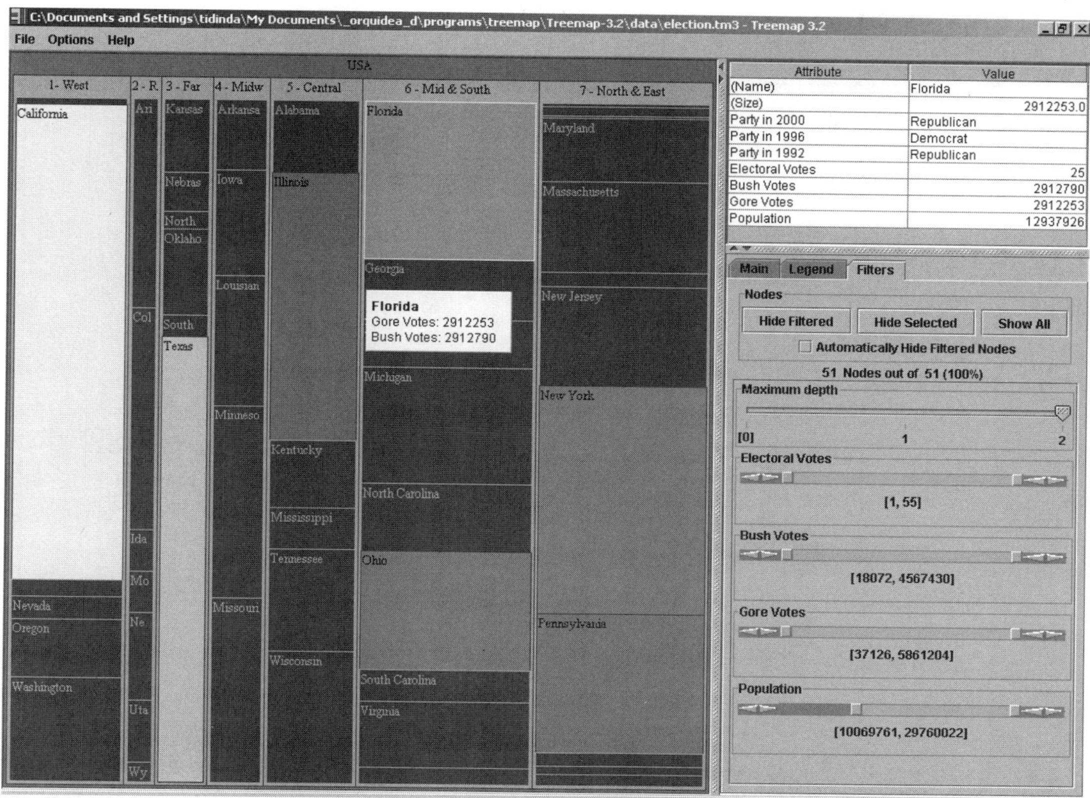

Figure 1.4
Direct manipulation and data visualization possibilities in Treemap© 3.2. Screen shot reprinted by courtesy of HCIL, University of Maryland, College Park (http://www.cs.umd.edu/hcil/Treemap/).

Intellectual tools deserve an appropriate presentation or introduction. Not only in operational terms (which is the most popular kind of online help users get from software manufacturers), but also (and perhaps more interestingly) about the problem-solving strategies that the designers had in mind when they produced the software. A detailed example of how users would benefit from a more careful introduction to knowledge associated with the product will help us draw some conclusions about the intellectual aspects of software production and use that nonpredictive theories such as semiotic engineering can bring to light and help explore. To this end I will employ a use scenario from Adobe® Acrobat® 5.0.5.

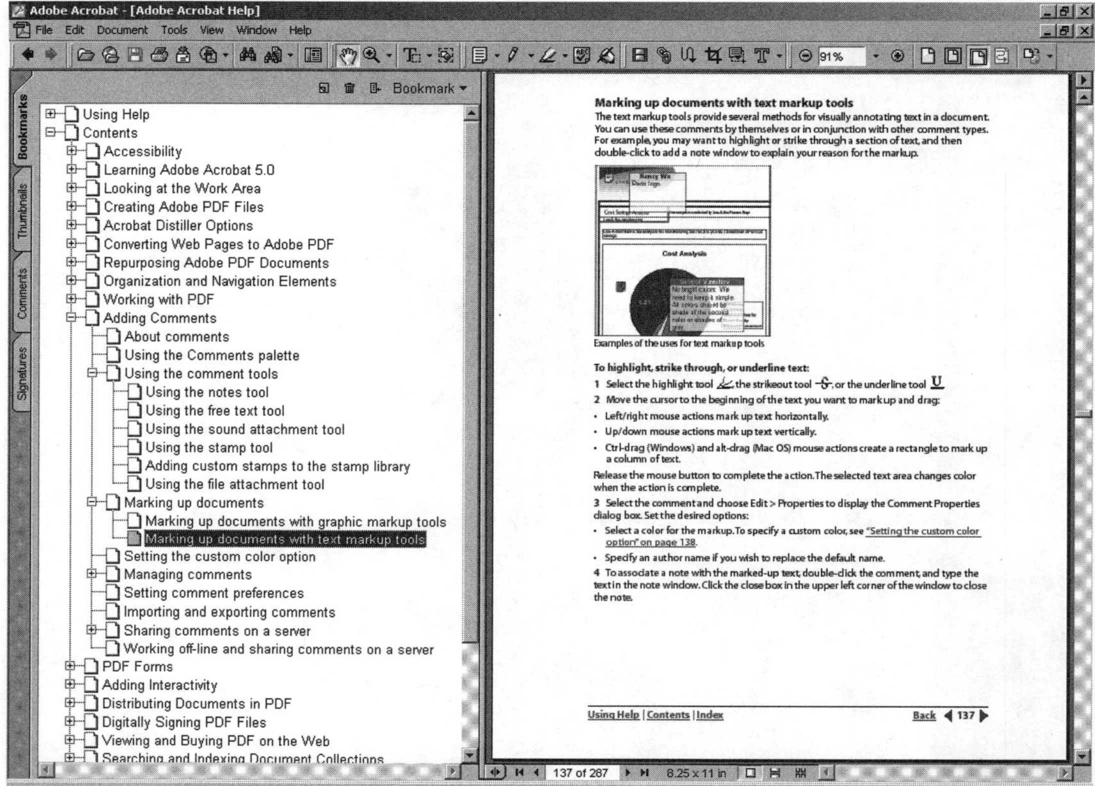

Figure 1.5
Acrobat® 5.0.5 standard interface. Adobe® product screen shot reprinted with permission from Adobe Systems Incorporated.

Acrobat offers to users a set of powerful tools for reviewing documents. Among the most useful are "commenting tools" and "markup tools." In figure 1.5 we see a screen shot of Acrobat showing its own help documentation as a PDF file that can be commented and marked up. On the top of the screen is the usual menu bar and tool bars. On the left-hand side are the bookmarks, which in this case contain a detailed summary of the document. And on the right-hand side is a document page linked to the highlighted entry of the summary ("marking up documents with text markup tools"). The "note tool" is an example of a commenting tool, and the "highlight tool" is an example of a markup tool. The analogy with concrete artifacts such as notes and highlight markers is emphasized by the visual signs appearing on the toolbars on top of the screen. Thus, users can write notes and highlight portions of text while they are reviewing documents.

Following the UCD cannons, the system image directly projects the idea that users can call a document's reader's attention to portions of the text and write comments about them. So, for instance, a reasonable reviewing strategy that most users are likely to adopt is to highlight parts of the text that need to be reviewed and then write a note with suggestions and justifications or questions. The steps to achieve this goal are as follows:

1. to select the highlight tool
2. to press down the mouse button at the beginning of the text portion to be highlighted
3. to drag the mouse to the end of the text portion to be highlighted
4. to release the mouse button
5. to select the note tool
6. to click on the document page close to the highlighted portion
7. to double-click on the note icon
8. to type in comments and suggestions
9. to close the note (optional)

The visual effect of these steps can be seen in figure 1.6. The first two lines of the top paragraph on the page are highlighted, and next to them is a note where the user comments that she never knew highlights were comments. This user has been using Acrobat for over a year now, and her reviewing strategy has always been what she calls the "highlight-and-add-note" strategy. But she learned a few things about this strategy. For example, the spatial contiguity of the note and the highlighted text is of course critical. Otherwise, sentences like "This is new to me" cannot be correctly interpreted. *This* must always refer to an object that is spatially contiguous to it. Another important lesson is about producing a summary of her comments, which she often does using the "summarize tool" (see figure 1.7). This tool generates a listing of comments made by the user. The comments can be filtered and sorted in various ways, but the default situation is to list comments and markups in sequential order of creation. Therefore, when this user generates a summary of her document, the content of a note she wrote following steps 6 to 8 comes right next to the text she has highlighted in steps 2 to 4. As a result, she can still interpret *this* in the listing as referring to the contents of the two highlighted sentences. The referent of *this* is shown in the previous entry of the summary.

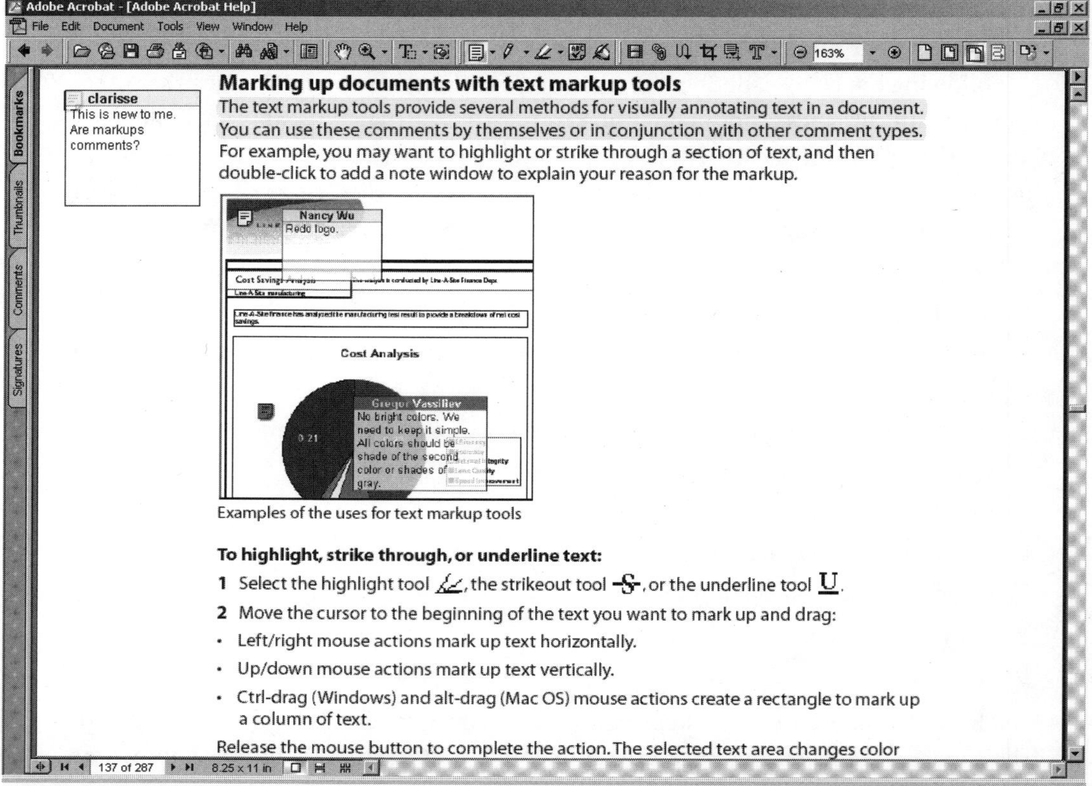

Figure 1.6
Notes and highlights in Acrobat® documents. Adobe® product screen shot reprinted with permission from Adobe Systems Incorporated.

At times, when checking all of her comments, she has tried to extend the highlighted portion of text to which comments refer. For instance, suppose that after doing a lot of reviewing on Acrobat's help document, the user highlights the other two lines of the first paragraph. Assuming that no other comments and markups have been made on this page, this becomes the third summary entry, and is listed after the note contents. As a result, although visually the note contents correctly refer to the four lines in the first paragraph on the page seen in figures 1.6 and 1.7, textually the reference is lost in the summary (see figure 1.8). The note comment is inserted between the first and the second two lines of the paragraph, and *this* seems to refer only to the part of the text, although it really refers to all of it.

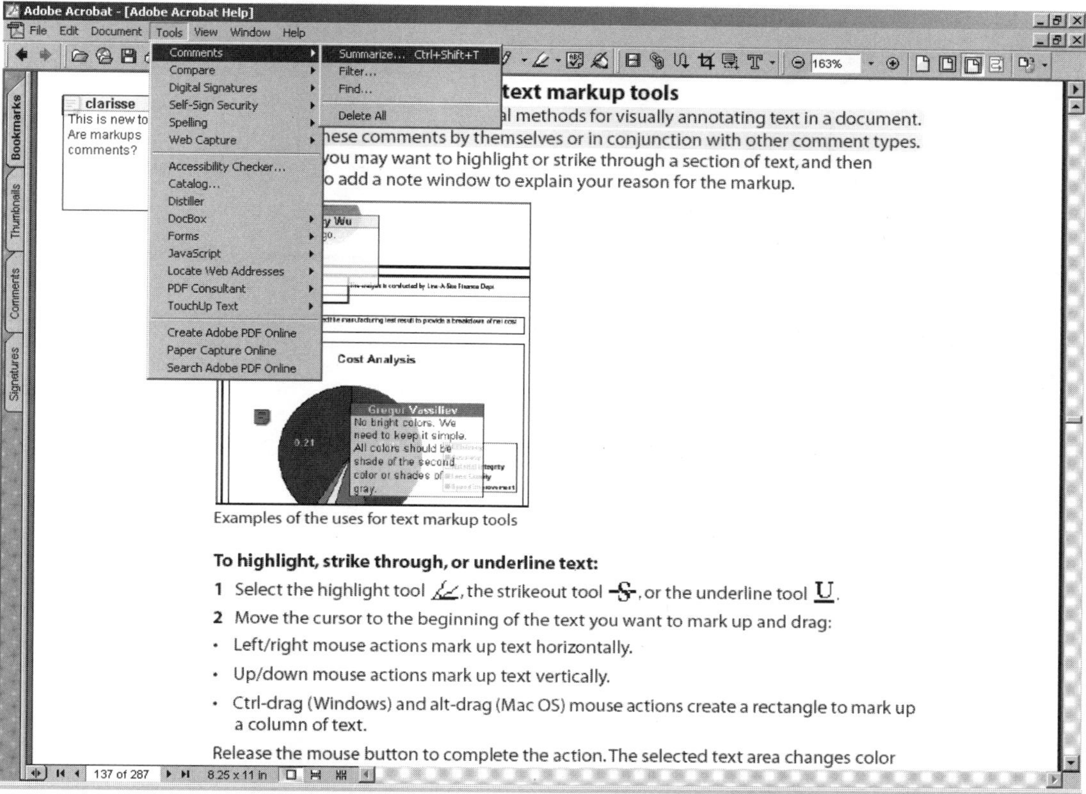

Figure 1.7
Menu choices for Comments in Acrobat®. Adobe® product screen shot reprinted with permission from Adobe Systems Incorporated.

The trick in Acrobat's interface is that, given how the system image is projected, the highlight-and-add-note strategy is the most obvious to users. And this may lead to problems in generating summaries. However, as the Acrobat's help documentation is saying, the highlight-and-add-note strategy is not exactly the design vision for efficient commenting and reviewing. As can be read in figure 1.5, designers do believe that users "may want to highlight or strike through a section of text, and . . . add a note . . . to explain [the] reason for the markup." However, the way to do this, in their view, is not to use the note tool but to "double-click [on the highlight or strike-through] to add a note window." But the system image does not suggest that this is a possibility, or that "highlights" and "notes" are both "comments"

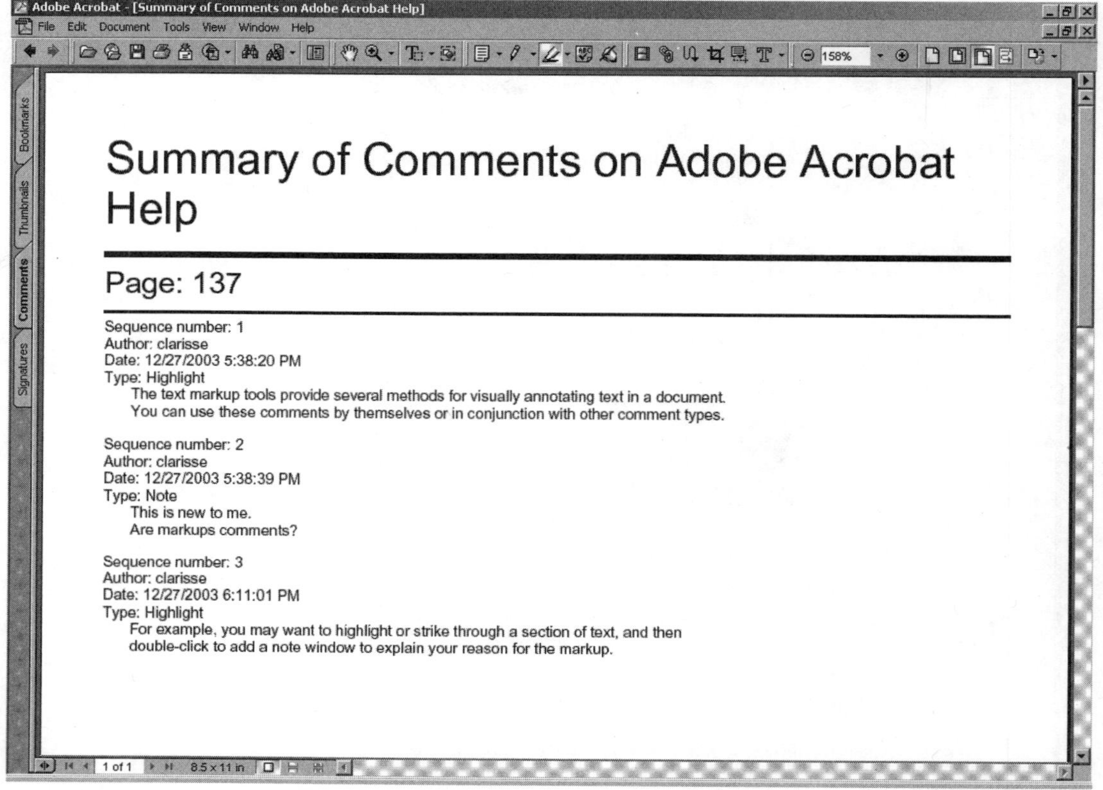

Figure 1.8
Textual discontinuity of visually continuous highlighted text in comment summary. Adobe® product screen shot reprinted with permission from Adobe Systems Incorporated.

(which is precisely what the user is surprised to learn in the documentation). In the physical world, these are different things.

If Acrobat's default configurations are changed, however, the system image gives the user a hint that maybe notes and highlights have indeed something in common. The user can change her preferences and choose to see the sequence number of every comment. The visual effect of this change can be seen in figure 1.9. Note that both notes and highlights have "comment sequence numbers" (this is how this configuration parameter is named in the preference dialog). So, they are both comments. And, since we can double-click on note icons to open small windows and type in

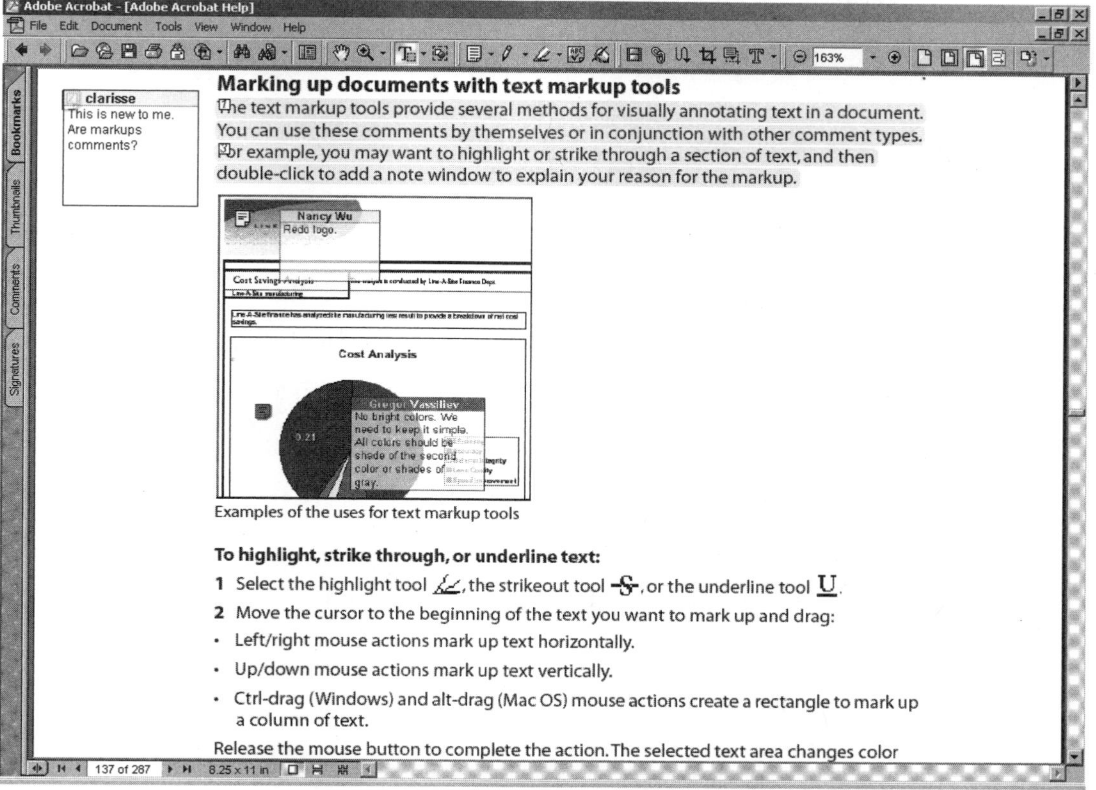

Figure 1.9
Visual similarities between comments and markups as a result of changing preferences. Adobe® product screen shot reprinted with permission from Adobe Systems Incorporated.

comments, we can also expect to double-click on highlighted texts in order to open the same kind of windows and type in comments.

The effect of this discovery on our user is much deeper than we may at first suspect. In fact, when she realizes that every highlight is a comment, just like a note, it dawns on her that she does not need to create a note to comment every highlight in the document. She can write her suggestion, justification, or question directly in the comment window associated with the highlight. And as she begins to do this, she realizes that the note window referred to in Acrobat's documentation indeed contains the whole extent of marked-up text. If she chooses the following interactive steps:

1. to select the highlight tool
2. to press down the mouse button at the beginning of the text portion to be highlighted
3. to drag the mouse to the end of the text portion to be highlighted
4. to release the mouse button
5. to double-click on the highlighted text
6. to type in comments and suggestions
7. to close the note (optional)

the summary of comments will look smaller and more readable like this:

```
"Sequence number: 1
Author: clarisse
Date: 12/27/2003 6:57:22 PM
Type: Highlight
The text markup tools provide several methods for visually annotating text in a document. You can use these comments by themselves or in conjunction with other comment types. For example, you may want to highlight or strike through a section of text, and then double-click to add a note window to explain your reason for the markup.
This is new to me. Are markups comments?"
```

---

and not like what is shown in figure 1.8. The design vision, according to what can be read in Acrobat's online documentation, aligns with the "comment-on-highlight" strategy, although the system image projects the highlight-and-add-note strategy with greater salience. Moreover, spatial contiguity problems disappear in the textual summary.

Without getting into a "bug or feature" discussion with respect to this example (i.e., assuming that similarities in visualizations of notes and highlights is a feature and not an unanticipated side effect of parameter-setting implementation), the truth is that operating with comment sequence numbers on and off communicates different meanings in Acrobat. And not all of these values have a logical connection with numbering comments. In particular, if the user knows that highlights (and other markup tools) automatically generate a comment, this can make reviewing more agile and consistent. If she doesn't, not only does this introduce unnecessary redundancies in the reviewing process, but this may also cause loss of information (as when the reader must interpret a word like *this*, referring to something other than what is spatially contiguous to it). Users are simply not likely to guess the best strategy from just looking at Acrobat's interface and focusing on the system image.

It is useful now to contrast two design objectives—producing and introducing an application that meets certain requirements. If Acrobat's designers had been given the goal to produce an application that allows users to operate in different ways and customize it to meet their needs, the problem with this interface would be that the system image does not portray equally well all of the product's features. In other words, the flexibility to tailor the application to different users' profiles is there, but it is poorly communicated. However, if designers had been given the goal to introduce such application, they wouldn't have even partially met their goal. Acrobat's more sophisticated uses are far from self-evident and do not speak for themselves. They may not go without an explicit introduction. In particular, tactical and strategic choices that users may or should make to increase their productivity and/or satisfaction cannot be derived from the strict meaning of the tools that they see in the application's interface. Tools tell them a number of things about Acrobat's operational features, but nothing about how this technology may bring about desirable changes in work strategies or tactics.

1.4 New Nonpredictive Theories for HCI

Nonpredictive theories of HCI, such as the semiotic theories that have guided the analyses of the examples above, can help us gain access to some relevant issues. The first is to add a new perspective on usability and focus on some factors influencing usability that are not totally obvious from design guidelines. For example, if we take Shneiderman's eight golden rules (Shneiderman 1998):

1. strive for consistency
2. enable frequent users to use shortcuts
3. offer informative feedback
4. design dialogs to yield closure
5. offer error prevention and simple error handling
6. permit easy reversal of actions
7. support internal locus of control
8. reduce short-term memory load

we see that they concur to helping users understand the application, of course, but they may not be sufficient to help designers communicate efficiently the intellectual value added in software tools. Acrobat's interface (with respect to our example) can be said to follow the eight golden rules, but yet it fails to *tell* the users about some relevant features of this technology regarding the various reviewing strategies that users can adopt. So, what do we mean by "telling users about the design vision"?

By shifting the design goal statement from producing to introducing technology, we can approach the answer. Introducing technology aims at making adopters understand valuable strategic aspects of it, and not only learning how to operate the system. Users must be told how technology can add value to their work and activities. Note that the eight golden rules refer to operational aspects: to what kinds of actions the user must perform, and the resources he needs in order to interact smoothly with the system. They do not refer to the strategic aspects of the technology, as for example to the relative advantages of choosing one interactive path over other possible ones. In the Acrobat example we see that users can easily achieve their reviewing goals using the highlight-and-add-note strategy (which can be said to comply with Shneiderman's golden rules). But they would very probably be much more efficient (and would prefer to be so) if they were aware of the comment-on-highlight strategy that can be adopted by changing preference parameters.

One could argue that changing the label of the "show comment sequence number" parameter to something like "show comment icons and numbers" might improve the interface and evoke the strategic value of this alternative mode of operation. But this line of solution is not good enough, for two reasons. One is that it is episodic and ad hoc, a kind of solution that depends on the designer's capacity to foresee when and why it should be extended to other portions of the interface. In other words, by keeping with the goal of producing usable interfaces, and using operational usability metrics to assess the quality of the interface, a designer is not prompted to think systematically about the strategic decisions of the users. The other reason is that only by replacing the overall HCI design goal with one of introducing technology, strategic aspects naturally come first. If one cannot see why one should learn a new technology, one can easily choose not to learn it at all. Or, as seems to be the case with Acrobat, if one doesn't see that certain operations open the avenue for alternative strategies that can be considerably more efficient than others, the value of the technology is not fully understood.

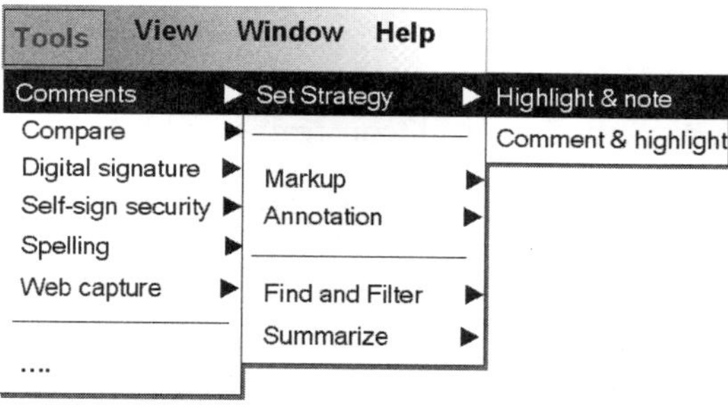

Figure 1.10
Communicating strategies to a user—a redesign of Acrobat®'s original menu structure.

So, by shifting focus in stating design goals, we are simultaneously shifting communication priorities in the interface. Strategies come first, then operations. This does not necessarily mean that we must have a two-stage communication structure in the interface, first telling users everything about the strategies and then, depending on their choice, telling them all about operations. Neither does it mean that interfaces must be verbose and loaded with text and explanations. Semiotics can be used to explore how we can convey both using one and the same sign structure. Just as an example of how strategies can be communicated along with operations, consider the proposed redesign of Acrobat's Tools menu structure, shown in figure 1.10.

Communicating strategies of use is an important factor in making users understand the design vision. The kind of communication suggested in figure 1.10 would benefit other system's interfaces such as Treemap's and WinVi's, illustrated earlier in this chapter.

1.5 The Contribution of Semiotic Engineering

What effects does a semiotic perspective bring about for HCI research and practice, and what is the value of semiotic theories in this discipline? To answer these questions we must analyze how semiotic engineering relates to the other theories—is it detrimental to others? is it prone to being complemented or supplemented by others? In the following subsections we will discuss

- the semiotic engineering homogeneous model for users' and designers' activities in HCI;
- its ontological, epistemological, and methodological constraints and commitments; and
- the consequences of having homogeneous models.

1.5.1 A Homogeneous Model for Users' and Designers' Activities in HCI

Semiotic engineering views HCI as a particular case of computer-mediated human interaction. This perspective is invariant across most semiotic approaches to HCI (e.g., Kammersgaard 1988; Nadin 1988; Andersen 1997), but the specificity of semiotic engineering is to characterize interactive computer applications as metacommunication artifacts (de Souza 1993; Leite 1998). Metacommunication artifacts communicate a message about communication itself. The message is elaborated and composed by designers and intended for the users. This is the first stance in which HCI designers and users are brought together under the same communicative process. In order to decode and interpret the designers' message, users proceed to communicate with the message, which gradually unfolds to them all the meanings encoded in it by the designers.[1] The message actually speaks for the designers in the sense that it contains all the meanings and supports all meaning manipulations that the designers have rationally chosen to incorporate in the application in order to have it do what it has been designed to do. In semiotic engineering terms, the message serves as the designer's deputy, presenting not only an artifact that can perform a certain range of functions and be used within a certain range of contexts, but also the rationale and design principles that have been followed while synthesizing this product. Rational decisions and choices relative to meaning and meaning manipulation are the best evidence that interactive computer applications are intellectual in nature. And as is the case of any other intellectual object its meaning can only be fully grasped and understood when conveyed in an appropriate semiotic discourse—one in which basic metalinguistic functions are available for mutual communication.

The four-stage evolutionary schema of metacommunication involving designers and users in HCI involves the following steps:

- The designer studies users, their activities, and their environment;
- The designer expresses, in the form of computer technology, his views about how the users, their activities and environment may or must change (because users so wish);

- Users unfold the designer's message through interacting with the system; and
- Users finally make full sense of the designer's message and respond to it accordingly.

The whole process thus starts with the designer studying the users, their activity, and their environment. He takes into account ergonomic, cognitive, social, and cultural factors that can affect usability and adoption of the technology being built. He consolidates all this knowledge into his interpretation of who the users are, what they need, what they like and prefer, and so on. The second stage in the process is an articulation of the knowledge gained in the first stage with the technical knowledge and creativity of the designer, who then produces an artifact that tells his mind in the form of an interactive message. The third stage corresponds to the user's unfolding of the designer's message, gradually making sense of the various meanings encoded in the artifact. The fourth and last stage in this particular type of computer-mediated human communication corresponds to the user's final elaboration of the meanings unfolded during interaction, a stage when the user finally makes full sense of the message. At this stage the user's response to the technology is mature and complete. The user knows the technology, no matter if he is fully satisfied with it or not. Semiotic engineering focuses on optimal communication, not on other crucial aspects of design such as aesthetics, productivity, and user satisfaction, to name but a few.

The metacommunication artifact is thus a designer-to-user message, whose meaning can be roughly paraphrased in the following textual schema:

> Here is my understanding of who you are, what I've learned you want or need to do, in which preferred ways, and why. This is the system that I have therefore designed for you, and this is the way you can or should use it in order to fulfill a range of purposes that fall within this vision.

Notice that this overall content of the designers' message to users holds true in single-user and multi-user applications, stationary and mobile applications, fixed and extensible applications, Web-based or non-Web-based applications, basically visual or basically textual applications, virtual reality, work and fun applications, and so on. It is a robust characterization of HCI across media, domains, and technology, which is a promising feature for a prospect foundational theory.

1.5.2 Ontological, Epistemological, and Methodological Constraints and Commitments

By underwriting a semiotic approach, the semiotic engineering of human–computer interaction is bound to live with certain ontological, epistemological and methodological constraints and commitments that may or may not exist in other alternative theories. We should start this discussion by committing to a definition of semiotics itself. Our choice is to adopt Eco's definition (Eco 1976, 1984), according to which semiotics is the discipline devoted to investigating signification and communication. Signification is the process through which certain systems of signs are established by virtue of social and cultural conventions adopted by the users, who are the interpreters and producers of such signs. Communication is the process through which, for a variety of purposes, sign producers (i.e., signification system users in this specific role) choose to express intended meanings by exploring the possibilities of existing signification systems or, occasionally, by resorting to non-systematized signs, which they invent or use in unpredicted ways.

Eco's definition of semiotics can easily justify why HCI is legitimately an object for semiotic investigation. It also supports the prevalent view in semiotic approaches to HCI, namely, that HCI is a particular case of computer-mediated human communication. All interactive computer-based artifacts are meant to express a design vision according to an engineered signification system. And it finally reveals the nuances of the semiotic engineering notion of metacommunication artifacts by helping us see that the signification system used by designers to communicate their vision to users must become instrumental for the users to express their particular intent and content back to the application (lest interaction becomes impossible).

But Eco, as many other leading semioticians, fully embraces the fundamental notion of unlimited semiosis, proposed by the American nineteenth-century philosopher and co-founder of contemporary semiotics, Charles Sanders Peirce. This notion rests on the idea that a sign is not just a relational structure—binding together a representation, an object that warrants it the status of being a representation, and a mental interpretation triggered by it. It is a recursive function which can be applied to itself any number of times, yielding interpretations that become the argument of the next function application. The recursive process of its application is called unlimited semiosis.

In spite of its apparently convoluted formulation, the meaning of unlimited semiosis is relatively easy to grasp. In practice, it amounts to a number of interesting formulations of intuitive facts involved in human communication. It says that the meaning of a representation cannot be defined as a fixed object or class of objects, although, for there being a representation at all, there must be an object or class of objects that requires a representation. For example, for the word *HCI* to be a representation (at all) there must be an object or class of objects that directly determine its codification into a signification system. In the absence of these, nothing can be a representation "of" anything. The existence of a mental stance directly determined by the presence of a representation, but only indirectly determined by the presence of an object or class of objects, opens the possibility of subjective (internal) ingredients to interplay with objective (external) ones, generating arbitrary interpretations for any given representation. So, there are three components to a sign: representation, object, and interpretation (often called *meaning*). For mutual understanding to be possible, there must be (a) regulatory mechanisms that can determine if and when shared meanings have been achieved, and (b) generative mechanisms that can produce other mental stances of meaning when the first triadic configuration of semiosis proves to be insufficient for achieving shared meanings. The principle of unlimited semiosis states that in communication, for instance, semiosis will continue for as long as communicating parties are actively engaged in mutual understanding. Because there is no way to predict the length of this process, and because in theory it can last for as long as one cares to carry it on, semiosis is unlimited (although it is finite on an individual scale, given the finitude of our existence). The same can occur in noncommunicational semiosis, when the human mind ponders reflectively over the meaning of things. This is the very nature of philosophical activity, and by definition it can extend to any length of time, even beyond the limits of an individual's life span, if we consider schools of thought to behave as a collective mind. Culture, ideology, archetypal myths are yet other instances of unlimited semiosis in action.

So, a semiotic theory of HCI, such as the one proposed by semiotic engineering, has to incorporate signification, communication, and unlimited semiosis in its ontology, no matter how uncomfortable the consequences of this move in epistemological and methodological terms.

At the ontological level, semiotic engineering splits meaning into two very diverse categories. Human meanings (that of designers and users) are produced and interpreted in accordance with the unlimited semiosis principle. Computer meanings (human meanings encoded in programs), however, cannot be so produced and interpreted. For a computer program, the meaning of a "symbol" (a kind of degraded sign, in this context) is no more than an object, or class of objects, encoded into another symbol system (or directly into a physical state of a physical device). Theoretical constraints on algorithmic computation cannot support the notion of unlimited semiosis (Nake and Grabowski 2001) and thus set the borderline between human and computer semiotics (see section 7.1 for an extensive discussion of this issue). Moreover, computer interpretation is itself a sign of human interpretations about meaning and meaning-related processes. The way programs assign meanings to symbols is a reflection, or representation, of how programmers believe meanings are logically assigned to symbols.

At the epistemological level, some important constraints must be spelled out. First, in a semiotic perspective, there is no room for a purely objective and stable account of meaning, whether the designers' or the users'. Meaning carries inherent subjective and evolutionary ingredients determined by unlimited semiosis that cast a shadow of doubt upon the idea that the users' context, requirements, and capacities can be fully captured by any human interpreter at any given time. Even when we let go of the idea of capturing all meanings, the choice of which are the relevant ones is equally prone to misjudgment and incompleteness. Consequently, in this sort of epistemological context, a researcher cannot possibly assume a positivist attitude, commonly adopted by many who aim to build predictive theories. From a semiotic perspective one cannot observe and interpret empirical phenomena without being affected by his or her own subjectivity, and the sociocultural context around him or her. Therefore, the value of observation and interpretation cannot be dissociated from the purposes the empirical study is designed to serve in the first place.

In order to preserve the theory from being declared anarchic and ultimately useless, for scientific purposes in general and for HCI design in particular, this epistemological challenge must be counterbalanced by sound methodological choices. They must enable researchers to identify the limits of subjectivity, the power of cultural determination, the conditions of social contracts in communicative phenomena, and, in the particular domain of HCI, the effects of computer technology upon human signification and communication processes. Sound choices will protect researchers and professional practitioners against adopting a naïve idealized view in which interactive computer-based artifacts can be built according to laws that are similar to the ones that allow civil engineers to build bridges. And they will also keep them from adopting a nihilist view in that, because users can never be fully understood and systems must always be built, any approximation of the actual use situation is as good as any other. One of the peculiar aspects of this theory is that it carries in itself a certain ethics of design, which other theories don't explicitly discuss or assume to exist.

In sum, semiotic engineering operates on a homogeneous continuum of analysis, where designers, users, and computer artifacts have a role in an overarching communicative process. The unit of analysis is a metacommunication artifact—an interactive computer-based system engineered to communicate to its users the rationale behind it and the interactive principles through which the artifact can itself be used to help users achieve a certain range of goals. However, the adoption of a semiotic ontology of HCI calls for strict epistemological and methodological vigilance. We believe that this situation pays off for two main reasons. One is that the range of phenomena encompassed by a semiotic perspective is considerably wider than that covered by the main theoretical alternatives backing up HCI today. It suffices to mention, as a justification, that none of them brings together designers, computer artifacts and users under the same observable unit of investigation. The other is that we cannot be sure, given the lack of explicit statements about epistemological and methodological commitments in research work produced by alternative theories, that similar challenges would not be faced by cognitive, ethnographic, psychosocial, ergonomic, or purely computational traditions in HCI research. Therefore, it may well be the case that a stricter vigilance of this sort may yield novel and important knowledge about the nature of HCI, with positive impacts for both research and professional practice.

1.5.3 The Consequences of Having Homogeneous Models

A homogeneous continuum of analysis in HCI brings about a certain number of consequences. First, as we have already mentioned, because users and designers are involved in the same communicative phenomenon, semiotic engineering becomes a reflective theory. In other words, if designers use semiotic engineering to build interactive applications, they must think about their own role and intent in HCI, and about how their role and intent affect and are affected by those of the users. The theory is well-suited for problem situations in which introducing interactive technology seems more important or more precisely the case than producing it.

Second, this homogeneity brings about different possibilities not only for interpreting design problems, but also for structuring the solution space and exploring the comparative value of alternative solutions. These possibilities stem from our knowledge about signification and communication phenomena, and their relationship with culture and computer technology. As a consequence, a number of constraints and concerns stand out in the design process. For example, when HCI design is cast as signification system engineering, we realize that this system must be used in three different situations. To begin, in order to communicate with users via the designer's deputy, designers themselves must use it. This is the context of the one-shot unidirectional communication voiced by the interactive discourse possibilities programmed into the application. It must also be used by the designer's deputy (or "system"), which will concretely interact with the user, systematically generating and interpreting signs according to the semiotic rules embedded in the program. And finally it must be learned and used by the users, who can only come to understand, apply, and enjoy a computer application if its signification system can effectively support communication.

Third, design intent is brought forth as a first-class citizen in this scenario. Because designers are actually communicating to users, the purpose of communication must be achieved. Two consequences follow from this. One is that designers must have a clear idea of what they want to do and why. The other is that they must be able to tell this to users in ways that are computable, easy to learn and remember, efficient and effective. Note that they are not talking about telling the users which button to press to activate this and that function, or what is the meaning of this and that visual form on the screen. They are telling them why the application makes sense to them, and why they expect that it will make sense to users, too. One of the leading reasons why designers expect that users will be pleased with the application, and make an effort to learn the specifics of it, is that they know who users are and have designed the application especially for them. If designers can't tell this—that is, if they don't know who the users are and have designed an application that has some inherent qualities that they expect will be intuitively perceived and naturally approved—they must still acknowledge that these qualities are there and help the users appropriate such qualities.

Fourth, a homogeneous communicative framework for HCI where designers, users, and computer artifacts are brought together can be used to inspect the nature and the quality of design processes and products. The latter can be further analyzed both per se and in situ—that is, outside and inside the contexts of use. Since communication is such a pervasive activity in this semiotic perspective, we have the tools to answer a number of questions. For instance, we can analyze the following:

- What signs are being used to compose the signification system that will carry the one-shot message to users, and also support ongoing communication between the user and the designer's deputy?

- How does the signification system encode design intent? Is this encoding likely to be understood by the users? Why?
- Once the users understand design intent, how can they put this intent into operation for their own benefit?
- What kinds of semiosic processes triggered by the signs that compose the engineered signification system does the designer anticipate? Which ones can the designer's deputy process? Which ones can it not?
- If the users' semiosic processes evolve in directions that have not been anticipated by the designer, which signs will express this communicative breakdown? What remedial resources can be used to reestablish productive communication? Can users extend the signification system? How?

Finally, by including designers in the unit of investigation of HCI-related phenomena, semiotic engineering opens the door to an examination of its own limitations. In the process of analyzing this specific kind of computer-mediated human communication, designers may realize that they need tools, knowledge, or other resources that this theory is not able to provide. And as soon as they realize it, they can look for other theories that will complement semiotic engineering (i.e., provide the additions that will lead to a *complete* fulfillment of needs), supplement it (i.e., provide additions that will lead to an *increased* fulfillment of needs), or simply replace it (because others can yield better results altogether).

1.6 Expected Contributions for Professional Practice

Novel theoretical approaches to HCI have been repeatedly called for to advance research and contribute to improve the quality of information technology artifacts (see, e.g., opinions expressed in Barnard et al. 2000; Hollan, Hutchins, and Kirsh 2000; Shneiderman et al. 2002; Sutcliffe 2000). As we have already mentioned, however, the latter has been the object of some debate, since studies have reported that practitioners disagree with the view that theoretical research can have positive and timely impacts on the quality of HCI product design (e.g., Gugerty [1993]).

Donald Schön (1983) reviewed and critiqued alternative views on the relationship between scientific and practical knowledge, and proposed that there are two paradigmatic positions in this field. One is the technical rationality perspective, according to which practical knowledge is applied science. In this view, technical professionals should be trained in basic sciences that provide them with generally applicable problem-solving methods, and then develop the necessary skills to select and apply the best-fit method to the problems they are likely to encounter (Simon 1981). The other is a reflection-in-action perspective, according to which practical knowledge involves the capacity to name the elements present in problematic situations and frame them as problems. These problems are often unique and usually unstable, unlike the general kinds of problems assumed to exist in the other paradigm. In the reflection-in-action view, technical professionals must be equipped with epistemological tools that can help them raise useful hypotheses, experiment with different candidate solutions and evaluate results. As a consequence, Schön suggests that the education of professional designers can benefit from more epistemic approaches to practice. Schön's message to HCI designers in particular (Schön and Bennett 1996), is that they should ask themselves what is the artifact they are about to design, and not only how they can make the artifact usable. The answer to the first question, as in the case of engineering models, for example, can be found by "interacting with [a] model, getting surprising results, trying to make sense of the results, and then inventing new strategies of action on the basis of the new interpretation" (181).

If we look at HCI research over the last decade or so, we see that a very large portion of the results it has produced falls in the category of predictive methods or explanatory models of users' behavior (Shneiderman et al. 2002). The products of research have typically taken the form of design guidelines and heuristic rules. Tacitly assuming that designers are faced with recurring problem types, many researchers struggle to articulate guidelines and rules into generalizable principles. Principles, in their turn, can be used to support the methods with which design problems can be skillfully resolved. Perhaps the most enduring instance of how theories can be used in this direction is Card, Moran, and Newell's model (1983) of the human information processor. For nearly two decades, this theory has influenced a considerable portion of HCI designers who view interaction as a cognitive problem whose solution can be found with the application of appropriate task and user modeling techniques derived from the original theory or some of its derivatives.

There are, however, some problems with the technical rationality perspective. Experimental validation of the methods derived from the various theoretical stances is difficult if not impossible to carry out. Keeping rigorous control over statistically relevant corpora of design situations in current HCI professional practice would not only involve enormous costs (having different design teams developing the same "real world" application by using different comparable methods; tracing every step of their progress; and performing statistically significant product evaluation tests in the end), but involve methodologically dubious procedures (deciding whether an implemented program strictly follows a design specification; deciding whether a particular design specification represents all dimensions of design intent and content).

Another kind of difficulty with technical rationality is that the purposes and requirements that justify and trigger the design of various interactive software artifacts are constantly changing. Many HCI practitioners believe that users don't know what they want. But this isn't necessarily the case. Users may know very well what they want and yet change their minds every time they are asked about requirements and purposes. As everybody else, the more they think about the problem, the more they understand about it. So, new insights are constantly arising from their reflection. This situation makes it again very difficult to practice HCI design as applied science, because the problem to apply it to is intrinsically unstable (and not amenable to the kinds of generalizations targeted by technical rationality).

In spite of these difficulties, and the resonance of Schön's ideas in a number of HCI research centers, researchers have not turned to epistemic theories of HCI, or to producing epistemic tools. An epistemic tool is one that is not used to yield directly the answer to the problem, but to increase the problem-solver's understanding of the problem itself and the implications it brings about. In the same spirit as Kirsh and Maglio's account of epistemic actions performed by Tetris® players (1995), epistemic design tools are those that will not necessarily address the problem solution, but the problem's space and nature, and the constraints on candidate solutions for it. Suchman's ideas (1987) and Winograd and Flores's account (1986) both called attention to the fact that intelligent human behavior uses freely exploratory interpretation of signs belonging to the context of activity in order to take goal-related action. And good computer tools should help people do this more and better.

Given the objectives that we set out to achieve with semiotic engineering, we can say that the main theoretic contribution we intend to make is to address the epistemic needs of both designers and users when communicating through or with computer-based technologies. With a semiotic perspective on HCI, we intend to open the road for eventually producing epistemic design tools that will help designers deal with 'knowledge' itself. The reflective nature of semiotic engineering is particularly suited for the task. It can be easily articulated with Schön's reflection-in-action perspective on design, and can strive to compensate the difficulties brought about by the technical rationality perspective by raising the designers' epistemological awareness on what they are doing and on how this affects what users are doing.

This book is organized in three parts. Part I offers an introductory overview of our goals and assumptions, followed by a concise presentation of some theoretical concepts used in semiotics that are necessary for understanding semiotic engineering. It ends with a detailed presentation of our theory of HCI. Part II shows how the theory can be applied to inform the evaluation and design of HCI products in three specific contexts. I start with communicability evaluation and the construction of online help systems. Then I explore customization and extension of applications in the context of end-user programming. And I conclude the second part of the book with a discussion of the semiotic engineering of multi-user applications. Part III contains a single chapter, in which I share with readers my questions, beliefs and expectations about the potential and the immediate opportunities for research in semiotic engineering. Because the theory is itself a sign that readers may add to their ongoing semiosis, there is no ultimate conclusion or prediction about what semiotic engineering means. This book is only my current discourse about what it means to me, hoping that it will be a useful and stimulating reading for those who like to think about HCI.

2

Fundamental Concepts in Semiotics

In this chapter I present a small set of semiotic concepts, all related to each other, which form the theoretical basis of semiotic engineering. The chapter is neither a summary of any existing semiotic theory, nor is it a comprehensive overview of semiotics as an entire field of study or discipline. It is rather a reading of certain semiotic theories, aimed at building the foundation for a semiotic theory of HCI. All the selected concepts play a fundamental role in semiotic engineering. Other unmentioned concepts have been or may be useful for advancing theoretical aspects of HCI, but the selected set is intentionally small and cohesive (ideally minimal), so that the targeted theory can be more easily understood.

Semiotics covers a vast territory of scholarly theorization and debate. It is generally concerned with "meaning-making and representation in many forms" (Chandler 2002) and with "everything that can be taken as a sign" (Eco 1976). Depending on the domain of meanings, on meaning-makers and meaning-takers, semiotics crosses disciplinary intersections such as those with psychology, anthropology, biology, logic, linguistics, philosophy, and many other applied areas of study and professional practice, like media studies and even software engineering. The themes of semiotic interest have been the object of investigation for as long as philosophy exists. A search for the meaning of meaning and the nature and purpose of representations is the legacy of Greek philosophers to all those engaged or interested in asking what they know, and why or how it is that they know what they know. Therefore semiotic engineering favors a philosophical perspective on investigating, teaching, designing, evaluating, and even practicing HCI.

I introduce and illustrate the following relevant topics:

- semiology and semiotics
- signs, semiosis, and abduction

- sign classifications, their origin, and their use
- pragmatics, speech acts, and culture
- sign production, communication, and discursive competence
- metaphors and metonymies

All definitions will be given in a format that suits the application of the corresponding concepts in HCI. Consequently, they do not reflect existing (and often heated) contention among theorists who have opposing views or see further distinctions in their account of sign-related phenomena. My goal is to be consistent and concise in presenting a semiotic interpretation of HCI, not to provide an exhaustive account of all possible interpretations.

It has already been said that semioticians obscure rather than illuminate a novice's understanding of the field (Chandler 2002). One of the characteristics in their writing that thoroughly contributed to this reputation is their esoteric use of terminology. In this introduction to semiotics, I have made a deliberate effort to clear at least some terminological obstacles. Whenever possible, more familiar words have been used to convey the essence of the theory.

2.1 Semiology and Semiotics

Modern semiotics is the result of the independent intellectual efforts of two remarkable thinkers, Ferdinand de Saussure (1857–1913) and Charles Sanders Peirce (1839–1914). Although they were contemporaries and both devoted to unveiling the mysteries of signification—one in Europe, the other in North America—they developed distinct and independent theories. De Saussure's semiology appeared in Switzerland, out of his interest in the study of language and linguistics (de Saussure 1972). Peirce's semiotic, known today as semiotics, appeared in the United States, out of his interest in the study of logic and the philosophy of science. Much of the variety in semiotics today is due to the individual power of de Saussure's and Peirce's thinking and the breadth of their theories along such different lines.

De Saussure's theory of signs emerged from his perspective on language as a system of arbitrary signifying units. His main concern was to account for the general mechanisms by which such units—or *signs*—were organized into abstract constructs that individuals put to use in a variety of social contexts. He called the abstract system *langue*, and its realization in specific instances of sign usage, *parole*. This distinction opened the way to the structural study of language as an autonomous object of investigation, regardless of the particular physical or psychosocial constraints to which individual behavior is exposed (like mental capacity, speech production limitations, or cultural regulations). *Langue* was viewed as the result of consistent distinctions and principled distribution of system units whose value (atomic or combinatorial) was determined by the values of all other units in the system. As a consequence, the study of language as *langue* required, from a Saussurean perspective, the concurrent examination of all units (simple and compound) in the system. This holistic "synchronic" view of language provided the appropriate background for the study of linguistic varieties (individual, social, geographic, historical, rhetorical, etc.) and served as inspiration for *structuralism*—a particular perspective on scientific analysis made famous by the anthropological studies of Claude Lévi-Strauss and the psychoanalytic theories of Jacques Lacan, for example.

Another capital feature of the Saussurean *signs* is that they were postulated as *arbitrary*—that is, not causally determined by that which they signify. This postulation underlines the nature of representation in its widest sense. To "re-present" something is not to "replicate" or "re-produce" it, keeping all the determinations applicable in its contexts of occurrence in physical or mental reality. Rather, to "re-present" something is to bring it up again in another dimension (the representational one), where causation and truth yield to the possibilities of signification. One of the extreme consequences of the arbitrariness of signs with respect to what they signify is the possibility of using language to tell lies. Lies are only possible because representations are not linguistic reinstantiations of the world. This apparently obvious point about the noncausal nature of signs reemphasized the independence between meaning and truth, a recurrent philosophical issue throughout the centuries that is often overlooked both in theory and practice.

One of the various connections that can be established between the basics of semiology and HCI is that, although de Saussure's focal system of signification was natural language, he explicitly stated that his theoretical framework could be applied to the analysis of any other system. Thus, computer applications' interfaces can be viewed as an object of semiological investigation. However, some of the structuralist concepts presented previously are substantially modified in a computer environment. For example, the distinction between *langue* and *parole* virtually doesn't exist from the perspective of a computer program. Unlike humans, a computer program does not produce nongrammatical sentences or mispronounced words because it is under psychological pressure or physical stress. Computer language generation is not *parole*, but an algorithmic instantiation of the rules of *langue*. Attempts to incorporate individual variations of *parole* into the computer's *langue* results in major complexities for design, in particular because *parole* is not just a peculiar individual way to use a socially established system of signs. It is the very seat of psychosocial and cultural determinations of sign systems, whose *algebraic* abstraction, so to speak, is the *langue*. Therefore, as soon as psychosocial and cultural determinations are merged with algebraic specifications of computer languages, the theoretical distinction is lost, and with it the ability to account for (and simulate) our *fault tolerance*, and awareness of it, in using language and other natural sign systems.

Another illuminating connection between HCI and de Saussure's semiology is related to the *arbitrariness* of signs. As has been mentioned, natural language and other human sign systems allow you to represent things that are not true, such as (intentional or unintentional) lies and wishes. It is thus related to your capacity to imagine and create things that you do not verify in reality. However, computer systems cannot produce signs *unless* they are the result of some algorithmic symbolic manipulation, and are thus causally related to base signs programmed into applications. Therefore, not only are interactive systems unable to wonder, imagine, or lie in any legitimate sense of these words, but also they cannot appropriately handle a user's imaginative or humorous behavior. This is an important realization for the design of intelligent and adaptive user interfaces. Intelligent computer programs cannot be expected to handle the full range of human signification processes, and users should be aware of where limitations lie.

The Peircean perspective on signs was not motivated by natural language, but by Peirce's interest in logic and epistemology. Peirce's philosophical perspective was much broader than de Saussure's, so much so that among the themes of his writings are the nature of mind and knowledge, the appropriate methods for scientific inquiry, the basic phenomenological categories that mind can perceive, and even the influence of love or sympathy on the evolution of the universe (see The Peirce Edition Project). Semiotics was then geared toward epistemological, rather than linguistic, concerns. Peirce was convinced that all advanced forms of thought (especially scientific thought) were fundamentally based on conventions and rule-based representations. So, to him, an epistemology of science was ultimately an account of such conventions and rules, an account of the underlying signification systems in which and through which knowledge was built.

His definition of a sign—*anything that stands for something else, to somebody, in some respect or capacity* (Peirce, 1931–1958)—underlined the fundamental role of interpretation (what somebody takes something to *mean*) in semiotics. Nothing is a sign *unless* (or *until*) it is interpreted by somebody. It follows from this definition that the same signs may have very different valid meanings, that mutual intelligibility widely depends on cultural conventions and mechanisms to negotiate shared meanings, and that ultimately there is no such thing as *the meaning* of a sign (not even in the equivalent of de Saussure's *langue*). The consequences of this theory, not only for logic and linguistics, but also for all disciplines where meaning is central, cannot be underestimated. For example, in a semiotic perspective meaning cannot be framed as a fixed and permanent entity—it is a process. Consequently, all theories built on the existence of unchanging meaningful objects suddenly become incompatible with this perspective and are automatically challenged by it. However, the concept of a continuing semiotic interpretation of signs does not stand unless it can be made compatible with our finite minds and finite resources. Therefore, an account of how and why the ongoing interpretive process is halted and (temporarily) instantiated as *the meaning* of a sign was a crucial requirement for the scientific plausibility of Peirce's theory.

Peirce's response to this challenge came as a method for hypothetical reasoning, also known as abductive reasoning, or simply abduction. The gist of this method (which will be presented in further detail in this chapter) was the idea that mind assigns meaning to things by building plausible hypotheses about the sign that is taken to represent them. As long as these hypotheses are confirmed by positive evidence, they concur to build the meaning of the sign being interpreted. If and when negative evidence is found, hypotheses (and meanings) are modified or replaced by more plausible ones. For instance, when going back home at the end of the day, if you see that the lights of your house are on you take this to *mean* (i.e., you assume, or hypothesize) that there is somebody home. But if you open the door and see nobody, then you may assume (or take the lights on to *mean*) that somebody has forgotten to turn the lights off before leaving. In the absence of counterevidence, you stabilize your interpretive process at this point. It may be resumed, however, if a few hours later everybody else in the family is absolutely sure that they turned the lights off before they left, or if you realize that some of your valuables are missing (in which case the lights on would be a sign of burglary).

With more or less explicit acknowledgement from researchers, Peirce's theories have contributed to artificial intelligence and machine learning, especially with respect to frame-like knowledge representation techniques (Eco 1984; Eco, Santambrogio, and Violi 1988) and automatic reasoning methods (Josephson and

Josephson 1994). Their fundamental contribution to HCI was pointed out by Mihai Nadin as early as 1988 (Nadin 1988), but the only relatively popular (and often misunderstood) use of Peircean semiotics concepts in HCI is his classification of signs into icons, indices, and symbols. As will be seen in other parts of this chapter and other chapters of this book, semiotic engineering makes extensive use of Peircean concepts in its account of HCI design and evaluation. This is why I privilege the term *semiotics* over *semiology*.

Other semioticians have influenced our conception of semiotic engineering as a theory of HCI. First comes Umberto Eco—described by Chandler (2002) as a theorist who bridges both the structuralist and the Peircean traditions. His view of semiotics as "the logic of culture" (Eco 1976, 3), as its name suggests, brings together the human (culture) and the computational (logic) underpinnings of HCI and supports a new breed of theoretical formulations and methodological tools for researchers and practitioners. Additionally, Charles Morris's view (1938, 2) of semiotics as "an instrument for science" has helped me elaborate relevant epistemological aspects of semiotic engineering. Although Morris's perspective does not fully acknowledge its Peircean origins, his reading and presentation of Peirce's theory is clearer and more direct than its sources. Thus, Morris has provided insightful interpretations of how semiotics can be used as a metalanguage for scientific descriptions.

2.2 Signs, Semiosis, and Abduction

Signs, semiosis, and abduction are the three most basic semiotic concepts used in semiotic engineering. Signs, as we know, have been defined by Peirce as *anything that stands for something else, to somebody, in some respect or capacity* (Peirce, 1931–1958). However, unlike many of his predecessors throughout the history of philosophy, Peirce did not describe the structure of a sign as twofold. Unlike de Saussure, for example, who followed this tradition and proposed that signs were a relational structure binding a representation (a perceptible *form*) to what it represents (a conceivable *content*), Peirce proposed that signs had a threefold structure and, as seen previously, *functioned* as a process. The three constituents of the Peircean sign were the representation (called the *representamen*), its referent (called the *object*), and its meaning (called the *interpretant*). The triangular representation of this structure has become popular in semiotics. In figure 2.1 two important aspects of this structure are underlined. First, that there is no necessary direct con-

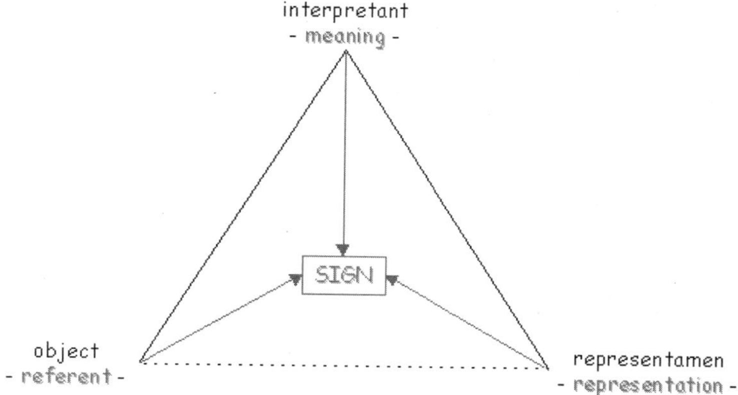

Figure 2.1
The structure of the Peircean sign.

nection between a representation and that which it refers to. This connection *may* be there (as is the case of a photograph on a driver's license), but it doesn't *have to*. Second, meaning is always a mediator between a representation and what it refers to. In other words, there is actually no representation unless there is a meaning binding it to what it refers to, which is another way of saying that there is no sign unless some interpreter takes a representation to *mean* something else. So a sign requires the concurrent presence of these three constituents. From a semiotic perspective one cannot talk about representations without talking about their referent and meaning. Nothing is a representation except by virtue of a sign that ties it to referent and meaning.

We intuitively know that representations have meaning and that it doesn't make much sense to talk about them independent of what they mean. But the news brought by Peirce was that representations and meanings are still not enough (where he diverges from de Saussure's opinion). The presence of three constituents directs our attention to much confusion about what representations really mean. A complete understanding of this nuance cannot be reached without an appropriate definition of the *interpretant* and its connection to semiosis.

The meaning of a representation, technically called the *interpretant*, or by extension the meaning of the sign, is defined by Peirce as *another sign*. Consequently, for every sign there is another sign that corresponds to its meaning. Interpretation being the process by which meanings are associated to signs, it follows from Peirce's definition that this process is theoretically infinite. Although the idea is intuitively contradictory with the finiteness of human minds, we can have a glance at its psychological plausibility in reflective mental processes. For instance, the more we think about some significant thing, the more meanings we associate to it (essential or accidental). Therefore, there are indefinitely many meanings (a psychologically more palatable version of infinity) to a sign, and it is impossible to predict the exact path and length of meaningful associations that will be made during interpretation. This interpretive process has been originally called semiosis, and later unlimited semiosis (Eco 1984).

In order to illustrate the practical implications of unlimited semiosis, let us assume that a customer goes into a small shop and sees the sign of a hammer (🔨) hanging from one of the shelves where goods are displayed. We may rightfully assume that the 🔨 representation refers to a hammer, but we shouldn't assume that the meaning of 🔨 is "a hammer." From a sign-maker's perspective (e.g., the owner of the shop), the meaning of this representation may well include such signs as "we sell hammers," "here is where hammers can be found," "have a look at our hammers," and so on. From a sign-taker's perspective (e.g., the customer who has just come into the shop), the 🔨 may mean not only such things as "they sell hammers" or "this is where their hammers are," but also things like "they sell nails" or "I need to buy a hammer." Notice that the latter two are associated with 🔨 as a result of inference and episodic memory associations, not of strictly semantic relations (a popular source of definitions for the meaning of representations in other theories).

The particular kind of inference involved in interpreting 🔨 as a sign that the small shop also sells nails is a case of abductive reasoning. Compared to deductive reasoning (see figure 2.2), abduction is practically a reversed reasoning path. Deduction cannot start *unless* there is a set of known rules and facts about the world. Not only are they known, but they are also true and unchanging. For instance, it is a known fact that all physical objects fall (a naïve version of the law of gravity). Because a hammer is a physical object, if we let one go from our hand it will surely fall. Abduction, however, does not require that rules and facts be known and true from the beginning. Rules and facts are hypothesized whenever they can contribute to explaining (or making sense of) some observation in the world. In the small shop example, the presence of 🔨 can be explained, or makes sense, if we can assume the existence of a rule that says that all shops displaying the sign of a hammer sell hammers. If this rule existed, given that this particular one displays such a sign then it makes sense to think that 🔨 means that the shop does sell hammers. Notice that the hypothesized rule is not comparable to the law of gravity. It is only a plausible

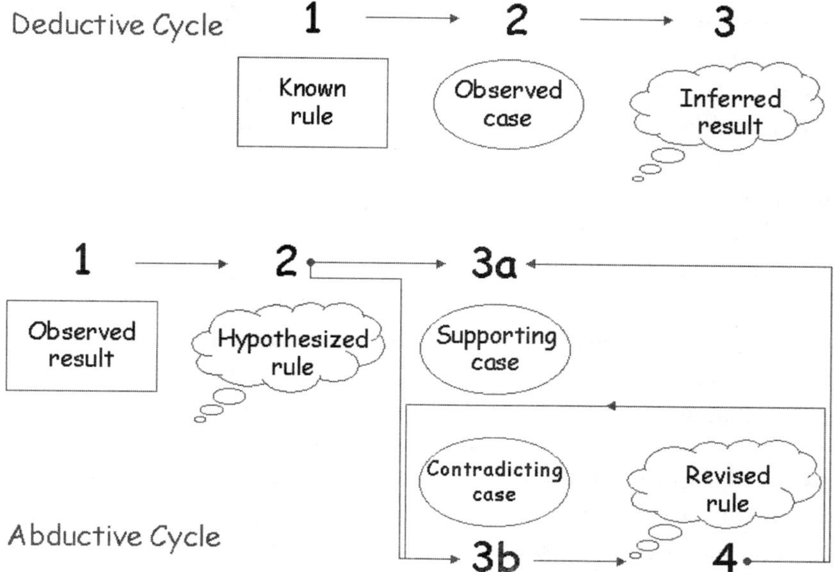

Figure 2.2
Abductive reasoning compared to deductive reasoning.

(commonsense) assumption. The 🔨 sign might in fact mean something else—that the shop repairs broken things, that the goods on that shelf are unbreakable, or whatever the sign-makers might have intended. Of course, the greater the distance between the intended meaning and the meaning that results from the most plausible rules, the lesser the chances that the meaning-takers will understand the sign as intended.

Assuming that 🔨 means that the shop also sells nails is a more elaborate abduction. It is the result of more than one abductive cycle. The first one leads to the conclusion that the shop sells hammers. The second one assumes that all shops that sell hammers also sell nails. Because this one (presumably) sells hammers, it must then sell nails as well. Once again, there is not a known true rule in the world saying so, but the meaning-taker's previous experience with signs and their meaning (semiosis) allows him or her to raise these hypotheses. The interesting fact, for computer science, is that abductive reasoning does not depend on the existence of known and stable primitives or axioms. The elements that function as primitives and axioms are hypothesized, produced on demand, and tested for suitability against the evidence collected by the human interpreter (or reasoner). This mode of operation cannot be accommodated by the classical Turing machine model, where symbol processing fundamentally depends on primitive symbols from which others can be causally derived by the effect of generative rules (for interesting critiques of the status of symbols and meaning and the limitations of the Turing machine model for computation, see Fetzer 1988 and Wegner 1995). So HCI is challenged by irreducibly different modes of sign interpretation and sign production. The consequences of such disparity for the communicative processes taking place in HCI constitute a central theme of semiotic engineering.

HCI provides us with clear evidence of users engaged in abductive reasoning. The following is an anecdotal scenario reported to the author by a user of Microsoft® Excel 2002. In it we can observe the power of sign interpretation and the kinds of plausible assumptions that users may make while interacting with computer applications.

John had prepared a spreadsheet with a large volume of data about his division's performance for the last three months. He then wanted to print it and take it to his manager in order to discuss some of his findings. He had to squeeze some of the columns in order to make some critical portions of the spreadsheet fit onto a single printed page. However, after having made a couple of changes to the original format, he suddenly realized that various "###" signs had appeared in the printable format (see figure 2.3 for a partial snapshot of John's screen). Being relatively familiar with various Excel error codes, he took the "###" to be error messages. But he was puzzled because he was sure that the spreadsheet had no errors before he started formatting it. Could the formatting have introduced errors in the spreadsheet?

In order to remedy the situation he restored the format he was using before he decided to print the spreadsheet (which took him a while), but to his surprise he could not see the ### signs anymore. And he could not quite remember where they had appeared—there were many of them. He concluded that he had inadvertently ruined something during the formatting process. So, he started it all over again, only to find the ### signs once more. Discouraged by the experience, he concluded that some formatting operations affect the data in large spreadsheets.

John's conclusion has its logic. Excel indeed uses the # sign to signal error messages such as, for example, a division by zero—#DIV/0!. And his previous experience with the # sign was all about errors in numerical operations. So he did not hypothesize that

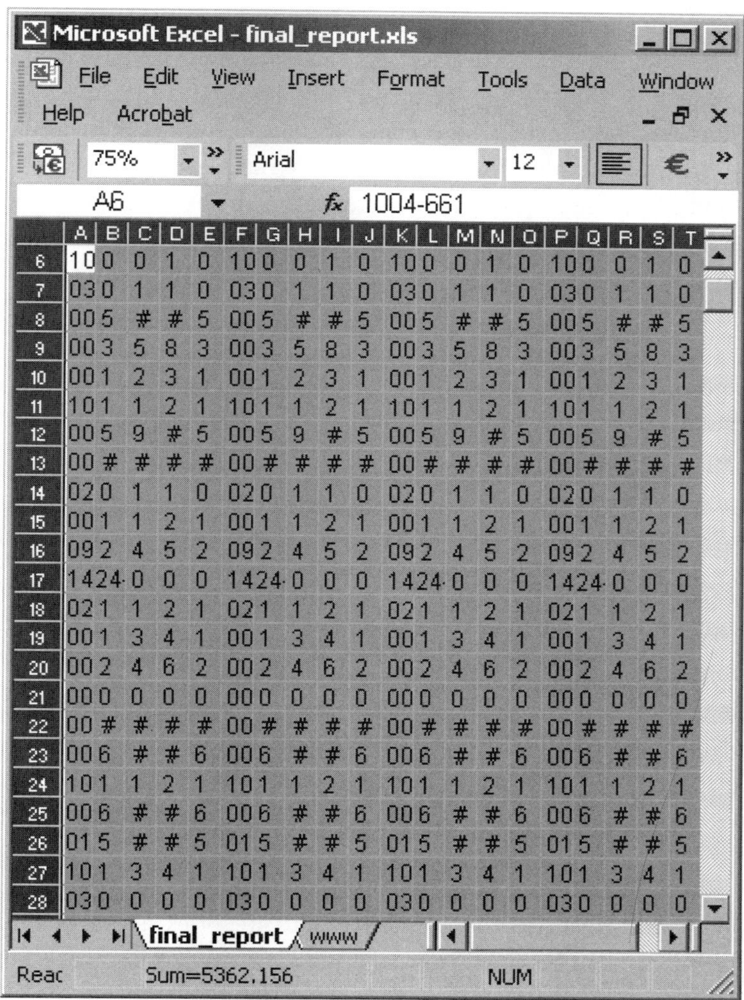

Figure 2.3
The # sign in Microsoft® Excel 2002 visualization. Screen shot reprinted by permission from Microsoft Corporation.

another kind of error—a data visualization error—was the case. Because John squeezed columns to fit in one page, the space necessary to visualize some of the data became smaller. Consequently, the ### sign appeared. But since John hypothesized the wrong rule (i.e., that data were lost), he never tried to solve the problem by using formatting tools (e.g., by using another font type, such as Arial Narrow, in his particular case). This would have enabled perfect visualization in the small scale he wanted to use. His semiosis took him away from the available solution. And Excel's help system was of no use in this case. The What's this? tool, graphically represented as **?**, when placed on the ### sign, simply said "No help topic is associated with this item." It failed to interpret "this" as a reference to ###. So although the tools to solve the problem were there and were not at all difficult to use (John himself says he uses the font type tool regularly), the right kinds of tools needed to support the formulation of appropriate hypotheses in this case were not.

2.3 Sign Classifications, Their Origin, and Their Use

One of the most popular references to Peircean semiotics in HCI is, as mentioned earlier, his famous classification of signs into *icons*, *indices*, and *symbols*. The liberal use of the word *icon* in HCI jargon, however, has contributed extensively to creating a great confusion about the original definition and purpose of this classification. A semiotic theory of HCI must only talk about sign classifications if they can be shown to enhance its descriptive, predictive, or explanatory power. In order to decide whether such classifications are useful or not, we should examine their origins.

Peirce's semiotics was intrinsically related to his greater philosophical project, which included fundamental postulates about the basic categories according to which all possible knowledge can be classified. Aristotle (1980), for instance, postulated the existence of ten categories: substance, quantity, quality, relation, place, time, position, possession, activity, and passivity. Radically committed to his *epistemology* (the study of what there is to be known and how such knowledge originates, expands, and collapses), Peirce postulated the existence of only three categories of semiotic interest—*firstness*, *secondness*, and *thirdness*. The minimalist names he assigned to them serve to dismiss confusions with other sets of categories known to philosophers.

Firstness is the category of undifferentiated qualitative experience. It encompasses all the phenomena that we are aware of experiencing but do not discriminate from, or associate with, anything else. We can intuitively align this category to sensations, perceptions, and *gut feelings* that we cannot put into words or express rationally. *Secondness* is the category of strict associations between two phenomena. Our capacity to relate one thing to another requires that we perceive an invariant or commonality between them. The name or reason of the invariant does not have to be known (for it would constitute a third "thing" in the observed relation); only the fact that there is an association is known. *Thirdness* is the category of mediated relations, involving at least three concepts. Going back to secondness, if the invariant between any two related things is itself a "thing" to the knower, than we have a case of thirdness. This is the category of rationality par excellence, because it allows us to formulate principles for relating things, for naming classes of things, and so on.

Concrete examples of firstness are often provided by young children when they don't feel well. Parents often have trouble trying to understand what is wrong with them in such situations, because the children do not know how to verbalize it. Following this line of illustration, the kids give signs that something is wrong—they cry, they are irritable, they have temperature, for instance. All of these are instances of secondness for parents (and for some kids, too). They are symptoms that something is wrong. And it is not until parents assign some acceptable *meaning* to these symptoms that we have a case of thirdness. The assigned meaning may be wrong, as we know, for it is typically the result of abductive (hypothetical) reasoning—not of a deduction. So, thirdness is the legitimate seat of rationality because it takes at least three phenomena to complete an inferential path (as seen in figure 2.2).

Peirce's definition of icons, indices, and symbols rests upon these three phenomenological categories and is much more elaborate than the definitions usually adopted in HCI. Originally, the threefold classification refers to how representations evoke their referents (not their meaning)—that is, to how the *representamen* manifests the *object* of a sign. Iconic signs are those where the representation brings out the firstness of its referent. Looser interpretations of this definition have popularized the view (used by Peirce himself as illustration) that icons are signs that "resemble" or "look like" that to which they refer. A preference for "visual resemblance" over all other possible sorts resemblance has contributed to the current equivocal view that an icon is a visual representation of something. Technically, an icon is a kind of representation that brings up the undifferentiated qualitative experience of sensing the referent. A sound may be an iconic representation (and we technically don't need the word *earcon* to refer to it), and so may a gesture or mimic.

Indexical signs are those where the representation brings out the secondness of its referent. The proverbial examples of smoke representing fire, snow representing cold, and so on, can easily illustrate the idea of secondness for causal associations between two concepts. But secondness does not refer only to causal associations. The term *contiguity* has been used to account for cases of co-occurrence in general. Thus, the representation of a train can bring out secondness if it refers to a railway, and that of a printer can bring out secondness if it refers to printing documents.

Symbolic signs are those in which the representation brings out the thirdness of its referent. Most of the words in any natural language are instances of symbolic representation. They are the most genuine case of de Saussure's *arbitrariness of signs*. They result from a regulating convention that relates them to their referent by virtue of an established meaning (see figure 2.1). There are other symbolic representations that are not words. For example, "∞" refers to infinity by virtue of a conventionalized notion of what "infinity" means. Some other symbolic representations, like , are actually quite visual (which does not turn them into an icon). The sign refers to a data file that some particular application can process. The variations of the verbal correlates of this visual representation are a telltale sign of its constitutive thirdness. "Document," "file," and even "project" are words frequently combined with "New" in menu options whose meaning systematically corresponds to that of this visual representation. is thus not technically an icon because the firstness it brings about is only that of a blank page, something only metaphorically associated to what users know it to mean.

Peirce's classification can thus, in its original sense, help us understand the semiotic complexity involved in producing or interpreting signs. It can be used to achieve the same kinds of analysis that Hutchins, Hollan, and Norman (1986) have achieved, for example, with their notion of articulatory and semantic directness. However, because the meaning (*interpretant*) of a sign is itself another sign, Peirce's categories can be applied recursively to examine the meanders of semiosic paths in a deeper degree of finesse than is achieved in traditional cognitive approaches such as that of Hutchins and colleagues. Semantic directness is a function of the distance between a user's conception of a goal or subgoal he wants to achieve and the corresponding structure of functions and procedures in the abstract model of the application. For instance, in most Windows® operating systems, the semantic directness involved in creating folders is greater than the semantic directness involved in partitioning a hard disk. In order to understand why partitioning a disk is much more complicated than creating folders, and why we usually partition a disk before we start installing applications and storing data, we must abandon the desktop metaphor. In a real desktop or office environment, we can divide and organize space quite freely by creating subdivisions on empty and occupied areas. In the computer version of a desktop, this can be done with folders and subfolders (in accordance with the metaphor), but usually not with hard disks (containers of all folders). The greater finesse of a semiotic analysis stems from the meaning of a sign being a function of ongoing semiosis. In other words, every sign appearing in the same domain, context, or mind as the one being interpreted affects the course of its interpretation. Thus, whereas from a semiotic perspective *all* the representations and meanings appearing in an application are necessarily involved in the analysis, the scope of analysis considered in semantic directness (as defined by Hutchins, Hollan, and Norman [1986]) is limited to that of the user's current goal or subgoal. Moreover, a semiotic analysis does not distinguish between semantic and articulatory directness. Articulatory directness is a function of the distance between the structure of functions and procedures in the abstract model of the application and the interface actions (the actual production of sign combinations) necessary to execute the user's goals or subgoals. The structure of the Peircean sign (which binds representations, referents, meanings, and meaning associations together) creates a *continuum* where semantics and sign articulation cannot be separated.

Peirce's sign classifications based on his fundamental categories can highlight the aspects Hutchins, Hollan, and Norman (1986) were interested in. The notion of *distance* that serves to establish semantic and articulatory directness can be replaced by firstness, secondness, and thirdness. Let us assume that a user of Treemap has a data set with the United States population for several years between 1981 and 1997. Her goal is to find out which state, in that period of time, had the largest population growth in absolute values. Treemap allows her to use different visualization styles and manipulations to interpret and compare data. An analysis of the semantic directness for achieving her goal with Treemap will show that there is no direct translation of her intent into a function that will return the result of a direct query (e.g., for all Y = state and all X = pop(Y in 1997) – pop(Y in 1981), show(sort(list of all X))). The user must translate her goal into the signs appearing in the semantic model of Treemap (e.g., "map color to attribute," "map size to attribute," "filter range of values," "visualize filtered values," and so on). What she decides to do (according to her personal interpretation of the application and of how it can help her achieve her goal) is to use filters. She guesses that the most significant changes would happen among the most populated states (an abductive step). So she starts by visualizing the five most populated states for every year for which data is available. In 1981, the five most populated states (in screen-reading order) are California, Texas, Illinois, New York, and Pennsylvania (see figure 2.4). In 1992,

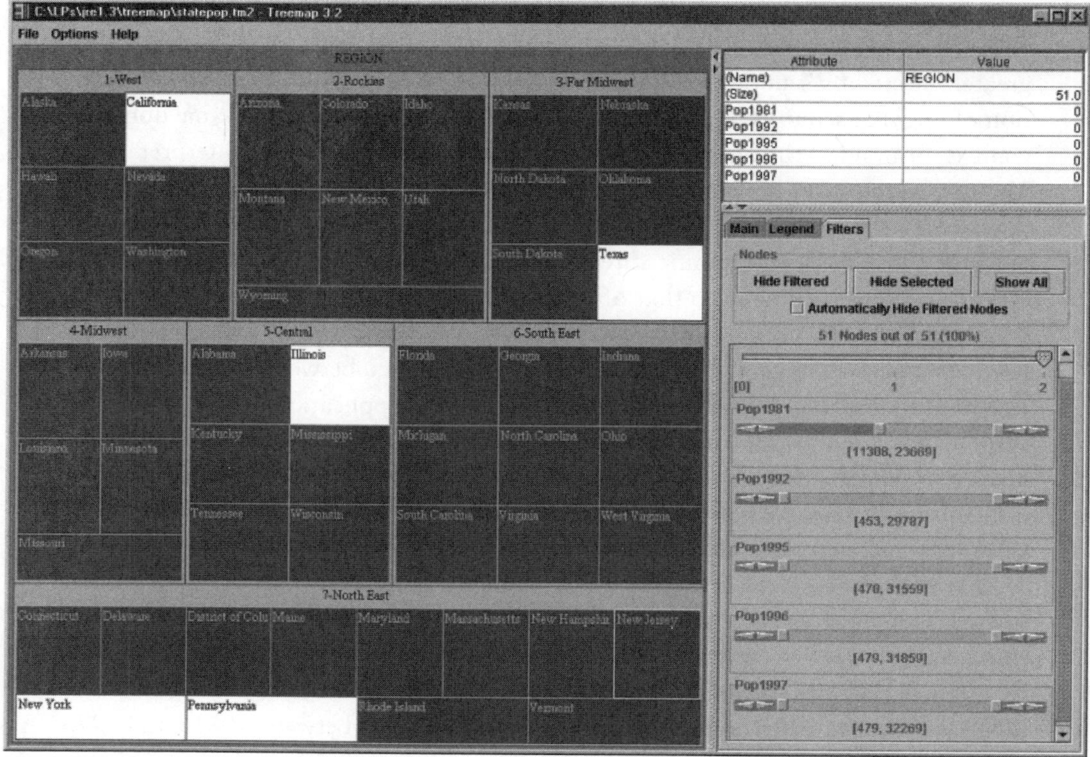

Figure 2.4
Visualizing the five most populated states in 1981 with Treemap© 3.2. Screen shot reprinted by courtesy of HCIL, University of Maryland, College Park (http://www.cs.umd.edu/hcil/Treemap/).

however, the five most populated states are California, Texas, *Florida*, New York, and Pennsylvania (see figure 2.5). She repeats the filtering for all years in the data set and finds out that Florida remains among the most populated states in all other visualizations.

The articulatory directness in Treemap (as the very idea of direct manipulation predicts [Shneiderman 1983]) is very high. Filtering data involves only a manipulation of sliders in the control panel on the right-hand side of the screen. But, unlike what a semiotic analysis can do, semantic and articulatory directness alone cannot account for what the user does next. She starts exploring direct manipulation to expand the scope of filtering and to discover, for example, the order in which states

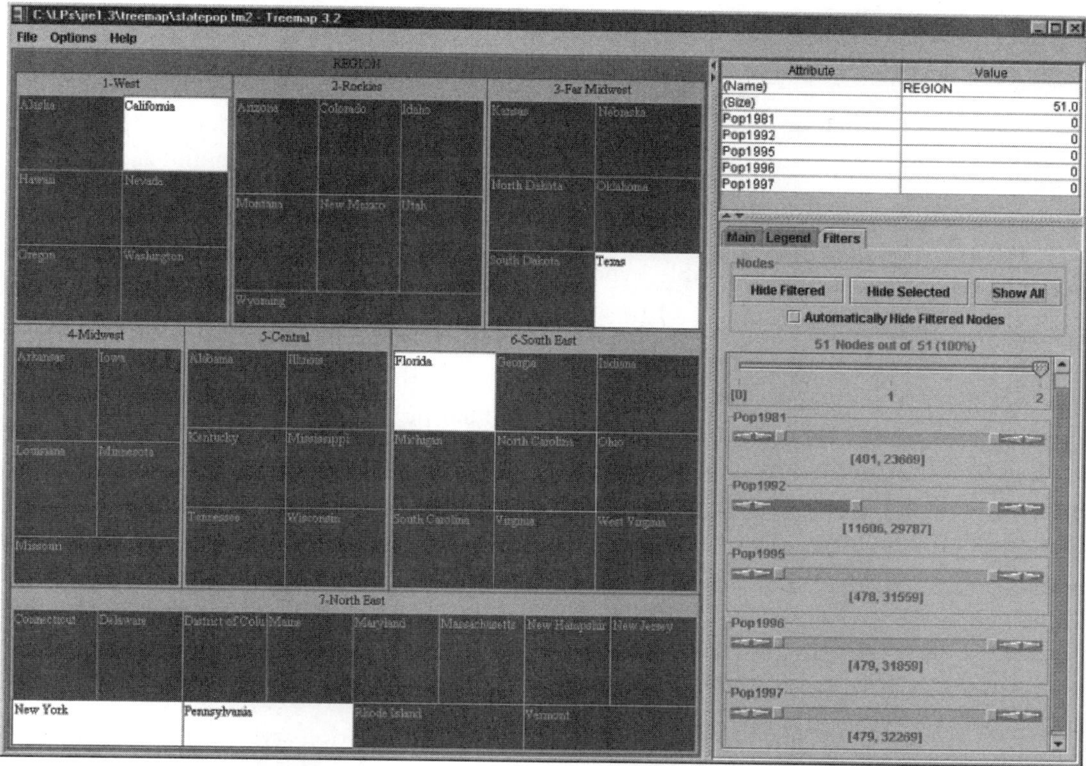

Figure 2.5
Visualizing the five most populated states in 1992 with Treemap© 3.2. Screen shot reprinted by courtesy of HCIL, University of Maryland, College Park (http://www.cs.umd.edu/hcil/Treemap/).

are visualized for each year (less populated states are darkened after the most populated ones). Her manipulation of available *signs* in the interface shows her that in 1981, for example, Florida was darkened even before Ohio. But in 1992, Ohio was darkened before Florida (which she takes as a sign of Florida's population growth, although this conclusion is not warranted by deductive reasoning methods, since Ohio's population could have technically decreased). She also finds out that, according to her data set, in 1981, when Florida was the seventh most populated state in the United States, Pennsylvania was the fourth. However, in 1992, Florida was the fourth most populated state in the United States, ahead of Pennsylvania.

When analyzed from a cognitive perspective using semantic and articulatory directness, Treemap seems to be very easy to use once the users succeed in translating their goals into the particular strategies that are implemented in this application, thanks to the specific visualization purposes that it aims to facilitate and demonstrate. A semiotic analysis can nevertheless go some steps further and account for a wider scope of interaction. For instance, why was it that the user chose to start from screening the five most populated states? Abductive reasoning and the process of generating plausible hypotheses can explain her use of common-sense information. Since her goal is to analyze growth in absolute terms, her first guess is that the answer will be found among the most populated states. This path leads her to spot the growth of Florida's population for that period of time. And once her semiosic path includes "screening" and "filtering" to produce other signs, she explores the idea of ranking, which eventually confirms (to her) that Florida is not only the state she is looking for, but that it had remarkable growth rates between 1981 and 1997. As semiosis goes on, the user is likely to ask herself why Florida became so populated, or maybe find out when Texas's population became larger than New York's, and so on.

Further semiotic analysis reveals that direct manipulation explores secondness (the contiguity aspects of representation with respect to its referent). It explains why semantic directness is lower in Treemap: The *thirdness* involved in the notion of "most populated state" is not privileged by the representation style of this application's interface. Moreover, a semiotic analysis can directly help us explore how technology influences problem-solving strategies and knowledge discovery. Just for the sake of exemplification, we can say that interfaces that choose to emphasize secondness over thirdness are likely to promote associative knowledge discovery and manipulation with greater ease than conceptual knowledge discovery and manipulation.

The idea that category-based semiotic analysis can explain (and anticipate) the success of some HCI styles and strategies over others has been explored in a case study about learningware (de Souza and Sedig 2001). Super Tangrams© is an application built to help children learn and retain the knowledge involved in translation, rotation, and mirroring of geometric objects (Sedig, Klawe, and Westrom 2001). Three different styles of interaction—direct object manipulation (DOM), direct concept manipulation (DCM), and reflective direct concept manipulation (RDCM)—promote different conceptualizations (semiosis) about 2-D operations on

Figure 2.6.a
Super Tangrams© direct object manipulation for rotations. Screen shot reprinted by courtesy of Kamran Sedig.

geometric objects and can make it easier or harder for students to learn the principles of Euclidean geometry.

Super Tangrams DOM interface works like most graphic editors (see figure 2.6a). Children can rotate objects to the left or right. They can flip them vertically or horizontally. And they can drag and drop them anywhere on the canvas. In accordance with findings from previous studies, Sedig and colleagues found out that children using the DOM interface were often confused about geometric operations. For instance, the drag-and-drop interaction often concealed the straight path constraint for geometric translations, leading children to think that geometric translation can follow an arbitrary curvilinear path.

DCM calls the children's attention to geometric concepts (vertices, axes, angles) by representing them visually and by allowing children to manipulate them instead of the generic shapes appearing in DOM (see figure 2.6b). This style of interaction also shows ghost images anticipating the effect of the operation being performed

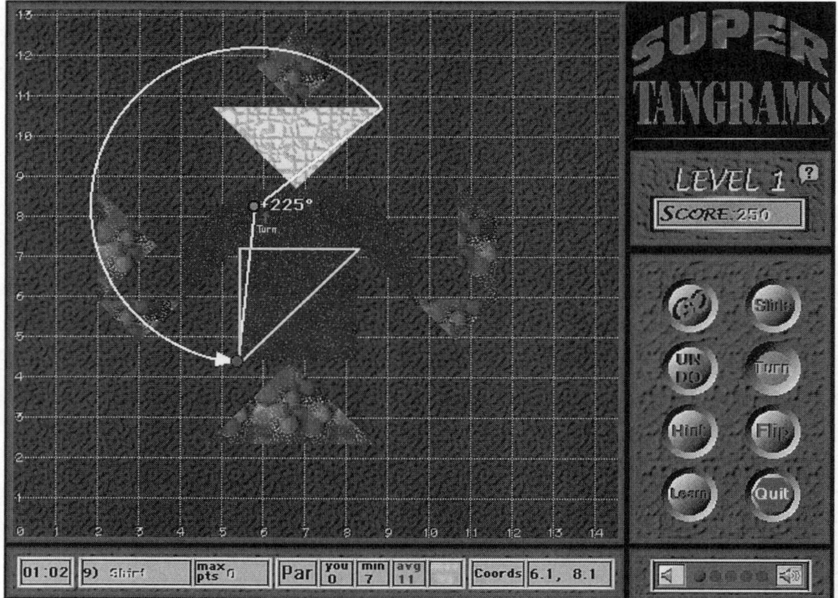

Figure 2.6.b
Super Tangrams© direct concept manipulation interface for rotations. Screen shot reprinted by courtesy of Kamran Sedig.

(e.g., the empty frame of a triangle, standing for the result of rotation, the arc corresponding to the path traveled by a particular vertex, and handles for changing the rotation angle). Not surprisingly, DCM interaction promoted better learning than DOM. Children were far more aware of geometric concepts (because they were explicitly represented and manipulated in the interface). Yet the verbal elaboration of the principle, closer to the algebraic formulations at the appropriate level of abstraction typical of good domain knowledge in geometry was only achieved with RDCM (Sedig 1998; Sedig, Klawe, and Westron 2001).

The RDCM interface also allows children to manipulate concepts associated with geometric operations, but they do so in a progressive manner. In the case of translations, for example, they can start from the most generalized notion of translation (DCM) and move to the next stage. The interface stops showing the ghost image of the object being translated. Children have to pay attention to the translation vector's extremities and their relation to the targeted final state of the operation. At the last stage, not only is the ghost image gone but one of the vector's extremities

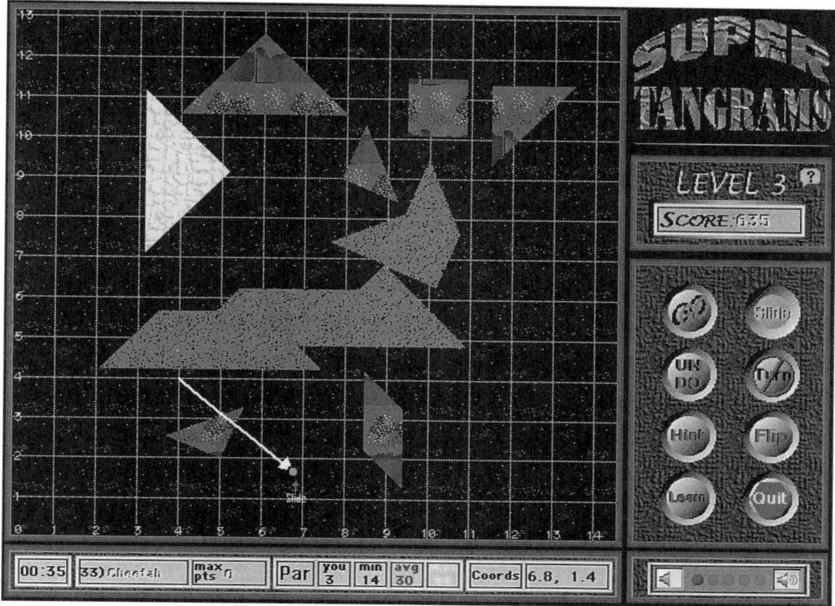

Figure 2.7
Super Tangrams© reflective direct concept manipulation interface for translation. Screen shot reprinted by courtesy of Kamran Sedig.

is fixed to a coordinate. The children then have to pay careful attention to the grid and think about the length and direction of the translation vector given the result they want to achieve. Figure 2.7 shows a snapshot of Super Tangrams at the most challenging stage of RDCM for a translation operation.

Semiotic theory provides an interesting account of Sedig's results (de Souza and Sedig 2001). DOM, DCM, and RDCM are progressively complex semiotic systems where the types of representation (with respect to their referent *and* meaning) have different levels of efficacy in communicating the principles of Euclidean geometry. The equivocal perception that direct manipulation interfaces are not good for learning purposes (Golightly and Gilmore 1997; Holst 1996; Rappin et al. 1997) can be avoided by an increased degree of semiotic awareness. The problem is not the style of the interface, but the signs appearing on the interface and the meanings that sign-maker and sign-taker give to them. Peirce's thirdness is the category of mediated phenomena. Mediation by principles and laws is one of the clearest instances of signification through linguistic formulation. Therefore, if the final goal of learning is to help learners formulate linguistically the rules of geometric translation and rotation in 2-D space, *visual* representations can never do the whole job themselves. They can (and do) serve as learning scaffolds for establishing solid interpretations (building the appropriate meanings) that can (and should) be used in the abstract formulation of the targeted principles. But symbols form the basis of all disciplinary discourse. Therefore, if a given interface style constrains semiosis to indexical representations of the meanings that one wants to communicate (as was happening in DOM and DCM), it will not (by itself) support symbolic formulations. RDCM was more successful than DOM and DCM because the interface included a true visual language, with the appropriate encoding for angles, axes, vertices, and so on, as well as for the operations on them. The complex articulation of such signs into which "sentences" (operation + parameters) corresponds to an algebraic formulation of the principles involved in translation and rotation.

We can see that a semiotic theory not only provides supplemental explanations for Sedig's findings (and supports his claims that DOM is not a problem per se in software applications for learning purposes), but supports useful generalizations. The ultimate target of learning is the formation of specific *interpretants* and the acquisition of specific signification systems. In Sedig's studies, learners were expected to master a specific signification system corresponding to a portion of Euclidean geometry. Other signification systems might refer to (parts of) arithmetic, logic, physics, biology, history, or poetry. All these disciplines have specific concepts and principled ways to combine them in order to describe, explain, construct, or discover other concepts. The elaboration of an appropriate signification system whose referent is, itself, another signification system (a discipline, or part of it) is a major semiotic task. The greater a designer's semiotic awareness, the greater his chances to build successful computer applications to support learning. A useful semiotic generalization is that if one such application's interface does not include signs of the targeted signification system or does not include an interpreter for valid sign combinations in this system, the learners won't be exposed to the ultimate target of learning.

So the design of learningware should start by a semiotic analysis of the targeted signification system (corresponding to the domain knowledge) and an exploration of the interactive and computational possibilities of other signification systems that can be used to represent the targeted system. Some formal characteristics of signification systems (e.g., the types and modes of representation they support with respect to the signs, their objects, and interpretants) will *mean* that the designer will have to combine different styles of interaction (as in Sedig's experiment), use a comprehensive formal language for interaction (e.g., the language of arithmetic or algebra used in calculators), or reframe his design target and build a different application for every distinct stage along the learning process.

2.4 Pragmatics, Speech Acts, and Culture

Pragmatics and semiotics have intimately related origins, although this is not as widely recognized as we might expect. Peirce was among the founders of *pragmatism*, a particular philosophical perspective that related the meaning of signs to the effects they had on other signs (pertaining to one's own individual semiosis, or to a broader scope of collective semiosis). Pragmatism has "assessed more profoundly than ever before the relevance of [the relation of signs to their users] in understanding intellectual activities" (Morris 1938, 29). Hence its importance for semiotic engineering and its targeted account of how users interact with intellectual artifacts. The work of pragmatist philosophers gave rise to pragmatics, characterized by Morris as a branch of semiotics, whose main goal is to account for the relation between two specific constituent parts of the sign: representation (*representamen*) and its meaning (*interpretant*). This goal involves dealing with what Morris calls the "biotic" aspects of semiosis—the psychological, the biological, and the sociological phenomena that influence interpretation. Notice here a hint to some misconceived notions, implicit in some HCI approaches to meaning, that we should be looking for a theory of the relation between representation (*representamen*) and referent (object). Such theory would miss the biotic dimensions Morris is talking about, or mistake them for what they are not. The idea that there might be pragmatic rules to describe biotic relations, which some pragmaticians and logicians would be happy to discover, is actually a derivation from one of Peirce's late conclusions—that *interpretants* are a habit, a habitual response to the presence of signs more or less closely related to their referent. This response can be such that the objective presence (or even the objective existence) of the referent is irrelevant for the achievement of the effects associated to the sign. Everyday examples of how world news broadcast in the media (specific spoken words and selected images) affects people, markets, and politics serve as supporting evidence for the early pragmatists' claim.

If the relation between sign users and the meanings they produce (with or without access to objective referents) could be described by rules, human interpretive and cognitive behavior would be a matter of mechanics. Away from the ethical implications of a mechanized view of human mind and human culture, this hypothesis has tempted a number of researchers in artificial intelligence (AI), since it carries the promise of computational tractability (even if partial). If such rules could be found, we would, for example, be able to build cooperative agents with which users would interact extensively and productively to achieve a wide range of purposes. But research in pragmatics has brought some bad news for the computationally inclined. One of the problems with the idea of pragmatic rules is the leap from the individual to the social scale of meaning-assignment processes. If rules were to account for the relation between the sign and its interpreter by way of the meaning he attributes to the sign, what would it *mean* if I interpreted a 🔨 sign in a small store as "this store sells hammers" and somebody else interpreted it as "this is where hammers are sold"? Are we using the same rules? Different variations of the same rule? Different rules? And how about the interpretations of other hundreds of customers? How would the ultimate set of rules be generalized from individual experience? Or is there no such thing as a truly *individual* experience? Are we all just enacting some kind of behavior determined by universal rules?

One of the most interesting examples of how researchers working with natural language processing (NLP) in the early days of AI explored the possibilities of using such rules is Schank's conceptual dependency (Schank 1975). In this perspective, such different interpretations of 🔨 as "this store sells hammers" and "this is where hammers are sold" would be related to each other in an associative network of conceptualizations (*interpretants*) whose relations to each other could be computed in terms of semantic primitives and case structures. What was not so clear to many adopters of Schank's conceptual dependency theory is that the meanings encoded in NLP applications were only a particular preestablished and unchanging semiosic path. It could at best stand for the knowledge engineering group's particular interpretation of a domain, but certainly not for the *semantics* or *pragmatics* of natural language utterances whose referent belonged to that domain. Communication between users and systems under these conditions was not only a matter of linguistic competence but, perhaps more important, a matter of having users restrain themselves to following always and only the preestablished semiosic paths a system could handle. And because this is totally unnatural for any human being, early NLP dreams have been gradually abandoned.

However, especially for the purposes of HCI, NLP kindled a long-standing philosophical debate: How can any two people understand each other if meaning has such deep roots in individual experience?

In modern pragmatics and semiotics the answer to this question is often formulated in terms of culture. Brown comments that the function of education, which extends over many years of our lives, is to expose us repeatedly to the same structured kinds of experience in such a way that all of us who are exposed to it develop a common pattern of usage for all meanings involved in those situations (Brown 1995). Although Brown doesn't mention semiotics in her account of communication—her focus is on understanding the cognitive basis of language use—her analysis is fully compatible with Peirce's views. By and large, it is our repeated exposure to the kinds of signs that are privileged in our culture and intricately related to each other that determines the conditions of convergent semiosis, necessary for any two people to communicate. Danesi and Perron (1999) claim that cultures provide the signifying order that affects the path of individual semiosic processes. But it is Umberto Eco (1976) who has championed the view that culture and semiotics must be so intimately related that the latter is in fact the logic of the former.

Pragmatic concepts and theories have influenced HCI and HCI-related areas. One of the enduring examples in HCI, especially relative to computer-supported collaborative work (CSCW) applications and computer-mediated communication (CMC), is that of speech acts (Austin 1962; Searle 1969, 1979). The essence of speech act theory is that language is not only used to represent (perceived) states of reality, namely, to make statements about what and how the world is or is not, but also, and perhaps more extensively, to have some effect on this very world, to *do* things. It stems from a pragmatist tradition and has evolved into the study of patterns and principles that speakers adopt to accomplish various actions with words. Speech act theorists distinguish between different dimensions for analyzing and describing spoken communication. The distinction between the language user's *intent* (the *illocutionary act*) and the *resulting effect* of language use (the *perlocutionary act*) has added a considerable degree of finesse to the study of language and communication. Austin and Searle have both used classifications of speech acts in their account of how words affect the world (or are affected by it). Searle's classification has influenced the *language-action perspective* (LAP) for systems design (Winograd 1987), which guided the development of The Coordinator® (Flores et al. 1988), possibly the most widely discussed CSCW application to date. The five basic classes of speech acts proposed by Searle are

- assertives (speech acts that commit the speaker to the truth of what is being said);
- directives (speech acts that aim at causing the hearer to do something);
- declaratives (speech acts that change the status of the world by virtue of what is said, by whom and to whom);
- commissives (speech acts that commit the speaker to taking some particular course of action in the future); and
- expressive (speech acts that aim at drawing the hearer's attention to the speaker's psychological state or attitude).

Popular illustrations of the five classes of speech acts typically align: assertives to informative statements; directives to requests and orders; declaratives to (usually ceremonial or institutionalized) declarations, such as "You are now man and wife" when uttered by the celebrant of a religious wedding ceremony; commissives to promises; and expressives to a wide range of utterances where psychological or social factors determine and explain a particular use of language (such as in apologies, reprimands, or praise). Speech act theory has supported the use of computer systems to coordinate human action and communication. The Coordinator, for instance, was "used for everyday communications in sales, finance, general management, operations, and planning functions in organizations of a variety of sizes and types" (Winograd 1987, 87). The system viewed each communication as part of structured patterns of action, aligning illocutionary to perlocutionary acts. Thus, for instance, if a particular communication was emitted as a request (a directive act), the system would be able to compute the perlocutionary effect the speaker expected and thus prompt the hearer to respond to such expectation. Likewise, assertive and commissive speech acts had a particularly relevant effect in organizational environments (Flores et al. 1988), given the kinds of commitments implied by their use in communication.

Not surprisingly, first-generation systems that adhered so closely to speech act theory encountered resistance from users. The problem was not with the LAP, but with the relatively narrow focus on speech acts as interpreted by Searle. By that time, other pragmatic theorists, such as Leech (1983), for example, had already broadened the scope of how language is used in communication and shown that, among other things, politeness and even the principles of irony play a fundamental role in the success of interpersonal linguistic exchanges. Leech's account of pragmatics bridges speech act theory and Grice's cooperative principle (1975), whose purpose was to characterize the constraints under which a particular *logic of conversation* could be sketched.

The cooperative principle is defined by four maxims, freely paraphrased as

The Maxim of Quantity Participants in a conversation should make their contribution as informative as necessary; not more, not less.

The Maxim of Quality Participants in a conversation should only say what they honestly believe to be the case; they should acknowledge their doubts about what they don't know for a fact, and never tell a lie.

The Maxim of Relation Participants in a conversation should only talk about what is relevant for the ongoing conversation.

The Maxim of Manner Participants in a conversation should express their contribution clearly and unambiguously.

Even a superficial reading of these maxims should allow us to notice that in many casual types of conversations they are frequently disregarded. For instance, small talk includes a lot of irrelevant information and is most often not about information but about socializing. Nevertheless, the cooperative principle is crucially important in conversations for coordinating rational goal-oriented behavior in pair or group work. This is why it has been used in the design of many knowledge-based problem-solving systems. Another noteworthy aspect of the cooperative principle is its descriptive power (which acts somewhat in the opposite direction of the design situation just mentioned). For example, this principle can account for some popular HCI guidelines such as Shneiderman's (1998) "strive for consistency" (maxim of manner) and "offer informative feedback" (maxim of quantity), or Nielsen's (1994) "visibility of system status" (maxim of quality) and "aesthetic and minimalist design" (all four maxims).

Leech has conceptualized pragmatics in a slightly different way. In his view, pragmatics is about problem solving. Speakers have goals to achieve (cast as problems to solve) through the use of language. They exploit a variety of linguistic tools, which Leech formulates as principles. Unlike rules, principles are regulative: They apply variably to different contexts of use; they are assessed by "more or less" rather than "yes or no" values; they can conflict with each other; and they can be contravened without impeding the activity to which they concur (Leech 1983). Pragmatics is about problem solving because communication requires that language users make decisions (in a kind of means-ends analysis) about what and how they are going to communicate in order to fulfill their goals. Valued psychological and social goals, for instance, may create important relevant conflicts with one or more cooperative maxims. Maxims themselves can conflict with each other. A simple illustration of such conflicts is the role of white lies in sparing the feelings of hearers. To tell a lie is a frontal violation of the Maxim of Quality. However, this violation may be less offensive or damaging than the consequences of telling the truth in various trivial matter situations.

But pragmatic principles don't usually cut across cultures. Leech's own formulation of his politeness principle is an interesting testimony of British culture, more evident, probably, to an observer from a non–Anglo-Saxon culture. The following six maxims that constitute Leech's politeness principle have a strong and weak form, the latter shown in parentheses.

The Tact Maxim (Applicable to *Directive* and *Commissive Speech Acts)* When using language to give orders or make promises, it is polite to minimize the cost to interlocutors (or to maximize interlocutors' benefit).

The Generosity Maxim (Applicable to Directive and Commissive Speech Acts) When using language to give orders or make promises, it is polite to minimize the speaker's benefit (or to maximize the speaker's cost).

The Approbation Maxim (Applicable to Expressive and Assertive Speech Acts) When using language to express or state something that affects interlocutors, it is polite to minimize dispraise of things having to do with them (or to maximize praise of such things).

The Modesty Maxim (Applicable to Assertive Speech Acts) When using language to express or state something that affects interlocutors, it is polite to minimize praise of things having to do with us (or to maximize dispraise of such things).

The Agreement Maxim (Applicable to Expressive and Assertive Speech Acts) When using language to make a statement about something that affects interlocutors, it is polite to minimize disagreement (or to maximize agreement).

The Sympathy Maxim (Applicable to Expressive and Assertive Speech Acts) When using language to make a statement, it is polite to minimize antipathy toward interlocutors (or to maximize sympathy toward them).

If we take the modesty maxim, for example, in some cultures maximizing dispraise of one's doing (the weak formulation of the maxim, whose strong formulation is "minimize praise of one's doing") has the opposite effect. Speakers who insist on dispraising their good achievements provoke a negative reaction from the hearers (who interpret the speakers' strategy as a scheme to elicit praise from the others). The same is true for other politeness maxims, which points to the fact that there probably aren't *universal* pragmatic principles of this sort.

Many tricky challenges in HCI design are thus explained by the influence of culture on interpretation and, more important, by the fact that pragmatics is a matter of principles, not rules. Principles apply "more or less" to different situations. Productive conversation results from good decision making, more than from competent linguistic and domain knowledge. Consequently, HCI design should emphatically aim at supporting the users' decisions about how to interact with systems and other users. Supporting decisions is not the same as supporting understanding and cognition, although the latter undeniably contributes to the former. One of the clearest distinctions between the two is perhaps that knowledge and action to support understanding is usually formatted in *positive* terms—explanations about how to achieve goals, how to carry out tasks and perform operations; information about the meaning of terms, the function and behavior of objects; and so on. Knowledge and action to support decisions is usually formatted in *comparative*, and sometimes even *negative*, terms—analyses of costs and benefits involved in making choices, troubleshooting hypotheses, instructions for how to diagnose failure, and so on. Back in the mid-eighties, Lewis and Norman (1986) talked about "designing for errors," an idea that was later condensed into design guidelines about helping users diagnose and recover from errors quickly and easily. But there is more involved in users' decision making, as I point out in the example that follows.

Qualcomm's email software, Eudora® 5.0.2, includes a special feature called Moodwatch® to scan incoming and outgoing email for potentially offensive words and phrases. Users can configure different levels of sensitivity, signaled by a range of one to three chili peppers (see figure 2.8). Moodwatch has been developed based on the work of David Kaufer, an English professor at Carnegie Mellon University. He and Qualcomm's spokesman Jeremy James reportedly say that "the feature isn't foolproof, but the English language is complex. Sending the message 'You are a moron and complete idiot' will rank three chilies. But 'You are a tiresome buffoon' doesn't raise Moodwatch's hackles one bit" (Shankland 2000).

Moodwatch is an attempt to address an important social issue brought about by the Internet—our vulnerability in face of flamed verbal attacks coming through email, chat, discussion lists, or any other kind of computer-mediated communication technology available today. The solution offered by Qualcomm is based on

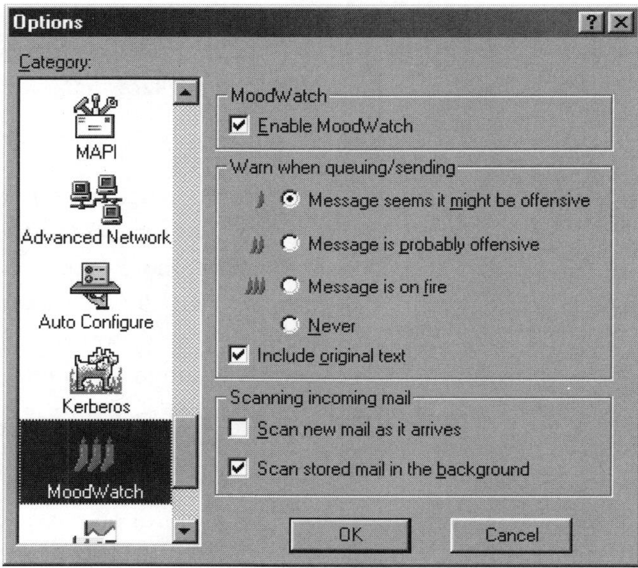

Figure 2.8
Screening flamed email in Eudora® 5.0.2. Screen shot reprinted by courtesy of Qualcomm Incorporated.

lexical and phrasal entries found in a kind of flamed speech dictionary of "aggressive, demeaning, or rude language, that typically appear in flames—or abusive electronic communications" (Delio 2000). Although Moodwatch lacks the kind of pragmatic competence needed for identifying really aggressive, demeaning, or rude communication, it helps users avoid inadvertent uses of language that may sound offensive.

This situation brings up an interesting opportunity for pragmatic decision-support tools that most of the popular CMC applications haven't been extensively exploring to date—online resources for helping users reach for social and cultural adequacy when addressing hearers in a foreign language. Many users (as speakers) have doubts about the right way to open and close email exchanges with senior professionals that they have never met, for instance. Is *netiquette* the same as *etiquette*? What are the do's and don'ts of politeness in the new media? And etiquette applies to HCI as well. One of the early versions of the Mac OS® Finder offers a good example of the effect of politeness and cooperation (or lack of either) in designer-to-user communication. If users inadvertently started typing without having set an appropriate active application to receive the input, the "system" would send a message saying "No one is listening to keystrokes at the moment so you might as well stop typing." This example shows that, independent of the advent of Internet and all the recognized interpersonal exchanges that it now affords, HCI design itself can benefit from listening to the concerns of CMC.

2.5 Sign Production, Communication, and Discursive Competence

Although semiotics and communication have a wide intersection in terms of the general phenomena they investigate, the various theories of communication may end up having little or no intersection at all with the fundamental semiotic concepts presented in this chapter. Probably the best known and most frequently invoked example of how big the differences in perspective can be is Shannon and Weaver's model of communication (1949), which accounts for communicative processes in terms of probabilistic properties of information source codes and message transmission. No mental, social, or cultural factors intervene in their theory, which has understandably appealed to engineers engaged in building information retrieval systems. The Shannon–Weaver model, however, has been confusing for those outside the strict mathematical boundaries within which the theory was proposed. According to Eco, the model can be interpreted as referring to a structural theory of the statistical properties of an information source; a structural theory of the generative properties of a source code; a study of how nonsignificant signals are transmitted through a channel; or a study of how significant pieces of information are transmitted for purposes of communication (Eco 1976). The second and fourth perspectives, for example, are much more useful for semiotics than the first and third are.

One of the first "semiotic" rereadings of the Shannon–Weaver communication model was proposed by Roman Jakobson (1960), who talked about channels, messages, senders, receivers, and codes like his predecessors, but in the context of *communicative functions* (including psychological and social). Jakobson structured the space of communication in terms of six related elements: context, sender, receiver, message, code, and channel (see figure 2.9). A *sender* transmits a *message* to a *receiver* through a *channel*. The *message* is expressed in a *code* and refers to a *context*. In communication, *sender* and *receiver* are alternate roles taken on by interlocutors. Although this model is unclear about a number of crucial issues in communication—such as, for example, whether the context of the message is that of

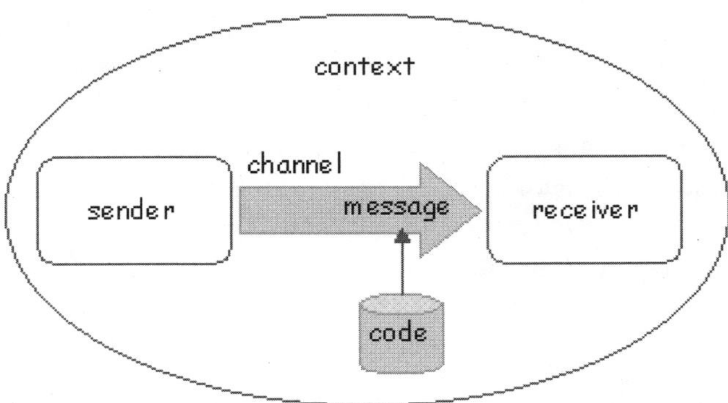

Figure 2.9
Jakobson's model of the communication space.

the sender's, the receiver's, or both—Jakobson's contribution to semiotic studies was to shed light on how language can be used to draw the hearer's attention to certain elements of this communication model.

Jakobson further defined six functions of language in communication, each corresponding to one element of the model. The functions are not mutually exclusive in a communicative act, which means that a particular message can serve more than one purpose. The *expressive* function focuses communication on the *sender* of the message; the *conative* function, on its receiver; the *referential* function, on its context; the *phatic* function, on the channel; the *metalinguistic function*, on the message's code; and finally the *poetic* function, on the message itself (what it says and how it says it). Semiotic engineering uses this model extensively to structure the design space of HCI (see chapter 3), based on the examples and correspondences shown here. Each linguistic example of how the function can be expressed is paired with an HCI example (figure 2.10a–f).

Expressive When the speaker says "In my humble opinion, this is the best choice," he is stressing his own attitude vis-à-vis what he is stating. In the HCI example in figure 2.10a, notice the use of "me" and "we" in the "system's" message, calling Eudora 5.0.2 users' attention to the sender's need for help.

Conative When the speaker says "Hi, there. Anybody home?," he is checking to see if his listener is present and alert in the communicative setting. In the HCI example in figure 2.10b, notice the SWI Prolog© user's attempts to make the Prolog interpreter respond by typing ⟨ENTER⟩ four times. The sign "|" is returned, not the

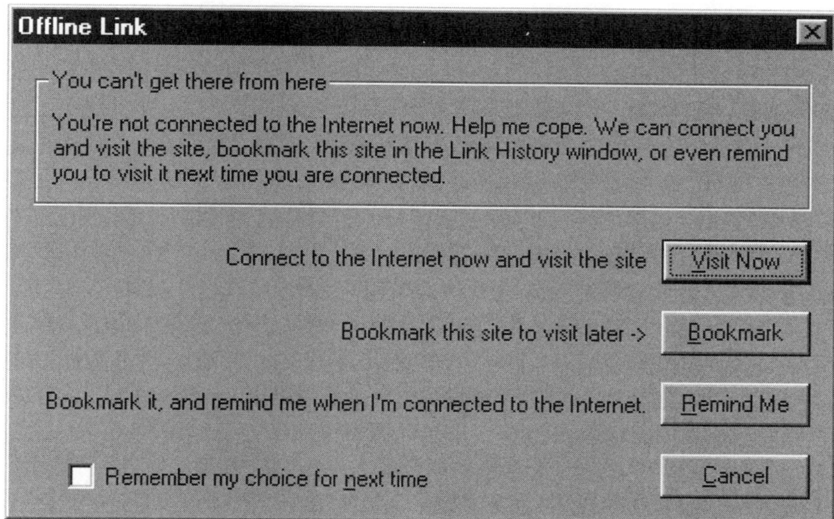

Figure 2.10.a
Expressive function in Eudora® 5.0.2 dialogs. Screen shot reprinted by courtesy of Qualcomm Incorporated.

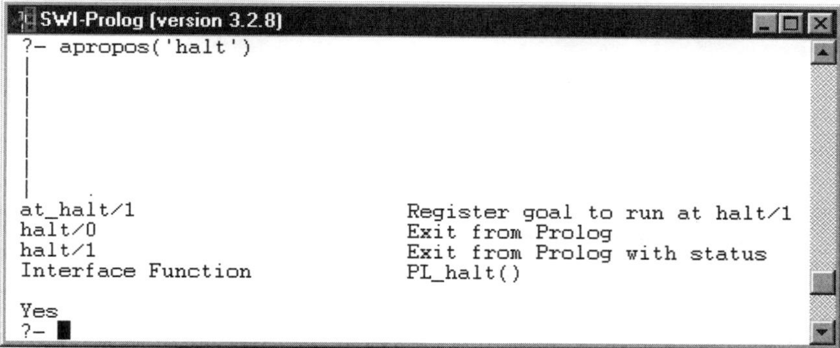

Figure 2.10.b
Conative function in SWI Prolog© dialogs. Screen shot reprinted by courtesy of Jan Wielemaker (http://www.swi-prolog.org).

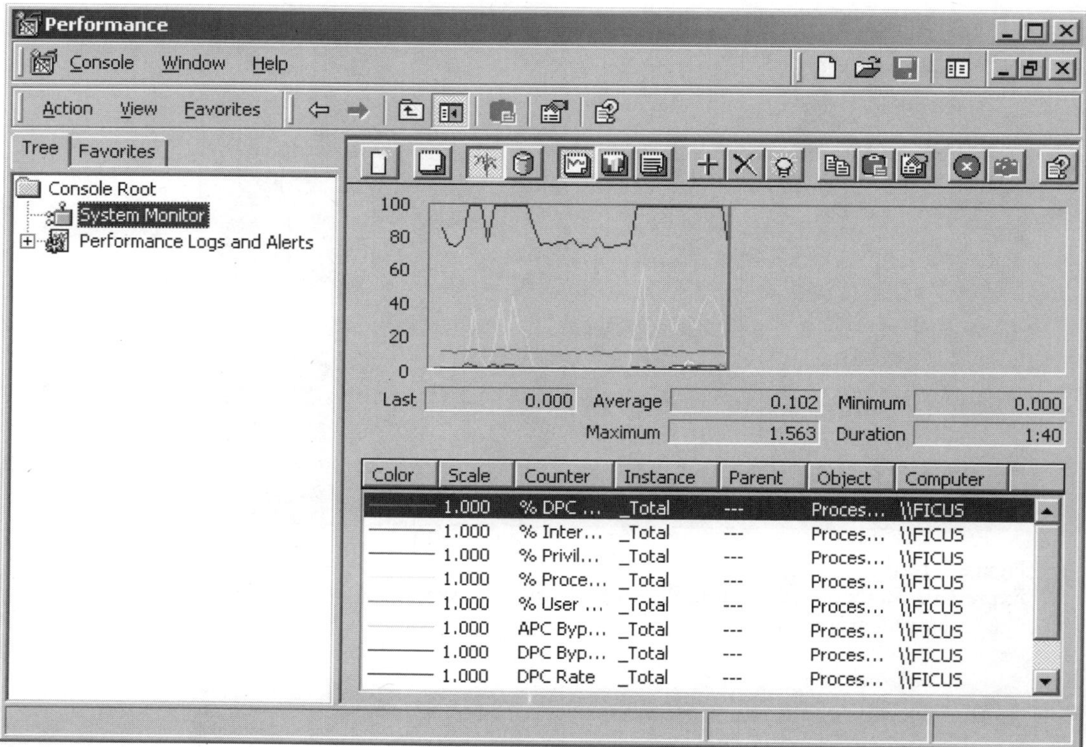

Figure 2.10.c
Referential function in Windows® 2000. Screen shot reprinted by permission from Microsoft Corporation.

answer to the Apropos command. After repeated unsuccessful *calls* to the system, the user realizes that a "." was expected. The "." makes the system respond to the user's command.

Referential When the speaker says "It is cold and windy today," he is directing the listener's attention to an element of the context when their communication is taking place. In the HCI example in figure 2.10c, notice the information about CPU use in Windows® 2000, which calls the user's attention to details of the machine's state.

Phatic When the speaker says "Can you hear me?," he is directing the listener's attention to the status of the channel (or *medium*) through which communication is carried out. In the HCI example that follows, notice that Windows® NetMeet-

Figure 2.10.d
Phatic function in Windows® NetMeeting 3.0. Screen shot reprinted by permission from Microsoft Corporation.

ing users can check the quality of video channel transmission in a separate window named My Video.

Metalinguistic When the speaker says "What does *interpretant* mean?," he is directing the listener's attention to the content of the message(s) exchanged during communication. He is checking the meaning of a message component. In the HCI example that follows, notice the explanatory message of StuffIt® Expander® about what happens to files and archives when they are dragged onto the box.

Figure 2.10.e
Metalinguistic function in StuffIt® Expander®. Screen shot reprinted by courtesy of Aladdin Systems, Inc. StuffIt Expander and StuffIt are registered trademarks.

Figure 2.10.f
Poetic function in Windows® Media Player. Screen shot reprinted by permission from Microsoft Corporation.

Poetic When the speaker says "What do you think is the meaning of meaning?," he is playing with the possibilities of the code used in communication (a play on words). In the HCI example in figure 2.10f, notice how this Windows® Media Player® visualization pattern (a star shape) has been set to go with the music being played (a Christmas medley).

The interest of transposing Jakobson's functions to an HCI environment is to explore the communicative dimensions and resources that HCI designers can use to facilitate their own communication with users and the user-system exchanges. In each of the previous examples, the function introducing the example is the most salient. As is the case in linguistic communication, a particular communicative event may involve more than one of Jakobson's functions. Senders always choose where they want to place the focus of communication by making one of the functions stand out more clearly than the others.

Jakobson's model can also help designers understand and make the best use of some communicative events. For example, the uncooperative and impolite Macintosh message shows that the system was designed to diagnose correctly a problem with the communication channel. By saying that "No one is listening to keystrokes at the moment so you might as well stop typing," the system is telling the user that it somehow knows that the appropriate channel for communication hasn't been established. Since establishing the channel is a requirement for any successful communication, the pragmatically appropriate and expected behavior is that the system would advance a solution (like asking which of all active receivers, or active applications, the user wants to address). The system could also anticipate the problem, as some applications do in certain contexts, by controlling the focus of interaction in such a way that there is always a receiver for keyboard communication. Jakobson's model is important because it tells us that all six elements are involved in any communicative act and that all six functions can be used (in design, in our case) to prevent or remedy communicative breakdowns.

Whereas Jakobson elaborated on the structure of the communicative space and the various functions that language can perform in bringing attention to one or more of the elements in this space, Eco (1976) elaborated on sign functions (not communicative functions), which he defined as those that correlate elements of an expression plane to elements of a content plane. The power of this notion lies in its ability to distinguish between signs and signals, which Jakobson does not set out to tackle. This distinction allows us to speak of signals as potential elements of the expression plane—that is, elements that have not been systematically or circumstantially correlated to any other element of the content plane but have the potential to be. Linguistic examples are easily grasped: for instance, *wod* is not a word in English, but it has the potential to be one. *wrsit* is also not a word in English but it does not have the phonemic potential to be one (because the sound combinations in it are not part of the English sound patterns).

When it comes to designing (artificial) semiotic systems, as is the case in HCI, it would be helpful to have a theory of sign functions (actual or potential) that designers could use. Eco's semiotic theory includes a theory of sign production (TSP), whose goal is precisely to account for all types of sign functions, conventionalized or not, linguistic or not, previously instantiated or not. This last point is specifically important for HCI, given that many of the concepts and contexts that users have to talk about or interact with in HCI do not have a parallel outside the computer system where they occur. Inasmuch as the characterization provided by TSP can help designers of semiotic systems anticipate the quality of communication supported by the various types of sign functions, this theory can actually advance a theory of HCI design.

Sign functions are the fulcrum of Eco's theory. Sign functions serve to distinguish between two major dimensions of study—signification systems and communication processes. Signification systems are the result of culturally conventionalized sign functions. In other words, whenever culture produces a convention that correlates a certain set of expressive elements to a certain set of contents, a signification system is in place. Signification systems constitute the codes available for communication processes. These processes, however, are not constrained to expressions that belong to a signification system. Communication processes explore and elaborate on existing signification systems, but communicators may choose to use innovative or latent sign functions allowed by signals of the expressive plane that have the potential to participate in sign functions. The need to use such potential sign functions in communication is well known in artistic communications, of course, but also in the sort of creative communication that is required when we want to express a novel concept or idea.

Eco proposes a typology of modes for sign production. Four parameters are used to distinguish the various modes of sign production (Eco 1976):

- the physical labor needed to produce an expression
- the type-token ratio of the expression
- the type of continuum to be shaped
- the mode and complexity of articulation

The physical labor needed to produce an expression corresponds to the *cost* of choosing and articulating an element of the expressive plane (e.g., uttering a word, drawing an image, mimicking a gesture, and so many intentional forms of expression). Values of this parameter range from *recognition*, when it suffices to pick a preexisting conventionalized expression for the intended content, to *invention*, when there isn't any preexisting convention to express the intended content. Intermediary values are, for instance, *ostention* (the act of bringing up the content from its original content plane to the expression plane) and *replica* (the act of producing a copy of the content in the expression plane).

The type-token ratio of the expression is related but not identical to physical labor. It refers to the agreement between a particular expressive element (an expression *token*) and a class of expressive elements to which it belongs (the expressive *type*). Thus, whenever there is an expression system enforced by cultural practices, communicating with expressive elements taken from this system is easier than when this system is not available. The values taken on by this parameter range from *simple* (or "ratio facilis" in Eco's theory) to *complex* (or ratio difficilis). Complex cases of token-type expressive relations can be found when the expression type coincides with the semantics of the content. For example, most maps and diagrams, which are motivated by the *content* they convey, are signs expressively more difficult to produce in terms of token-type ratio because there is no ready-made convention that the sign producer who is not a professional can resort to. Instead, he or she must observe the determinations of the content and produce an expression token that can be directly related to its content. With this parameter, Eco (1984) is exploring the idea that expressive conventions (or types) facilitate communication. He also remarks that some intermediary token-type ratio values appear when, for example, diagrams are conventionalized (e.g., as a notation). The effectiveness of conventions in decreasing the complexity to produce diagrams as a means to communicate ideas is proportional to the cultural basis that supports the convention, often referred to as *critical mass*.

The type of continuum to be shaped distinguishes two important situations in sign production. In the first, the referent or content of expressions is made of the same material (*stuff*) as the expressions themselves. Natural language is abundant in instances of such homogeneous *continui*. For example, if we say "The past tense of regular verbs in English is formed by adding an '-ed' suffix to the infinitive form," the meaning of the expression "-ed" belongs to the same (linguistic) *continuum* as the expression itself. In fact, all of the other signs in the sentence can be argued to be a case of material homogeneity in sign production. The same is not the case with other linguistic or pictorial signs like hammer or  . These are cases of material heterogeneity. The interest of analyzing material congruence in communication is related to self-reference in artificial languages. Most programming languages, for instance, have the ability to process symbols whose referent are symbols in the language itself (e.g., and not in a lower-level machine code). This is why programming languages have been characterized as being *naming spaces*, among other things (Gelernter and Jagganathan 1990). When it comes to HCI, all applications where users can create new symbols in the semiotic systems they use for interaction (e.g., be it because of customization, end-user programming, or merely the creation of objects to which they can refer to while building expressions about other objects) can benefit from an analysis of material congruity between expressions and contents in the semiotic systems.

The mode and complexity of articulation Characterize the degree of *grammaticalization* of the sign being produced. Highly grammaticalized signs are produced according to complex rules, as is the case of natural language signs, for instance. Each natural language word follows certain phonemic (relative to sound patterns) and morphologic (relative to lexical and word-formation patterns) rules. Natural language sentences, made of words, follow syntactic and semantic rules. And finally communicative utterances and texts, typically made of phrases and sentences, follow pragmatic rules, some of which have been mentioned previously. Visual signs, on the other hand, have a much lower degree of grammaticalization. Icons, for instance, don't usually have any formation rules to combine their various constituent parts into a whole (i.e., to "articulate" them).

Inasmuch as computer science follows the Turing machine model, it becomes apparent that this parameter is highly productive as a means of characterizing computer programs in general and application interfaces in particular. Many design guidelines talk about "consistency" or "patterns" that designers must follow throughout an interface project. These notions are typically associated to principles, much weaker than rules, that provide a sense of unity to the interface. Mullet and Sano (1995), for example, explicitly invoke a semiotic background to propose design principles for representation and images. In their own words, "when developing multiple images, care must be taken to maintain cohesion within the image set to consider the physical, conceptual, and cultural context in which the images will ultimately be displayed. Mastery of these concepts is far more important than any innate 'artistic' ability in developing an effective image program" (175). For Eco, the principles followed in this program are a kind of quasi-grammatical code (for they lack the descriptive and generative power or grammatical rules), an idea known as "pattern languages" that has long been used by architects and designers (Alexander 1977).

Signs may thus be combined in different ways, and at different costs to the sign producer and consumer. Eco remarks that communication involves a *discursive competence*, the accumulated knowledge of repeated exposure to certain sign combinations that allows a hearer to know or anticipate what the speaker is going to say in numerous contexts. Discursive competence has a social dimension, knowledge that is experienced and reinforced collectively by a group of people, as well as a psychological one, knowledge that is built individually as a result of repeated experiences and interpretations. Discursive competence plays a major role in communication, both for success and failure. It contributes to the interpretation of messages as "intertwined contents" (Eco 1976), each partially dictated by certain abductive steps that belong to our discursive competence. In the HCI example that follows, the trace of discursive competence in determining a user's behavior is particularly illuminating for a semiotic analysis of interface signs.

This HCI scenario tells the story of a user who had to process her email and wanted to listen to music as she did so. It shows how she made sense of various interface signs she was exposed to over a period of time, and it provides a powerful illustration of semiosis, abductive reasoning, discursive competence, and various other concepts presented so far.

> Joan plans to spend about fifteen minutes with email and decides to program a listening session in Windows 98® CD Player. She wants to listen to Vivaldi's *The Winter*, which corresponds to the last three tracks in her *Vivaldi's Four Seasons* CD. Joan doesn't quite remember how to program a listening session using CD Player because it's been a while since she last did this with the help of a friend. But she thinks it should be easy. Her first step is to put the CD in the drive, and it automatically launches CD Player. She pushes the stop button as she listens to the first bars of *The Spring* concerto (in Track 1). She then chooses the option Edit Play List . . . in the Disc pull-down menu, and a dialog box pops up (see the right-hand side of figure 2.11). In it Joan sees various text boxes where she can type in information about her CD, but her attention goes to two list boxes, one named "Play List" (on the left-hand side of the dialog box) and another named "Available Tracks" (on the right-hand side). Between them there are four push buttons labeled ← Add, Remove →, Clear All, and Reset. After some struggling

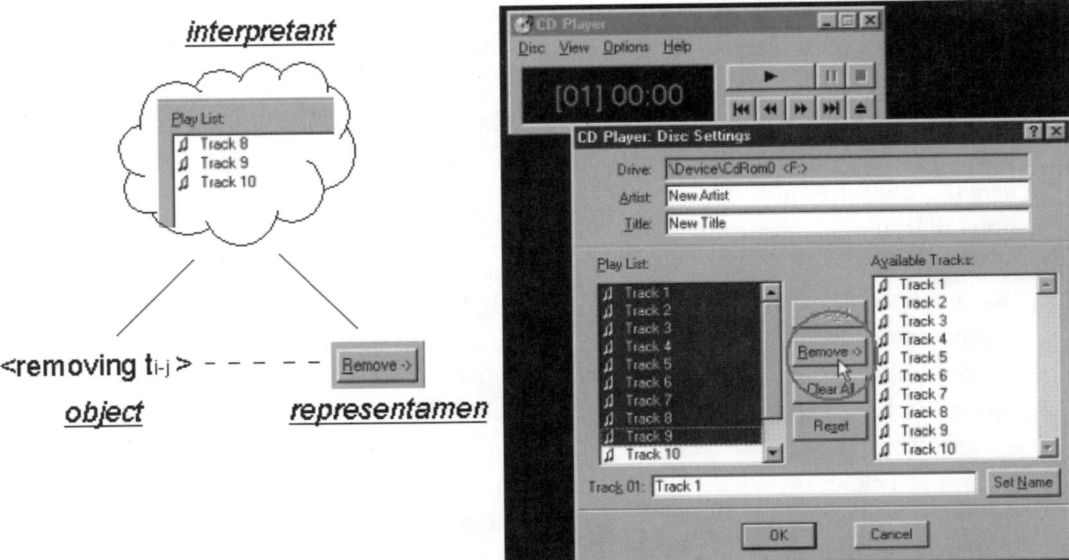

Figure 2.11
Signs and semiosis while interacting with Windows 98® CD Player. Screen shot reprinted by permission from Microsoft Corporation.

with the interface, she realizes that the listening selection results from removing the tracks she doesn't want to listen to from the playlist. In figure 2.11 we see the point where Joan has selected Tracks 1 through 9 (corresponding to the three concertos she does not want to listen to) and is about to remove them from the playlist. This is semiotically characterized by the instantiated sign components in the triangular sign diagram on the left-hand side of figure 2.11. However, she suddenly hesitates and wonders if that is what she did the last time. The directed arrow → next to the word Remove makes her wonder if those tracks will be removed from the list on the right-hand side. That she definitely doesn't want. She does not want the tracks to be removed from her CD!

After some ten seconds of hesitation, Joan decides that her only choice is to push the Remove → button, which she does. To her relief, the playlist on the left (not on the right, luckily) is shortened to three tracks only: Track 10, Track 11, and Track 12, which correspond to *The Winter* concerto. So she closes the dialog box, presses the Play button on the main window (upper part of the screen on the right-hand side of figure 2.11), and goes on to process her email.

> A few weeks later, Joan wants to listen to Vivaldi again, but now she wants to listen to all of the *Four Seasons*. So, she picks up her CD, puts it into the drive, and is surprised to listen to the first bars of . . . *The Winter*! Her surprise turns into panic when she searches next tracks on the CD and finds out that only Tracks 10, 11 and 12 are scanned. She must have removed the other tracks from her CD, then!

Discursive competence plays major role in this example. Of course the tracks on Joan's CD have not been erased, but the computer system is breaking an important principle of this user's (and of many others') discursive competence. The topic of some conversation about a particular computer object *does not* persist beyond the temporal limits of the particular conversation when it was first (or last) introduced. If this is the interlocutors' wish, they must explicitly signal that the topic is to be resumed. Phrases like "as we were saying last time" or some other equivalent sign combination in the communication code are typically used to this end.

This communicative failure on the part of the system adds to Joan's equivocal abduction (motivated by her doubts about the meaning of Remove →), and it leads her to think that she has positive evidence that she has ruined her CD. The connection between the meanings that the user thought of (in *semiosis*) but discarded for pragmatic reasons (her success with programming her first session) and the ones appearing much later, on another occasion, supports the view that the scope of interpretation exceeds the limits of particular tasks and situated goals. The interpretation of all signs is determined by *unlimited* and *ongoing* semiosis, which HCI designers seldom think of spontaneously.

Joan started to have problems when she first encountered the Remove → sign. She expected the button to be labeled Remove, and not Remove →. The directed arrow, strangely pointing to the list of Available Tracks, posed an interpretation problem to her. She could not be sure of the meaning of the arrow in the context of that particular interaction. However, she hypothesized that the arrow was somewhat spurious or irrelevant for that situation. When she pressed the button, she saw that the playlist looked okay and the playback too. At that point, she concluded (on the path of abductive reasoning) that the → sign was indeed misplaced. It was meaningless and had nothing to do with the action triggered by the button.

Here again the lack of discursive competence on the part of the system is the crux of the problem. The arrow does make some sense, but only in a particular conversational context when, in the process of programming a session, a user is sending a misselected track back to the list of available tracks. The effect is actually one of removing the wrong track from the playlist. The arrow comes, by analogy, from the ← Add button, which does seem to *transfer* (a copy of) a track from one list to the other. But if no transfer (adding) has been performed by the user in the context of the current discourse, the presence of the arrow is completely incohesive.

Eco's TSP parameters can also support a semiotic analysis of this interaction (and might have supported the semiotic design of this interface). The → was interpreted by the user as an articulated sign. Especially in the presence of the ← next to the word Add, it suggested to Joan that directionality could be combined with add and remove actions. But it can't. And she wonders why the arrow was there in the first place. At further inspection, Joan might have found out that there is a situation (or context) in which the arrows make some sense and do stand for directionality. In figure 2.12, we see that there are two items selected, one in each list, and all buttons

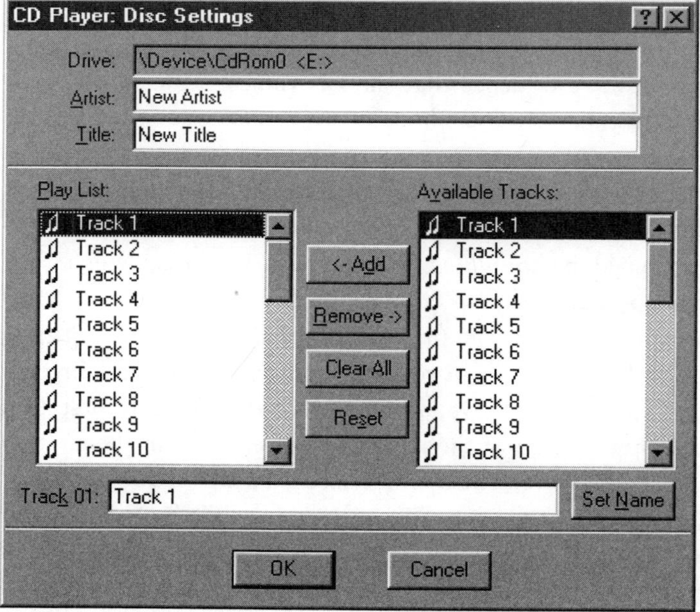

Figure 2.12
The meaning of arrows on Windows 98® CD Player buttons. Screen shot reprinted by permission from Microsoft Corporation.

are enabled. What does *add* mean in this context? Which of the two items is the object of the action? The arrows give the users a hint (although of arguable value). They may be loosely interpreted as "after the action is performed, the object it refers to will be available here." So, ← Add applies to the item on the right-hand side of the screen, since the one on the left is already in the location where the arrow points (to the list on the left-hand side). This reveals yet another articulation problem: The visualization proposed by this application suggests that there are two focal objects of discourse, when in fact there should be only one. Items on the right-hand side can only be the object of the add action, whereas those on the left can only be the object of the remove action. This is the correct articulation that this visualization so clearly betrays. A *simple* token-type ratio for this articulation is to use a single-focus strategy, as most interfaces do today. Thus, a selection from the Available Tracks list enables only the Add button, and conversely one from the Play List enables only the Remove button. Consequently, the correct syntactic combination could be supported by more refined focus control, instead of additional signs that have only a limited scope of interpretability.

2.6 Metaphors and Metonymies

Metaphors have been widely explored in HCI as a cognitive resource to help users understand new concepts by analogy. The historical "desktop metaphor" introduced by the Xerox Star station was meant to facilitate the users' understanding of file system actions in terms of everyday life analogs. However, a metaphor is a sophisticated means of expression in natural language (and other codes). It serves various rhetorical purposes, and it can very effectively enrich the discourse of a speaker, helping him or her achieve a wealth of pragmatic effects. For example, saying that "semiotics supports a new *breed* of HCI theories" motivates *semiosis* where such meanings as "cultivate," "raise," "reproduce," "offspring," "stock," and others are very likely to appear. Saying that it "supports a new type of HCI theories" does not evoke the same meanings, and the whole idea of a live and dynamic process of growth is lost. A speaker choosing the form "semiotics supports a host of new HCI theories" would have sacrificed the idea of homogeneity among the theories (preserved by the expressions "breed" and "type") in favor of stressing the quantity of new theories being talked about. "A breed of theories" and "a host of theories" are metaphorical expressions, although some hearers may not even realize it. Lakoff and Johnson's pioneer work (1981) in cognitive semantics has shown a wide spectrum of metaphors "we live by" and how they correspond to a few primitive notions that play a fundamental role in cognitive and linguistic competence.

Metaphors are essential for expressing creative thought and naming novel concepts. For instance, an *airplane's nose* is what English speakers have named the front part of an aircraft. In the early days of the aviation industry, the words *wing*, *tail*, and others were used in a metaphorical sense that later became a convention (or dead metaphor). The interesting aspect of these three metaphors—nose, wing, and tail—is that, when it comes to airplanes, the extent of analogy is not the same. Whereas an airplane's wings and tail have not only a similar (or prototypical) shape as those of many animals but also a similar function (to fly and control the direction of movement), an airplane's nose has nothing to do with the sense of smell. Only the shape and location are relevant for the metaphor. This principle allows us to understand expressions such as the 'airplane's belly' or its 'eyes', although the exact path of metaphorical relation is not always the same for all expressions.

Metonymies have historically been treated in association with metaphors (Aristotle 1984). Whereas the latter create a kind of semantic short circuit between two concepts (like animals and aircraft in the previous expressions), the former represent a concept by means of another that is semantically contiguous to it. Frequently used metonymies include representing: the part for the whole, or vice versa; the cause for the effect, or vice versa; the content for the container, or vice versa; and so on. For instance, when someone says "I like Bach" (i.e., Johann Sebastian Bach), he doesn't mean he likes the person, but his musical compositions. Likewise, it is literally impossible to "drink a glass or two" with a meal, but only to drink some liquid that will be contained in the glass.

Just like metaphors, metonymies serve many important rhetorical purposes. One of the most relevant ones for our purposes is that of expanding or restricting the focus of attention of the hearers. An expansion of the focus of attention results in generalizations like when we say that "Europe supported a decision made by the United States." Neither Europe nor the United States are "a person" who can make decisions about this or that. The metonymical rhetoric has the effect of highlighting the unity and homogeneity of action to the detriment of the diversity of opinions that typically characterizes a nation or a group of them. When we say or hear this sentence, we may be aware of but not paying any attention to the fact that not every citizen in Europe supports a decision that itself is probably not supported by every citizen in the United States. Our interpretation yields to the focused elements in the metonymical expression, and we may occasionally mistake figurative for literal meaning.

As was just said, examples of metaphors in HCI have become abundant since graphical user interfaces were created. The *desktop* is the most popular example of how metaphors have been explored to help users understand new concepts in terms of old known concepts. Metonymies are less frequently discussed, but no less abundant in HCI. Many text editors, like Microsoft® Word, for instance, make extensive use of metonymies in editing tasks. Specifically, many formatting operations on words do not require that the whole word be selected. In figure 2.13 we see that the boldface function is successfully applied to "word" both when the whole word is selected before the function is called and when only the cursor is placed "inside" the container word. The part (location inside the container) is taken for the whole (the full content within the container).

The same principle applies in many graphical editors, where operations commanded on parts extend to the whole and, interestingly enough, where operations commanded on a whole grouping of graphical elements (like "fill with color") apply only to the parts that "make sense" (e.g., polygons are filled with color, but text fonts are not).

The problem with both metaphors and metonymies is to decide whether they should be "grammaticalized"—namely, used as a systematic grammatical construct in the interface language—or not. Grammaticalized metaphors and metonymies, unlike what is the case in natural communication, become an organizing principle of the interface language. In other words, users "expect" the figure of speech to extend to all similar contexts. For example, Word users might be confused with the part-for-whole metonymy in the interactive situations illustrated in figure 2.14, where some commands apply while others don't.

The effects in figure 2.14 are related to the implementation of the program and to the hierarchy of objects from a "software engineering" perspective. Boldface functions apply to words, not to paragraphs; justification functions apply to paragraphs, not to words. However, the user may of course think of paragraphs written in boldface, or of paragraphs aligned to the left or right.

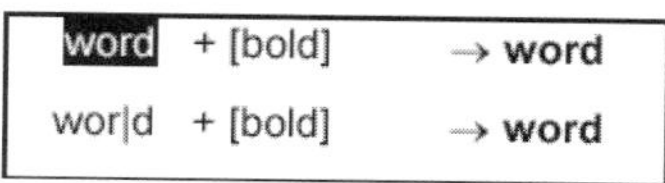

Figure 2.13
How metonymies are used for boldface formatting in Microsoft® Word.

This paragraph is being reformatted.	+ [align left]	→ This paragraph is being reformatted.
This paragraph is being |reformatted.	+ [align left]	→ This paragraph is being reformatted.
This paragraph is being reformatted.	+ [bold]	→ **This paragraph is being reformatted.**
This paragraph is being |reformatted.	+ [bold]	→ This paragraph is being reformatted.

Figure 2.14
Interactive inconsistencies with metonymical expressions in Microsoft® Word.

This example takes us back to our initial point about how in computation the difference between *langue* and *parole* is lost. Metaphors and metonymies are a matter of *parole*, not of *langue*. However, it is difficult, if not impossible, in any practical sense, to distinguish *parole* rules (that are not part of the "grammar") from *langue* rules (that constitute "the grammar") when it comes to specifying computer languages. This Word example shows that arbitrary decisions about which rules belong to the grammar and which don't may cause some confusion to users, for whom metaphors and metonymies are a natural and powerful communicative (and cognitive) resource.

3

Semiotic Engineering

The goals of semiotic engineering as a theory of HCI are to present an extensive and distinctive characterization of HCI, to provide a consistent ontology from which frameworks and models of particular aspects of HCI can be derived, and to spell out epistemological and methodological constraints and conditions applicable to the spectrum of research that the theory can be expected to support. This chapter presents the theoretical tenets of semiotic engineering and sets the basis for the three chapters of part II, where the theory is applied to evaluating the users' experience, to designing customizable and extensible applications, and to designing multi-user applications.

3.1 The Semiotic Characterization of HCI

HCI is a particular type of twofold computer-mediated metacommunication. Metacommunication is technically communication *about* (aspects of) communication itself. The most popular aspect explored in metacommunication is how it gives users a key for interpreting communication itself. Some messages give us a hint of how their senders mean them to be interpreted, as in the case of Magritte's famous painting *Betrayal of Images*. In it an explicit statement saying that *Ceci n'est pas une pipe* ("This is not a pipe") beneath a very realistic painting of a pipe calls the interpreter's attention to the representational aspects of the image and away from the referential and cognitive ones.

A similar type of metacommunication is to say that this is not a link. The message tells us how to interpret it. Unlike what these two examples may suggest, metacommunication does not need to be verbal. Nonverbal cues can also be crucial elements of metacommunication. For instance, the mere presence of a push button in an electronic document suggests that something will happen if the button is *pressed*.

In a printed document, however, the meaning of such metacommunication patterns becomes confusing.

HCI is a specific type of twofold computer-mediated metacommunication in which computer systems designers send systems users a *one-shot message*. The message tells the users how to communicate with it in order to accomplish a certain range of effects. It is a *one-shot* message because, from a design point of view, it conveys a complete and immutable content encoded in and made available by the system's interface. The message is designed to tell users what can be paraphrased as follows:

> Here is my understanding of who you are, what I've learned you want or need to do, in which preferred ways, and why. This is the system that I have therefore designed for you, and this is the way you can or should use it in order to fulfill a range of purposes that fall within this vision.

The "I"—first person of discourse—in this paraphrase is the system designer (or a spokesperson for the system design team). The metacommunication is twofold because it is only fully achieved if users communicate with the message. If they don't, the metacommunication is not achieved, because the sign standing for the designer's intent is not interpreted as such by the user. We deliberately talk about *interpretation* and not *understanding* because we want to draw attention to the fact that semiosic processes (see chapter 2) continuously generate meanings. Some of them may coincide with the designers', while some may not. Semiotic productivity in HCI is dictated by the success of designer-to-user metacommunication. As long as users generate meanings that are compatible with the designer's meanings encoded in their message, user-system communication is successful even if users don't interpret technology in the same way as designers do.

Three fundamental consequences follow from the semiotic engineering characterization of HCI. First, HCI designers are necessarily involved in the communicative exchanges between users and systems *at interaction time*. Second, the qualitative dimensions of HCI that semiotic engineering can help us appreciate must be anchored in the twofold metacommunication process described earlier. And third, the process of encoding the designer's metacommunication message as a computing system captures and freezes only a particular segment of the designer's semiosis about the product of his or her design. The actual meaning designers assign to a system they may have designed is much richer than what is encoded and will evolve overtime. So will the users' meaning. The computationally *encoded* portion of the designer's meaning constitutes and defines the one-shot metacommunication message sent to users. It can be generated and interpreted by computational procedures that will manipulate all and only the signs that have been implemented as symbols in the system's interface languages.

Together, these consequences uniquely determine the design space of HCI and introduce a new set of dimensions and categories for both design and evaluation of computer-based interactive artifacts.

3.2 The Semiotic Engineering Design Space

The semiotic engineering design space for HCI follows from how HCI is characterized in this theory. The designer-to-user metacommunication level determines the user-system communication. The designer's message determines both the system's stance as a sign (that can produce and interpret other signs) and the user's role in communication with the system. In the first case, the determination results in the system being a sign that *stands for* (and refers to) a particular segment of the designer's semiosis. An illustrative example will help us clarify that designers do *mean* to say things through the interface.

Arachnophilia© 3.9 is an HTML tag-based editor. In figure 3.1 the user has just pressed the button labeled EditImg (where the cursor still is) and the program pops up a message box saying that "it is good practice" to save files before attaching images. We can immediately see that this is in itself metacommunication (since the judgment of what is good practice obviously comes from the system's designer). Further evidence of how the designer-to-user communication determines the system's signs (including metacommunicative signs) can be captured in Arachnophilia's online help material, where the system's designer is the first person of discourse. He adopts an overtly tutorial attitude, and in the particular case of introducing an image in an HTML page, this is what he communicates to the users:

> Arachnophilia will now ask you whether you want to save your file. This is a very good idea for several reasons. One reason is that you might otherwise lose your work in the event of a system crash or power failure. Another is that, if you locate your Web page in a particular directory, Arachnophilia can automatically move all your resource choices to that directory also. This makes it very easy to move your completed Web page (or pages) to the Internet later on.
>
> After you have responded to the Save-File dialog box, hopefully by saving your file, Arachnophilia will ask you whether you want to automatically copy any files you select to this same directory. . . . Now navigate to a directory that contains some graphic files and select one. (Arachnophilia© 3.9, 1996–1998)

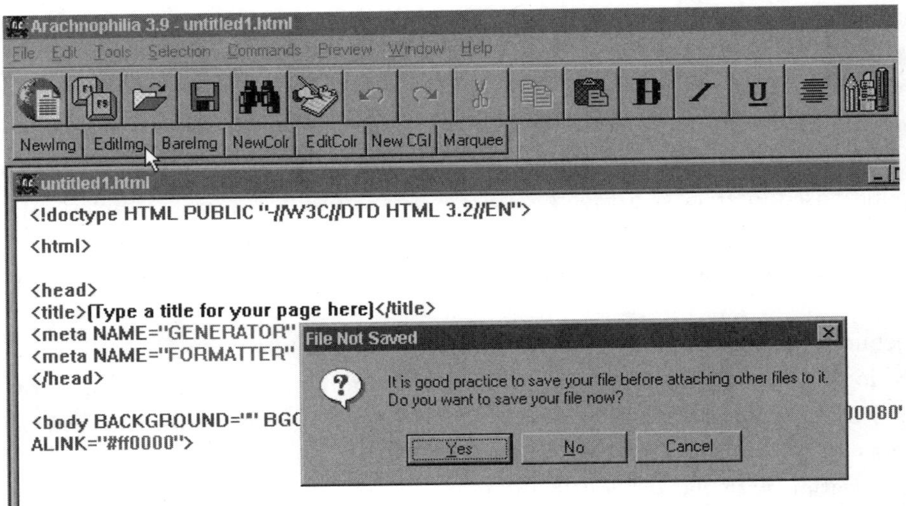

Figure 3.1
Metacommunication in Arachnophilia© 3.9. Screen shot reprinted by courtesy of Paul Lutus.

This passage provides numerous clues about Arachnophilia's designer's intent. Not only does it instruct the user at the operational level (saying how to insert the image), but it also gives tactical and strategic information about the application (the sound methods to achieve the insertion and the additional advantages of using the proposed method). Notice that the designer understands that the user may choose not to follow his advice (see the phrase "hopefully saving your file"), which explains the No button in the pop-up dialog in figure 3.1.

The metacommunication message also affects the way in which the users position themselves while communicating with the system. The rest of Arachnophilia's online help material shows that the designer has assumed a clearly tutorial, and even educational, attitude toward HTML editing. Phrases like "Now let's . . ."or "Now we . . ." express his engagement in promoting the user's learning experience. Eloquent evidence that users *sense* and *react to* this attitude even without resorting to online help was spontaneously given to us by one of the participants of an extensive evaluation experiment carried out with Arachnophilia (Prates, Souza, and Barbosa 2000a). He said: "This guy must think we are stupid. Why have these huge buttons in the toolbar?" Even without going into the details of who "this guy" is (the designer? the system?), this person (a graduate computer science student) expresses a negative reaction to taking on the user role reflected in the interface. In a post-experiment interview with the evaluator, this user said that the huge buttons suggested that he (the user) had never seen them before and/or did not have enough skill to be able to click on smaller ones. And he was annoyed by it.

Thus, the signs emitted by the system have fixed implemented semantics (**B**-labeled buttons denote "activate bold-face function") and algorithmically determined semiosic paths (the EditImg button in figure 3.1, which triggers the 'File not saved' dialog). However, the *meanings* of such signs, for both designer and user, may (and actually must, according to semiotics) evolve. For instance, after the user gets a few months of practice, the negative meanings associated with the large buttons may give way to more functional meanings, probably aligned to a task-centered semiosis. Likewise, as the designer revisits his decisions, he may come to realize that the large buttons are an unnecessary exception compared to the rest of the interface. This evolutionary nature of semiosis points in the direction that there is no such thing as *the* meaning of system's signs with respect to either the designer or the user. However, there is *one* implemented meaning of these signs, which pertain to computational processes that interpret them and/or produce them. And although it may be semiotically vacuous to expect that a particular meaning will be *the* user's meaning or *the* designer's meaning at any point in time, it is crucially important to evaluate how *a* user's or designer's meaning, contingent on the situation in which it is examined, compares to *the* implemented meaning of its corresponding interface sign.

Designing signs that can trigger converging semiosis around its implemented meaning is the primary goal of HCI design in a semiotic engineering perspective. This semiotic activity can be structured by means of Jakobson's model (1960) of communicative functions (see chapter 2). There are six elements to account for in the construction of metacommunication artifacts in HCI: the sender, the receiver, the context, the channel, the code, and the message. A designer must decide

- what aspects of his/her own constraints, motivations, beliefs, and preferences should be communicated to the user for the benefit of metacommunication (Who is the sender?);
- what aspects of the user's constraints, motivations, beliefs, and preferences, as conceived by the designer, should be communicated to the actual users to support their projection of themselves onto the role of system's interlocutor (Who is the receiver?);

- what elements of the user's expected spectrum of interactive contexts (psychological, sociocultural, technological, physical, etc.) must be processed by the system's semiotic computations and how (What is the context of communication?);
- what computable codes may or must be used to support effective metacommunication (including codes that can alternate with each other, codes that are deliberately redundant and should be used in synchrony, codes that complement each other, codes that supplement each other, etc.) (What is the communication code?);
- what channels of communication are available for designer-to-user metacommunication, and how they should or could be used (What is the channel?); and
- what he/she (the designer) wants to tell users and to what effect (What is the message?).

Figure 3.2 sketches the HCI design space structure in semiotic engineering. In it, the elements of Jakobson's model are identified for correspondence with the preceding list of decisions a designer must make when producing metacommunication artifacts for HCI.

Figure 3.2 also expresses the particular interpretation of the *computer as medium* concept and, by consequence, the type of computer-mediated human communication that is involved in my semiotic characterization of HCI. The computer is the channel through which both the higher-level designer-to-user one-shot message is conveyed, and the lower-level user-system communication is achieved as part of the metacommunication process. All messages (at higher and lower levels) are encoded in computational codes. Some of these messages unfold into other messages, while others may be atomic. Part of the global context of the designer-to-user metacommunication and the user-system communication can and must be encoded in the

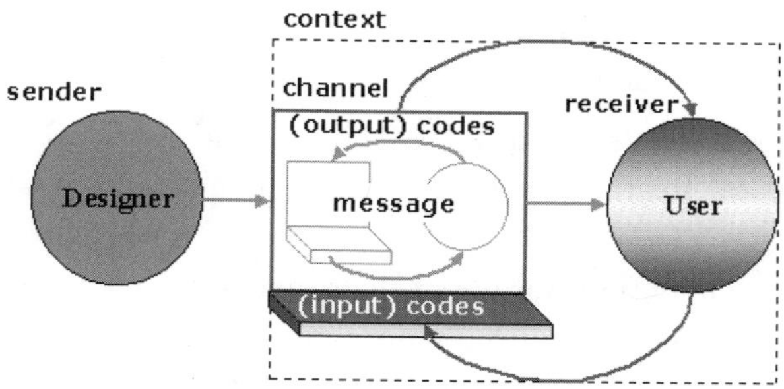

Figure 3.2
The HCI design space in semiotic engineering.

one-shot message from designers to users, so that it can play a role in the interpretation and production of signs pertaining to the user-system communication. The computational encoding of parts (or aspects) of the global context has the effect of filtering lenses. No matter how rich and dynamic the actual user's context may be, and in which directions it evolves, metacommunication can only picture a fixed set of meanings and semiotic processes encoded in the system's interface. Therefore, not only is the computer a *medium* for communication and metacommunication, but programs in the computer determine the codes, the channels, the messages, the contexts, and even the degree of freedom of interlocutors. In other words, we can expand the formula in many directions, saying that computers *are* the code, the channel, the message, the sender, and somehow even (especially in groupware applications) the user.

The problem with the metacommunication message characterization, so far, is its apparently passive ontological *status* and its unclear bond with its legitimate sender, the designer. Although I have said that the message sends and receives other messages, it is difficult to see why and when the unfolding communication would take place, and how it relates to the designer's intent. The concept of a *designer's deputy* completes the ontological underpinnings of HCI as viewed by semiotic engineering.

3.3 The Designer's Deputy

Semiotic engineering is committed to the view that software is an intellectual product. Just as Norman's theory of cognitive engineering (1986) underlined the fact that cognition is central to the user's activity, semiotic engineering is now emphasizing the fact that cognition is also central to the designer's activity. Both application designers and HCI designers are building artifacts that reflect their understanding and reasoning about a number of goals, constraints, opportunities, and challenges related to using computer technology to affect human life. Additionally, because the nature of software products is representational, both application designers and HCI designers are trying to *represent* their understanding and their intent in such a way that the users of their products can see what they mean. Hence the importance of pragmatics, and what Morris called biotic relations (see chapter 2), in an account of how users relate to computer artifacts.

The HCI designer is of course more closely involved in making users understand what he or she means. And, as has been shown so far in this chapter, the way to accomplish this task is through metacommunication. The designer's one-shot message to users is progressively unfolded and interpreted by the users as they communicate with the system. For metacommunication to proceed consistently and cohesively, the system must *speak for* the designer. If the system does not speak for the designer, either the designer's message is lost (supposing that users would be getting somebody else's message through the system) or metacommunication itself is canceled because some other agent (who is not speaking for the sender of the designer's message) suddenly gets in the way.

The system is thus the *designer's deputy*—a communicating agent that can tell the designer's message. Because the user communicates with the system, the designer's deputy must of course have elaborate communicative capacities. It must be able to communicate the contents of the one-shot message, which includes communication *about* what it can do.

The communicative (or discursive) competence of the designer's deputy must be analyzed in terms of *what* it can communicate and *how* it communicates it. The object of the designer's deputy discourse is exclusively related to the designer's one-shot message. For the sake of coherence and cohesion in the metacommunication process, no other topic of conversation should be allowed in user-system communication. Although this may seem to overconstrain the theoretical characterization of the designer's deputy (e.g., think of knowledge-based applications and learning systems that end up communicating about topics that were not foreseen by the designers of the original system), at closer examination we can see this must not be the case. AI applications are designed to "learn" or "acquire" predictable *kinds* of new knowledge (and no other). Therefore, in spite of not knowing the instances of new knowledge that an AI application will handle in real use situations, its designer certainly knows the types of knowledge involved (and how they are represented and processed by the system). Consequently, the cohesion and coherence of the designer's deputy's discourse in communication with the user can be maintained through the thread of knowledge types and instances.

The form of this communication may vary in many ways, but there are two opposite communicative orientations that roughly correspond to what has been previously referred to as *the model world* and *the conversation* paradigms in HCI (Hutchins, Hollan, and Norman 1986). The former assumes a *reified* designer's deputy (i.e., it is presented as a *thing*), and the latter assumes an *anthropomorphized* designer's deputy (i.e., it is presented as a human-like *agent*). Genuine all-reified or all-anthropomorphized designs are very rare, and they are hardly defensible in complex and extensive applications where the quality and quantity of tasks is large.

What we see in the vast majority of applications to date is a combination of both. Typically, some parts of the system reify the designer's deputy (which then appears in the guise of a tool or other physical object), whereas others anthropomorphize it (and the designer's deputy appears in the form of a guide, an expert, or some other sort of interface agent). The communicative challenges involved in choosing between the two alternatives center around the designer's answer to the following question: *How well will this deputy tell the users what I mean (including what I mean them to do)?* When combining alternatives (which amounts to splitting the designer's deputy's role into various specialized communicating entities, reified or anthropomorphized), the additional challenge is how to alternate them in such a way that the coherence and cohesion of the one-shot message discourse is not lost.

One of the advantages of introducing the designer's deputy as an ontological element in a theory of HCI is the explanatory power that is gained. The designer's deputy is a missing link in both traditional cognitive theories of HCI and in postcognitive theories as well. In the case of traditional theories, the missing link omits or rejects the effect of the designer's communicative intent. The fact that designers say that "they put affordances" in the system is less of a conceptual mistake (Norman 1999) than a strong intuition that the system is a *medium* for communication with users (de Souza, Prates, and Carey 2000). Notice that the designer's deputy handles design intent as a distinctive and crucially important part of its communications with users. In the semiotic engineering perspective, therefore, we do not need to talk about putting affordances in the interface, but we can certainly talk about the designer's goal of affording certain types of user experiences. And the expression of this intent can be elaborated and delivered through a variety of codes, depending on the selected guise of the designer's deputy.

Another interesting area in which the designer's deputy can play the role of a missing link is in many theories inspired by anthropology and social psychology (e.g., activity theory [Kaptelinin, Nardi, and Macauley 1999) or distributed cognition [Hollan, Hutchins, and Kirsh 2000]). The expansion that these theories have brought to the scope of analysis supported by traditional cognitive theories is considerable. They provided a rich account of the user's experience *in the world*, where the computer technology is present, and enlarged the designers' horizons about whom they were designing for and why. However, none of these theories has been particularly clear about how such expanded horizons translate into design products. The designer's deputy offers them a bridge into the nature of computer-based artifacts and an opportunity to explore the content and form of its interactive discourse in order to include the dimensions that each theory promotes as distinctive.

Empirical evidence of the designer's deputy's presence in HCI is scattered and incidental in many interfaces. Figure 3.1 provided such evidence. But a more common evidence that *someone* is speaking on the designer's behalf is, of course, online help. Another is the set of configuration dialogs present in most systems. In figure 3.3 we see a configuration dialog of the Opera© 7.11 browser. Notice how the designer's intent is being communicated when users are told about some particularly interesting things that can be done with the search string ("You can even store this sequence as a bookmark."). Other hints about how well the *system* knows the user come from the sentence in parentheses, talking about the place "where you normally enter Internet addresses." Of course it is the designer who knows the user, and the designer who is calling the user's attention to a neat feature of the system. But his or her

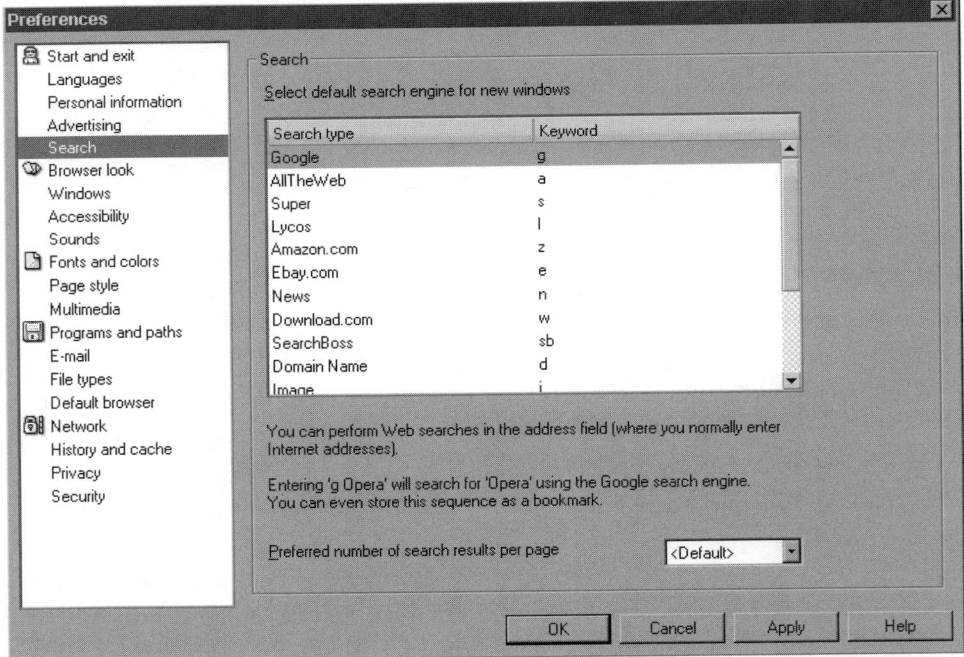

Figure 3.3
The designer's deputy discourse in Opera© 7.11's interface. Screen shot reprinted by courtesy of Opera Software ASA.

discourse *about* the system and *about* the user is being conveyed through the interface.

A full-fledged exploration of the designer's deputy's discourse can only be achieved if designers consciously recognize it as an element of HCI design. And because among the theories that have instructed the design of virtually all the existing interfaces to date none has explicitly included a designer's deputy or any equivalent element in its ontology, systematic evidence of how it affects HCI will only be obtained when semiotic engineering (or any other semiotic theory where the designer's deputy is accounted for) achieves critical mass. Internet applications, and e-commerce in particular, are very likely to be clients of this type of theory, for purposes of trust. The designer must convey the discourse of the system's *owner* along with his own. And we see traces of this explicit "first-person" discourse in statements like the one shown in figure 3.4. A condensed combination of trade owners, systems designers, and HCI designers produced the text offered to customers of Amazon.com. The opening sentence says that "Amazon knows that you care for how information about you is used." This is the trade owners' discourse. Later users are told to "Click here to see some examples." This is the HCI designer's discourse. A couple of lines after that, we see an explanation of "cookies" and how they are used to automatically extract information. This is the application's designers' discourse. The interesting point about this page is that it lets us anticipate the kinds of theories needed to support this type of design. Since communicating trust is such an important issue for the success of applications like this one, we need theories that can bring together all the various speakers who want to talk through the interface into an integrative framework for design. And semiotic engineering is a first step in this direction.

One last advantage of theorizing about the designer's deputy, before we move on to the semiotic engineering ontology of HCI, is to clarify some confusing aspects of *the computer as medium* approach (Reeves and Nass 1996; Andersen, Holmqvist, and Jensen 1993). In their work on who users think is the *source* of communication when they interact with computers, Sundar and Nass (2000) hypothesized that in the *computer as medium* paradigm, users would be talking to a *programmer*. Although I do not discuss Sundar and Nass's results here, the point of this reference is to show that the *computer as medium* paradigm does not imply that users are talking to programmers. They are most likely talking to designers (or perhaps the manufacturers and owners of technology), who know who the targeted users are, carefully analyze their intents, know their environment and requirements, and produce technology

Help > Privacy & Security > Privacy Notice

Amazon.com Privacy Notice

Last updated: April 3, 2003

Amazon.com knows that you care how information about you is used and shared, and we appreciate your trust that we will do so carefully and sensibly. This notice describes our privacy policy. **By visiting Amazon.com, you are accepting the practices described in this Privacy Notice.**

What Personal Information About Customers Does Amazon.com Gather?

The information we learn from customers helps us personalize and continually improve your shopping experience at Amazon.com. Here are the types of information we gather.

- **Information You Give Us:** We receive and store any information you enter on our Web site or give us in any other way. Click here to see examples of what we collect. You can choose not to provide certain information, but then you might not be able to take advantage of many of our features. We use the information that you provide for such purposes as responding to your requests, customizing future shopping for you, improving our stores, and communicating with you.
- **Automatic Information:** We receive and store certain types of information whenever you interact with us. For example, like many Web sites, we use "cookies," and we obtain certain types of information when your Web browser accesses Amazon.com. Click here to see examples of the information we receive. A number of companies offer utilities designed to help you visit Web sites anonymously. Although we will not be able to provide you with a personalized experience at Amazon.com if we cannot recognize you, we want you to be aware that these tools exist.
- **E-mail Communications:** To help us make e-mails more useful and interesting, we often receive a confirmation when you open e-mail from Amazon.com if your computer supports such capabilities. We also compare our customer list to lists received from other companies, in an effort to avoid sending unnecessary messages to our customers. If you do not want to receive e-mail or other mail from us, please adjust your Customer Communication Preferences.

Figure 3.4
Traces of many speakers talking through the Web interface of Amazon.com. Screen shot reprinted by courtesy of Amazon.com Inc.

that can meet the targeted users' needs and aspirations. Programmers need not have the least notion about any of these things. Second, the very idea of "the computer as source," which the study has tested and results have shown to be the favored hypothesis over "the computer as medium" one, might be refined into a "source in the computer" paradigm, which is more likely to be the precise case to test. The computer, in semiotic engineering terms, is the designer's deputy, which as we saw may appear in different guises. By introducing this element in the framework, we can possibly reconcile one of Sundar and Nass's caveats—that the participants of their experiment were computer-literate people who, of course, knew that "the computer" is not an autonomous source, although they responded to it in such a way as to exhibit social behavior that is typical of human interaction. This led them to conclude that a certain *anthropomorphism* of "the computer" happened even in the minds of savvy computer users. But the ontological stance of a designer's deputy may help us clarify the situation and proceed into finer distinctions about different representations of the designer's deputy and how people react to each of them.

3.4 A Semiotically Based Ontology of HCI

The sense in which I use the word *ontology* is not the one proposed by Gruber—*the specification of a conceptualization* (Gruber 1993). It is closer to the philosophical sense, in which an ontology expresses the categories of things that exist, from which follows a series of the relations among them. Since our subject matter, or domain, is specifically that of HCI, this *ontology* will be limited to the categories of interest for a comprehensive account of the phenomena that semiotic engineering tries to account for.

Four general categories comprise our ontology: namely, that of signification processes; that of communication processes; that of interlocutors involved in such processes; and that of the design space, from which HCI takes its shape. Signification processes will involve signs and semiosis. Communication processes will involve intent, content, and expression, as well as two differentiated levels of realization—direct user-system communication and mediated designer-to-user metacommunication. The interlocutors involved in HCI are designers, systems (the designers' deputies), and users. And finally the design space is characterized in terms of senders, receivers, contexts, codes, channels, and messages.

The ontology is intentionally minimal, condensing concepts like *human*, *machine*, *computer program*, *culture*, *grammar*, and others, in clusters like "user-system communication" or "metacommunication." The purpose of this condensation is to underline some very important epistemological and methodological commitments made by semiotic engineers and whoever uses this theory to understand more about HCI or to explore new possibilities in research and practice. The elements covered by the four categories are interrelated, as will be seen throughout the remainder of this book. In order to introduce the relations that will be explored in later chapters, I will define these elements in clusters.

3.4.1 Designer, System, and User

The designer, the system, and the user are the three necessary elements to frame HCI as a semiotic phenomenon. The majority of implicit or explicit ontologies assumed by other theories include only the system and the user. But if the designer is excluded from the root level of the ontology, systems must be postulated as autonomous signs—namely, signifying entities whose meaning exists exclusively by virtue of the user's semiosis. In this radical user-centered view, the system is devoid of many signifying dimensions that are intentionally added by the designer. As a consequence, curious ontological puzzles are encountered when it comes to explaining why people assign components of "human" semiosis (such as intent and beliefs) to *systems*. What is it about systems, as signs, that cause people to interpret them *as if* they belonged to another ontological category, namely, that of human beings? In semiotic engineering the system is a crystallization of a particular state (the final state) of the designer's semiosis with respect to what the user's expectations are and what the user's experience should be. And it conveys this crystallized semiosis to the user. During the process of HCI, the user spots traces of *some* human semiosis in the system and reacts accordingly. Although users may not (and typically do not) consciously identify the designer as the source of human semiosis in the system, the presence of the designer at the root level of an ontology of HCI allows us to theorize about how the system represents and achieves the designer's discourse in communicating with users.

3.4.2 Sender, Receiver, Message, Code, Channel, and Context

In a communicative process, a sender issues a message in order to achieve certain kinds of effects. The receiver is the one who gets the sender's message. The message is transmitted through a channel and must be encoded in a signification system that is shared by sender and receiver—the code. The message always refers to a context, which is the sum of all elements that affect the semiosis of sender and receiver involved in the same communication process. As mentioned in section 3.2, all of these components are causally related in the computer *medium*. And this has unique consequences for metacommunication in HCI.

3.4.3 Designer-to-User Metacommunication, User-System Communication, and Designer's Deputy

The designer-to-user metacommunication is a unidirectional and unique (one-shot) communication process in which the designer (sender) sends to the user (receiver) a message with the following content: "Here is my understanding of who you are, what I've learned you want or need to do, in which preferred ways, and why. This is the system that I have therefore designed for you, and this is the way you can or should use it in order to fulfill a range of purposes that fall within this vision." This message is encoded in one or more signification systems specially designed to enable user-system communication and is conveyed through the system (channel or *medium*) itself.

The view according to which message and medium collapse into one was popularized by Marshall McLuhan's aphorism *the medium is the message* (McLuhan [1964] 2002). His argument centered on the fact that each medium requires that messages sent through it be encoded and decoded in particular ways. In other words, in his perspective distinct cognitive styles for processing message contents are necessarily associated to different media, and this indissoluble determination of medium upon message allows us to conceptualize the two as one articulated whole. McLuhan has been criticized by some for his rather rhetorical formulation of the idea. An interesting critique came from Umberto Eco (1987), who used Jakobson's communication schema (the same used by semiotic engineering to structure the HCI design space) to show that McLuhan's evidence for his argument doesn't always refer to the channel. At times it refers to the code, and at other times it even refers to the form of the message (its expression). Eco's critique is particularly relevant for semiotic engineering because it points directly to how intricately the message (content and expression), the code, and the channel, in communication, may be associated to each other (and not only the message and the channel or the medium).

The user-system communication is a lower-level communicative process determined by higher-level metacommunication. In it a human being (the user, as sender or receiver) exchanges messages with a computer-based artifact (the system, as sender or receiver) using a constrained type of artificial codes—only those that can be processed by a computer program. Although the user, as a sender, may intend to achieve any number of effects and results by communicating with the system, the system is programmed to achieve only a fixed set of effects and results. Likewise, although the user's context for communication may vary freely, the system's "context" is structured around a fixed set of dimensions and elements that inexorably determine the way it processes the user's intent, content, and expression. This type of code ultimately determines the cognitive styles that must be used to process information and achieve successful communication. Furthermore, because these codes are themselves determined by the formal symbol-processing capacities of computer programs (the *medium*) through which messages are exchanged at all levels, McLuhan's broad statement that *the medium is the message* finds in HCI one of its finest pieces of evidence. And Eco's caveat about the mixture of dimensions that McLuhan seems to be talking about actually unveils the full complexity of HCI.

In a semiotic perspective the designer must be a root-level element in an ontology of HCI. But unless there is another ontological element that can channel the designer's metacommunicative intent to the users, there is no cohesive link between what the designer means to say through or with the system, and what the system means on the designer's behalf. The designer's deputy is the seat of the designer's intent and content at interaction time. It is thus a communicative constituent that legitimizes the system as a sender (i.e., an interlocutor endowed with intentional states) in user-system communication.[2]

3.4.4 Intent, Content, Expression, Signs, and Semiosis

The semiotic theory that provides the foundations for semiotic engineering discriminates between two basic processes: signification and communication. Signification is the process by which contents are systematically associated with expressions because of cultural determination. Communication is the process by which individuals use signification systems and other codes or signs (even ones that they may have invented) to achieve all sorts of purposes. It follows from this theory that intent, content, and expression are the fundamental constituents of communication.

In order to prevent important mistakes in knowledge built from this ontology, it is crucial to add one more element to it—semiosis. As was seen in chapter 2, semiosis is the unlimited sign-production process triggered by the presence of representations that stand for any quantity or quality of meanings. The process is unlimited in the sense that no one can fully predict its duration, its path, its content, and so on. Although some aspects of the process may be motivated (slanting duration, path, and content, e.g., in one direction rather than the other), the very nature of human mind and intelligence allows us to take another turn at any moment, and to halt it or resume at our will. So we see that computer programs are semiotically deprived of genuine semiosic capacities because semiosis violates the foundational Turing machine model. According to this model, a symbol-processing machine must obey a certain set of predetermined rules that dictate all and only the types of interpretations that the machine can assign to symbols. Thus, unlike humans, machine "semiosis" is predictable and limited by the rules that govern the machine's behavior. What this means in HCI is that the designer's deputy can only reproduce a limited (rule-governed) segment of the designer's semiosis. Therefore, in the process of user-system communication, the designer's deputy tells the user only a machine-processible version of what the designer really meant. And it tells it again and again, regardless of how the user's semiosis is freely evolving around the signs that are produced in this communication. From a semiotic perspective, this is the most important distinctive feature between the "H" and the "C" in HCI, one that can explain communicative breakdowns in human-computer interaction, but also—and more important—one that we can and must explore in design in order to expand the types of signification systems and artificial codes that we use to achieve the designer-to-user metacommunication with success and increase the quality of the user's experience in user-system communication.

3.5 Epistemological Considerations

The commitment of semiotic engineering to the concept of semiosis and its ontological status in a semiotic theory of HCI has very profound epistemological consequences. First, it requires more thorough examination of what we mean by *the user's meaning*, by *the designer's meaning*, and in truth by *meaning* altogether. The *meaning of meaning* has been the object of philosophical debate for many centuries. The classic work of Ogden and Richards (1946) contains this illuminating passage: "Normally, whenever we hear anything said we spring spontaneously to an immediate conclusion, namely, that the speaker is referring to what we should be referring to were we speaking the words ourselves. In some cases this interpretation may be correct; this will prove to be what he has referred to. But in most discussions which attempt greater subtleties than could be handled in a gesture language this will not be so" (15).

Since the early days of user-centered design, the goal of HCI design has hinged on the designer's ability to grasp a wide spectrum of the user's meanings with respect to a certain range of purposes and activities that the system should enable. For instance, the notions of "semantic and articulatory distance" were proposed by Hutchins, Hollan, and Norman as a way to measure the cognitive loads imposed to users by interface languages. The authors define such distances as follows: "Every expression in the interface language has meaning and form. Semantic distance reflects the relationship between the user intentions and the meaning of the expressions in the interface languages both for input and output. Articulatory distance reflects the relationship between the physical form of an expression in the interaction language and its meaning, again, both for input and output. The easier it is to go from the form or appearance of the input or output to meaning, the smaller the articulatory distance" (Hutchins, Hollan, and Norman 1986, 100).

We learn from semiotic theory that "the user's" side of these measures is not a fixed point. What the user (as a sender) *means* by an (input) expression and what the user (as a receiver) takes an (output) expression to *mean* is contingent on the communicative situation in which the expression arises. Although the authors correctly point out that any interface language has *a* (fixed) meaning (or a fixed set of discriminable meanings) that provides a static reference for measuring semantic and articulatory distances, it is not clear, either in their theory or in the voluminous work that has followed the cognitive engineering tradition, how semantic and articulatory distances are to be used in HCI design or evaluation. The *goal* of HCI design in this cognitive perspective is to build interface languages that are at a *small articulatory and semantic distance* from what the users *mean*. But, if the user's meaning can only be viewed as a transient state in an ongoing semiosic process, strongly determined by all its previous states, which design goal are we talking about? And what does it really mean to obtain one or another distance measure in a particular situation of use?

By embracing semiosis, semiotic engineering gives up the possibility of invoking the user's meaning to measure any *definitive* quality of HCI design. All measures of the user's meaning refer to the contingencies of the use situation where they were taken, and as such they point only to the factors that pertain to such contingencies. The unique advantage of such measures, if compared to similar measures in natural communication between humans, is that at one of its ends—the system's end—there is a semiotic agent who is only capable of reproducing exactly the same semiosic processes in the presence of a predictable and closed set of signs—the signs appearing in the interface language.

The role of culture in human communication is to function as a container of signs and meanings that "cohere in predictable ways into patterns of representation which individuals and groups can utilize to make or exchange messages" (Danesi and Perron 1999, 67). Such signs and meanings provide a signifying order that can be traced in individual and group semioses, although they are not the only factors determining how meaning is produced by individuals and groups, and consequently not the only factors determining how successful their communication will be. So, in an HCI context, there are two types of meanings whose distance from each other can be measured: interface language meanings (because they are fixed) and culturally determined meanings that appear in various segments of the users' semiosic processes.

What semiotic engineering enables us to *know* then is (a) the complete grammatical and semantic specification of the system's interface language (i.e., the system's signifying competence); (b) the complete specification of how the system functions as the designer's deputy (i.e., the system's communicating competence); (c) to what culturally determined signs and meanings the system's signifying and communicating competences are related; and (d) the role that this relation plays in contingent use situations. So, given what we can know, what should be the goal of HCI design? That we maximize the ratio of culturally determined signs and meanings in the system's signifying and communicating competence. This will prevent us from chasing moving targets if we really want to take semantic and articulatory distances as a basis for design and from misinterpreting contingent distance measures between the system's and the user's meanings as *definitive* evidence of the appropriateness of design.

In view of this reexamination of *meaning*, our next step in analyzing the epistemological commitments assumed by semiotic engineering is to raise a few questions about preliminary user studies and their role in requirements engineering. Ogden and Richards's caveat (1946) tells us that if we took sharing the same meaning as the fundamental criteria for successful human communication, we would possibly find out that human communication is, strictly speaking, never successful. To begin with, there is not a method to elicit the complete meaning of any sign from any human mind. Consequently, the notion of "same" should refer to only segments of the whole meaning. But which segments? Clearly, it is not the case that "any" segment will do. Our natural experience with human communication provides us with abundant examples of how partially shared meanings can lead us to serious trouble. Pragmatically oriented theories will try to determine the relevant segments by examining the receiver's reaction to the sender's message and what can be done with words (Austin 1962; Clark 1996; Hayakawa 1972; Searle 1979). All segments affecting the correspondence between the sender's intention and the receiver's reaction are relevant. But what may seem to be the expected behavior locally from a receiver in response to the sender's message may prove not to be so in a broader scope. For instance, let us revisit an HCI example presented in chapter 2 to illustrate how user and system are *not* communicating successfully from the beginning, although the problem only becomes evident further down the interactive path. In

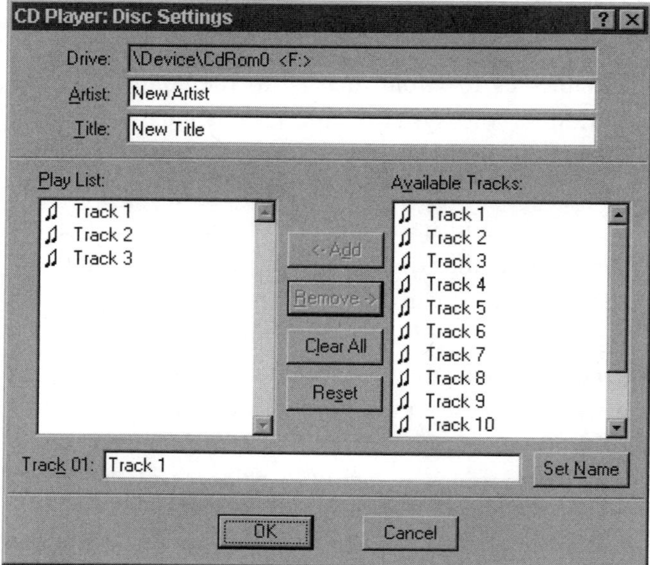

Figure 3.5
Programming playlists with Windows 98® CD Player. Screen shot reprinted by permission from Microsoft Corporation.

figure 3.5 we recall CD Player, a Windows application that plays CDs and allows us to program a listening session (see chapter 2). The dialog shown in the figure is the result of the following sequence of interactions:

1. The user inserts the CD in the CD-ROM drive (user's communication).

2. CD Player is launched and displays the number of tracks in the CD, a menu bar with various options, and a number of push buttons for playback control (system's communication).

3. The user opens the Disc pull-down menu and selects option Edit Play List (user's communication).

4. The system opens the dialog shown in figure 3.5 with the full list of tracks in both list boxes (Play List and Available Tracks), and four push buttons for adding, removing, clearing all, and resetting lists (system's communication).

5. The user selects the tracks that are to be removed from the playlist (user's communication).

6. The system enables the Remove →, the Clear All, and the Reset buttons (system's communication).
7. The user presses Remove → (user's communication).
8. The system shows the updated playlist on the left-hand side of the screen (system's communication).

At first sight, this might seem to be a successful piece of communication, since the system is doing what the user is asking for. But it may not be so (and often is not), as the example in chapter 2 shows. The user is not told by the system that the programming will extend to future listenings of the same CD. So, although we have a lot of local evidence that user and system are communicating successfully, another round of communication (days, weeks, months later) will probably show that something was wrong with this one.

So, going back to the epistemological issue under discussion, although pragmatic criteria for designating which segments of the user's semiosis must be captured in user studies, the scope of these segments is hard to determine. This example leads us to an important point about user studies and users' requirements analysis: Designers and analysts have their own semiosis going on before, during, and after they communicate with each other. So there is no such thing as a *complete* understanding of what the users mean, or of what the designers and analysts mean, when they seem to be talking *about the same thing*. Consequently, what seems to be the expected product of the requirements analysis and elicitation phases in many software development activities to date may in fact be a mirage. Rather than being a list of features and criteria that will make the system do what the user wants, it should be taken as a statement of the designers' and the analysts' interpretation of which elements of the user's semiosis should be accounted for by the system's semiosis. When they actually come to use the system, and live with it for a while, users will have different meanings and different situations to deal with, of course. And systems should be designed so as to respond productively and to communicate intelligibly in the presence of constant change.

A semiotic theory of HCI should then generate the necessary knowledge to help designers deal with patterns of change. Such patterns would be important in designing error messages, warnings, alerts, online help systems, and the like. All of these spring from the user's action being actually or potentially *different* from what the system *means* to say or do. In early user-centered design terms, we can say that semiotic engineering should provide the theoretical foundations for "designing for error" (Lewis and Norman 1986). But, not only this, patterns of change would also indicate how the system's semiosis could or should be adapted or extended to accommodate certain changes in the user's semiosis. Theoretical knowledge about how meaning evolves would then help designers produce systems with appropriate customization and end-user programming features, for example, two powerful mechanisms for handling contingencies of use situation in HCI.

The sum of these considerations is that semiotic engineering introduces a focal shift in what can be known in HCI and what designers can do with it. Whereas cognitive approaches focus almost exclusively on the users, and on what happens to them before and during interaction, our semiotic approach focuses on how the designer's semiosis (about the user's semiosis) can be crystallized in an interactive computer system that will communicate productively with users in the widest possible range of use situations. The types of knowledge pursued by semiotic engineering are then the ones that will identify the cultural underpinnings of semiosis, the patterns of change that can be represented and computed by means of interface language processors, the ways in which designers can express their design vision through computer-based metacommunication artifacts, and finally the ways in which the users' semiosis is affected by the designers' metacommunication at interaction time. This view is in line with Morris's perception (1938) that semiotics is an attractive instrument of science, because it forces us to address various aspects of meanings that may otherwise go unnoticed and undisputed in theoretical constructs.

3.6 Methodological Considerations

Psychological, anthropological, sociological, ergonomic, and computational theories should complement and supplement semiotic engineering with specific knowledge about human cognition and emotions, human activity, social structures and relations in groups and communities, the physical and environmental constraints for working with computers, and the kinds of symbol-processing machines that can be built. The main criterion for drawing a line between the contributions of semiotic engineering and those that must be complemented or supplemented by other theories is a methodological one.

First, semiotic engineering should not be used as a predictive theory. We can never fully predict how the users will get the designer's message. Although we can (as we do in human communication) raise expectations about the effect of certain communicative strategies and motivate semiosis along certain paths (and away from others), there is no way to determine exactly how somebody will interpret and use signs in communication, except in the case of highly rigid protocols (like login dialogs, physical interactions with the mouse, and so on) whose scope is too narrow to be of further interest.

Second, semiotic engineering should explain observable HCI phenomenon. The basic ontology in the theory contains the elements necessary to structure an explanation for any use situation of interest. The intrinsic quality of the explanation depends on the internal coherence of the explanatory discourse and on how observable evidence corresponds to the elements of such discourse. The extrinsic quality of the explanation depends, however, on the amount and the value of new information that it adds to explanations provided by other theories.

Third, semiotic engineering should provide the necessary means to formulate HCI design problems and questions and to elaborate the corresponding solutions and answers. Because meanings are always evolving, every HCI design problem is a unique design problem for which unique design solutions must be found. Therefore, one of the fundamental steps in HCI design is to be able to formulate and reformulate design problems, by asking relevant questions and exploring candidate answers productively. In a semiotic perspective, design should not be viewed as a matter of selecting the best matches between a repertory of design problems and a repertory of design solutions. Repertories of problems and solutions constitute the *culture* of design and provide signifying orders and signification systems for every unique design process.

It follows from this that the methods used in semiotic engineering research should always enhance the theory's explanatory power and increase the portions of HCI design culture that can be explicitly used in the elaboration and evaluation of unique designer-to-user metacommunication problems and solutions. Thus, the kinds of *design tools* that this theory is prepared to offer for professional design practice are essentially epistemic. They should help designers in constantly producing and analyzing new knowledge that is directly related to design issues. Semiotic engineering is totally aligned with Donald Schön's vision of what the design activity is and responds to his call for theories that will contribute to "an epistemology of practice" (Schön 1983). It provides researchers and designers alike with epistemic tools to expand their understanding of the nature of HCI and probe the possibilities of new metacommunication strategies.

3.7 Epistemic Tools for Semiotic Engineering

In Schön's view research and design are very similar. Both involve an iterative spiraling cycle of analysis and synthesis where knowledge plays the central role. Researchers and designers always participate in five major activities: problem approximation, problem formulation, generation of candidate solutions, evaluation of candidate solutions, and knowledge reorganization. Knowledge organization—determined by one's own current interpretation of his or her knowledge sources—feeds the other four activities and is itself fed by them. Every time an activity is successfully completed, it solidifies the knowledge that contributed to its success. And every time an activity is unsuccessful, it challenges the knowledge that was used to carry it on. Both researchers and designers are experienced practitioners of abductive reasoning (see chapter 2), although the goals and constraints involved in the abductive methods they use value different dimensions of the knowledge that is gained.

Every theory of HCI must contribute to the quality of HCI design products. Semiotic engineering has different types of epistemic tools that not only support research and expand its own frontiers, but also support the knowledge-centered activities in the design process. They are interpretive models, analytic principles, and analytic methods. From a research point of view, they all contribute to increasing the explanatory power of the theory and to synthesizing new epistemic tools. From a design point of view, they all contribute to naming and framing design problems, to synthesizing and evaluating solutions, and to elaborating metacommunicative strategies.

In figure 3.6 we see the main knowledge-based activities that are common to research and design processes, and where the preceding types of epistemic tools play a role in the knowledge process. Interpretive models are particularly important in going from design approximation to design formulation to the generation of solutions. Analytic principles are important in the generation and evaluation of solutions. And analytic methods are especially important for the evaluation of design solutions. All three types contribute to the (re)organization of knowledge, and all three relate to the ontological basis of semiotic engineering theory.

In the following chapters, interpretive models and analytical principles and methods will be illustrated with respect to three different areas of application for semiotic engineering: communicability evaluation and the organization of the designer's deputy discourse, the semiotic profile of interface and design languages

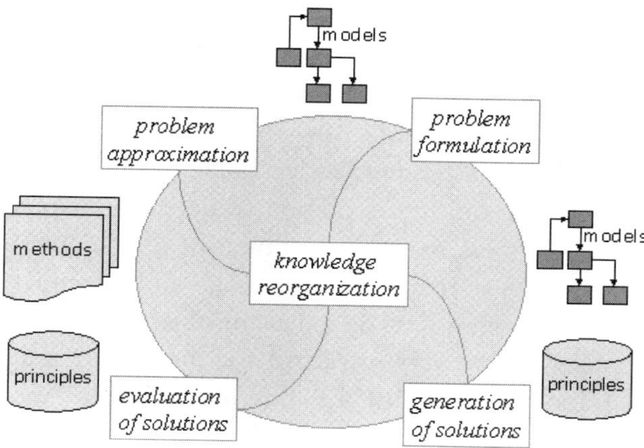

Figure 3.6
Epistemic tools and knowledge activities in research and design.

for end-user programming applications, and the structuring of communicative processes in multi-user applications.

As will be apparent, semiotic engineering is strongly committed to "representations." They are signs for those who produce them and those who interpret them. The most obvious signs I have discussed so far are the system itself and all the signs that appear in the system's interface language (either for input or for output). However, because the design vision is so crucially important for metacommunication in semiotic engineering, numerous representations that emerge along the design process are prime signs in HCI. The theory puts a special emphasis on models and other related representations of knowledge concepts that are produced and used in HCI.

In scientific research, models are one of the most useful tools for critiquing and advancing knowledge. But in design, especially in software design, models are often thought to be impractical for professional purposes. By adopting Schön's perspective on design, semiotic engineering views models as prime epistemic tools that must, nevertheless, be made more practical and efficient for the benefit of professional HCI design. Some portions of the models mentioned in the next chapters have been, and virtually all of them can be, programmed into computer tools to help designers accelerate the modeling process and document various parts of their semiosic processes. The important implication of the theory for design practice is that the latter is viewed by the former as a *rational* activity that continues during HCI itself, in smaller or larger scale. It is not that users are or should be eager to know the design rationale of the artifacts they interact with, because they are not, but that their semiosis must relate to the designer's semiosis, if communicative breakdowns are to be handled and resolved by systems at all. The ability of a system to "compute" the handling and resolution of communicative breakdowns directly depends on the designer's rationalization and representation of design principles, choices, assumptions, and goals. All of these must be the object of the designer's deputy explicit discourse. As a consequence, semiotic engineering will be an unattractive theory for those who do not or cannot view design as the object of rational explanatory discourse. But it is likely to be very attractive for those who want to bring concepts of AI to HCI and work toward the idea of "intelligent user interfaces."

II

Derivation

When your perception only equals that of your teacher,
you lessen the teacher's virtue by half.
When your perception goes beyond that of the teacher,
only then can you express the teacher's teaching.

—Zen saying

4

Communicability and the Designer's Deputy Discourse

There are many desirable "*-abilities*" in HCI: usability—the most famous, adaptability, applicability, extensibility, flexibility, reliability, predictability, sociability, and others. *Communicability* is the key quality of interactive computer-based artifacts for semiotic engineering. This does not mean that all other "*-abilities*" are unimportant or less important than communicability. It only means that, since our theory is specifically equipped to deal with communication and signification, our focal interest in HCI is the designers' ability to communicate the substance and qualities of their design through efficient and effective interface communication systems.

Cognitive theories of HCI have clarified some of the fundamental purposes of the kind of communication on which semiotic engineering focuses. For example, Norman's seven-stage model of user-centered HCI (1986) tells us that users have goals, which they achieve through seven iterated stages: (1) goal formation, (2) intention to act, (3) planning of actions, (4) physical execution of step(s), (5) perceiving the outcome, (6) interpreting perceptions, and (7) evaluating achievements in view of the original goal. HCI designers must therefore support users in achieving their aim by communicating: the range of goals that the system is centrally designed to achieve; the various methods that can be used to achieve them; the interface signs that can be used to activate the system to perform the various steps in a method; and the signs that tell users what the system's response is to their intervention.

But opportunistic behavior plays an important role in human achievement, and rational planning is not the only (and not necessarily the best) way of meeting our ends. Suchman, for instance, suggests that in every different situation we "negotiate" steps in the face of possibilities and adapt our plan sketches to the circumstances around us (Suchman 1987). This point is also raised in the context of activity theory (Bødker 1989), which calls our attention to the fact that activities are intrinsically dynamic. They change and evolve all the time, which makes it impossible to predict exactly how somebody will go about achieving even a customary goal. The message for HCI design is that strict plan-based problem-solving methods may be good for building algorithmic models of intelligent behavior (and AI applications), but they should not be used to model the users' behavior while interacting with computer artifacts.

A semiotic theory of HCI is particularly attractive because it contains the ingredients to address many important aspects of other theories and approaches. First, it unveils the fact that all *action* involved in HCI is primarily communicative. In other words, all that is achieved in HCI depends on *speech acts* (see chapter 2) uttered by the user or by the designer's deputy. As a consequence, the user's goals, plans, and activities have by necessity a semiotic extension. They must be cast in the form of signs. The most fundamental role of the designer's deputy is to *tell* the user which signs are available for the casting, which meanings they systematically take on in various interactive situations, and which range of responses to the user's speech acts can be communicated back to the user and how. Second, as a central concept in the theory, *semiosis* not only explains but in fact predicts that computationally encoded meanings pertaining to the signification system in any system's interface will trigger unlimited interpretation possibilities in the users' minds. Some of these possibilities will coincide with the original designer's expectations (and yield successful results), others will not. The latter are the prime object of HCI evaluation, either because they lead to failure during interaction, or because they point to productive resignification (a repurposing of the available signs). Interactive failures (and how to avoid them) are the focus of nearly every method of HCI evaluation. However, resignification indicates some interesting qualities of software applications like applicability (to how many different things can it be applied? [Fischer 1998]) and flexibility (in how many different ways can the users achieve a particular set of goals? [Shneiderman 1998]), for example. These qualities open the path to designing and evaluating interactive adequacy in accordance with the criteria favored by ethnographic studies and activity theory.

This chapter starts by showing how HCI designers can evaluate the communicability of the artifacts they design. It then shows how they can enhance communicability by elaborating the metacommunication discourse conveyed by various online help functions. The chapter also shows why and how the existence of explicit underlying models of the artifact (e.g., a user model, a task model, and an interaction model) can improve the user's experience from a communicative perspective (and hence improve it in a number of related dimensions).

4.1 Communicability Defined

Communicability is not a new term for the HCI community. Mullet and Sano have included it as one of their five principles for an efficient use of images in the design of visual interfaces (Mullet and Sano 1995). For them, "The communicability of any representation depends on a shared context between sender and receiver that allows signs to be interpreted within a pragmatics comparable to the one under which they were encoded" (188). For semiotic engineering, communicability extends beyond the realm of images. It applies to all the signs included in the various communication codes that constitute the system's interface. In other words, it extends to the whole signification system that enables HCI within the scope of a particular application.

In our theory, communicability is the distinctive quality of interactive computer-based systems that communicate efficiently and effectively to users their underlying design intent and interactive principles (Prates, de Souza, and Barbosa 2000). This is a metonymic formulation of the concept, which transfers to the design (the product) a capacity that is in fact expected from the design*er* (the producer). The metonymy is commonly used and has appeared, for example, in Brown and Duguid's understanding of the nature and goal of HCI design. See, for instance, the following passage:

> Ultimately, all artifacts have to be interpreted through some codes, which might encompass such relative but powerful intangibles as attitude, reputation, and intuition. Design must either try actively to engage in the construction and adoption of codes for interpretation or else passively accept the codes that users will themselves inevitably construct and engage. We do not claim that design can determine what codes are used. But it can, like all communications, attempt to cue relevant sets of codes and to dismiss others. (Brown and Duguid 1992, 170)

Brown and Duguid (1992), for whom "tools are cultural artifacts" (166), were discussing semiotic engineering *avant la lettre*, although they were trying to relate culture (or cultural codes) to artifact affordances. Communicability has everything to do with cueing relevant sets of interpretive codes and dismissing others, but it is less about affordances than about discourse. In semiotic terms, the task of HCI designers is to build a complex system of interactive *types* according to which users produce a potentially infinite set of interactive *tokens*. They must build a *language* for interaction. And because this *language* can be made of heterogeneous types of signs, it is more precisely characterized as an interactive *signification system* (with formally definable lexical, syntactic, semantic, and pragmatic components). High communicability discourse produced in accordance with this system cues a kind of semiosis (in the users' minds) that is compatible with the semantic and pragmatic definitions of the implemented interface language, whereas low communicability discourse cannot do it.

Moreover, communicability starts with interpretive codes but extends to expressive ones. Interactive discourse is produced by both the users and the designer's deputy. Both codes are hiding underneath the term *affordance*. For instance, the affordance of a sign type like 10 ▾ is "click & pull down." As part of an interpretive code, users will take it to mean something the designer's deputy is saying, such as "have a look at possibilities and choose one (or more)." But as part of an expressive code the same sign type will mean something the users can say themselves, such as "my choice is 10" or "see what I've chosen." The communicability of free text entries, for instance, is different from that of pull-down lists. Whereas in the latter the user is made aware of all existing choices the designer's deputy is able to interpret, in the former the impression he gets (though potentially erroneous) is that the designer's deputy can handle any sign that the user can produce through the available input devices. This simple illustration shows, additionally, that although designers cannot truly determine the interpretive codes that users will adopt during interaction, they can and do determine the expressive codes that users will employ to communicate with the system.

Communicability can thus be more technically defined as the designer's deputy capacity to achieve full metacommunication, conveying to users the gist of the original designer's message. This message, as seen in previous chapters, will tell the users what the designer's understanding of who they are is and what they want or need to do, in which preferred ways, and why. It will also tell them about the system that the designer has built for them based on what he knows, and how they can or should use it in order to fulfill a range of purposes that fall within the original designer's vision. Communicability applies to both interpretive and expressive codes that the designer's deputy handles for generating and interpreting messages during situated interaction with users.

4.2 Traces of Communicative Breakdowns during Interaction

No one can predict which is *the* precise meaning a user ascribes to any particular interface sign. Semiosis is an ongoing sign interpretation process that pragmatically settles around some meaning configuration when the interpreter no longer has the need, the impetus, the resources, or the means to continue. This situation poses an important epistemological challenge for evaluating the communicability of interface signs. When can we say that high communicability has been reached? Mullet and Sano's answer—when the user's interpretation is produced "within a pragmatics comparable to the one under which they were encoded" (1995, 188)—is correct but of little help if we think that the set of situations we are talking about is infinite. Not even statistical methods can be safely used when it comes to sampling the infinite. Therefore, we need something else. A simple example of what is at stake is the communicability of the sign that appears in current Windows applications. At times it will mean "close," at others "cancel," or even "abort process." But depending on what happens next to the user's clicking on it, it may also mean "no harm done" or "all data will be lost" (some old DOS applications running from Windows clearly capture this clicking event and warn the users against possible harm to their data). And even when data is lost, the type of data may be irrelevant to the user (which brings "all data will be lost" close to its obvious opposite "no harm done"). So what is "comparable pragmatics"? Or, more precisely stated, what does this criterion mean?

Instances of low communicability, however, are much easier to capture although the significance of the problem they are associated with may vary widely (as one would expect from an infinite set of pragmatic mismatches between what the user means or takes the system's signs to mean, and what is encoded in the underlying programs). These instances are signaled by numerous patterns of slips, mistakes, and failures that can be spotted during interaction. So communicability evaluation starts from examining communicative breakdowns, and from there certain aspects of communicability, not necessarily negative, are inferred. By necessity, this evaluation can only refer to situated interaction where the user's and the designer's deputy's discourse can be pragmatically interpreted in view of the actual circumstances of their mutual communication.

To illustrate the kinds of communicative breakdowns that semiotic engineering is prepared to evaluate, let us look at a very simple example of problematic designer-to-user communication through the designer's deputy discourse. The scenario for the illustration is the following:

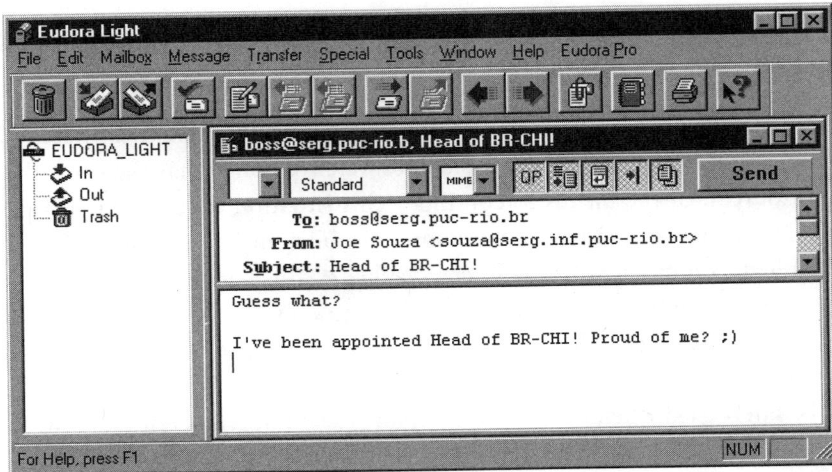

Figure 4.1
Composing messages with Eudora® 3.6. Screen shot reprinted by courtesy of Qualcomm Incorporated.

> Joe is using Eudora® 3.6 to handle his email. He has a standard signature that is automatically included at the end of the messages he sends, although he cannot see the signature text on screen while he composes a message. For example, the message he is about to send to his boss (see figure 4.1) will include Joe's standard signature, "Joe Souza—Usability Engineer (souza@serg.puc-rio .br)," right below the message body. But now that Joe has been appointed Head of BR-CHI, he wishes to create and use an alternate signature: "Joe Souza—Head of BR-CHI (souza@serg.puc-rio.br)." He easily finds out how to create the alternate signature (see figure 4.2), then sets out to switch signatures for the message he is about to send to his boss. He wants to sign it as Head of BR-CHI (new alternate signature) instead of as Usability Engineer (current standard signature).

In the illustrated narrative, we can follow Joe's interaction with Eudora 3.6 Light closely. The screen shots give the necessary context for interpreting our narrative of Joe's thoughts and actions. His reactions are occasionally expressed by special utterances ("Where is it?", "I can't do it this way," "I can do otherwise," and "Looks fine to me") that are used in the communicability evaluation method presented in

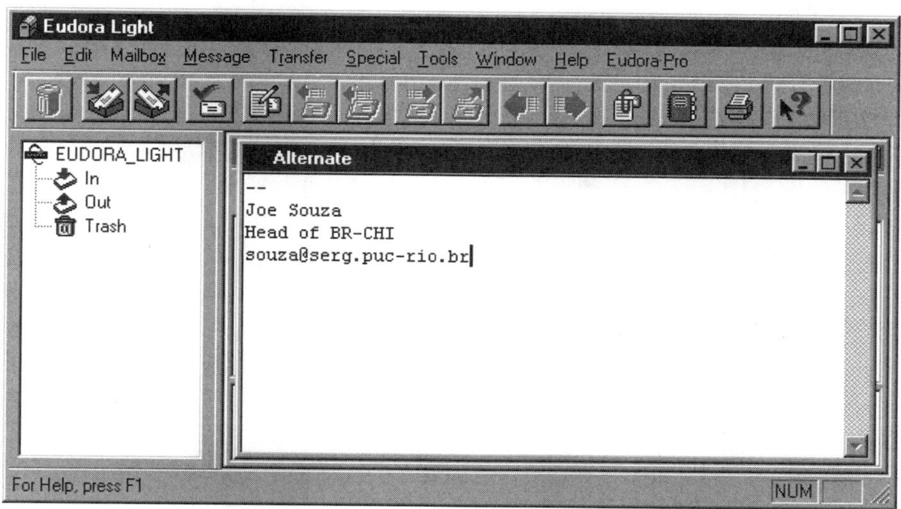

Figure 4.2a
An attempt to switch signatures using the Tools > Signature menu option. Screen shot reprinted by courtesy of Qualcomm Incorporated.

the next section. They characterize a hypothetical response of the user in face of the designer's deputy's discourse, and for now it suffices to take them at face value.

Joe goes back to the Tools menu in search of an option to switch his signature from standard to alternate. The menu options are the same he saw when he wanted to create an alternate signature, but he thinks that maybe now that he has already created one, choosing Signature should perhaps lead him to switching a function. But what he gets from the system is access to the same editing function he just used to create the alternate signature (see figure 4.2.a).

Oops!

Joe closes the editing window and starts over. He looks for an option switch signatures in other pull-down menus, like Special (see figure 4.2.b).

Where is it?

Since he cannot find what he wants in the Special menu options, he moves on to another menu. This time he tries the Message menu (see figure 4.2.c).

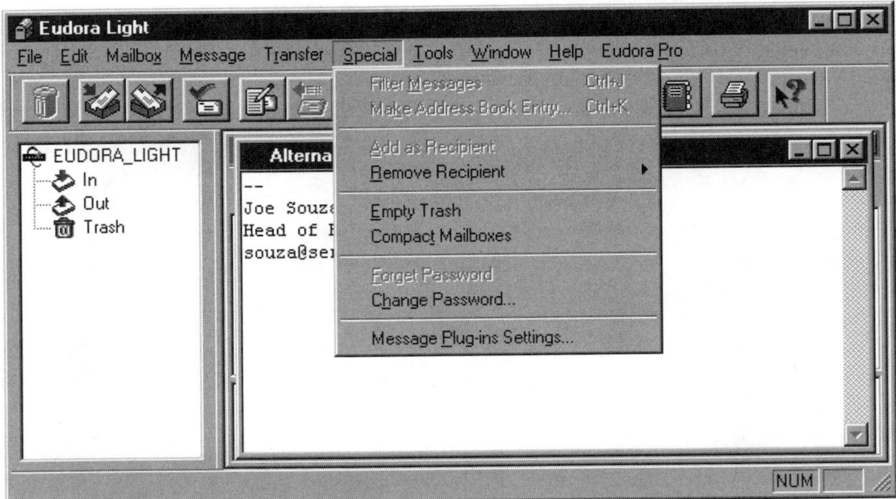

Figure 4.2b
Looking for an option to switch signatures in the Special menu. Screen shot reprinted by courtesy of Qualcomm Incorporated.

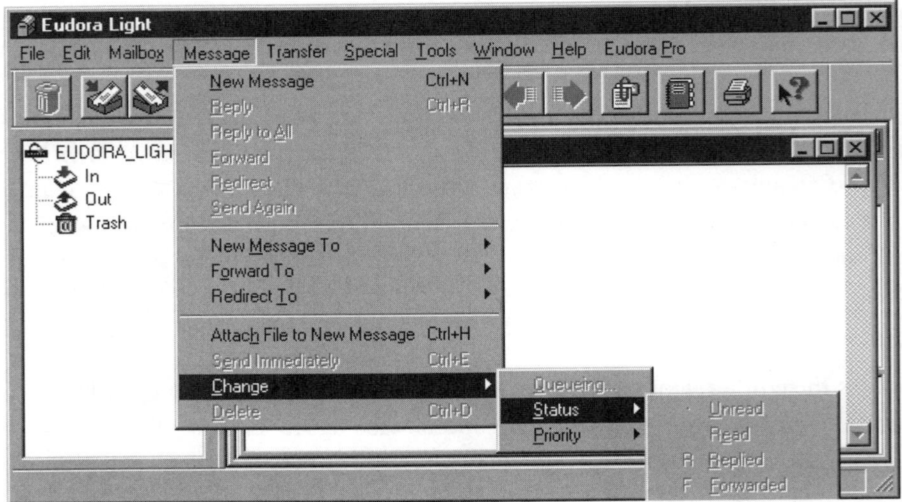

Figure 4.2c
Another frustrated attempt in the Message > Change > Status menu. Screen shot reprinted by courtesy of Qualcomm Incorporated.

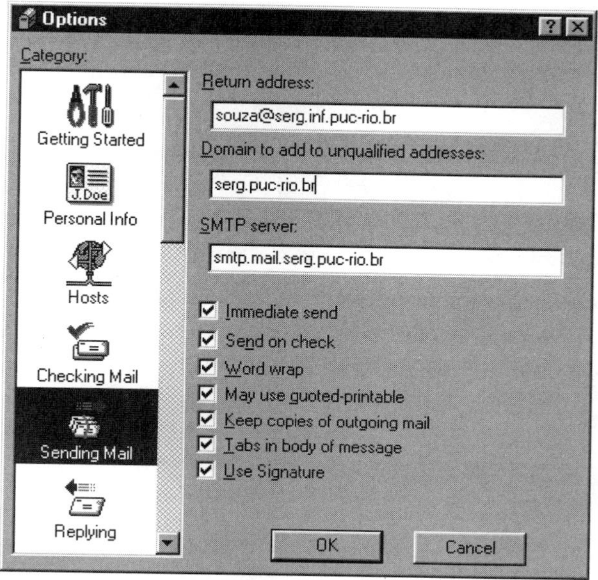

Figure 4.2d
Joe explores Options offered by Eudora®. Screen shot reprinted by courtesy of Qualcomm Incorporated.

There he inspects the Change option, and then Status, but finds nothing useful there either (see figure 4.2.c).

Where is it?

He looks into various menu options, but still cannot find it.

I can't do it this way.

He finally decides to change strategy and to frame his problem as a configuration one. So, he explores the Options menu. But . . . no hope there either (see figure 4.2.d).

I can do otherwise.

Frustrated by useless searches, Joe decides to take a radical step. He opens the alternate signature file (Tools > Signatures > Alternate), copies the new signature text, closes the editing window, switches to the message composition window, and pastes the alternate signature at the end of the message. There goes the message with a new signature! (see figure 4.2.e).

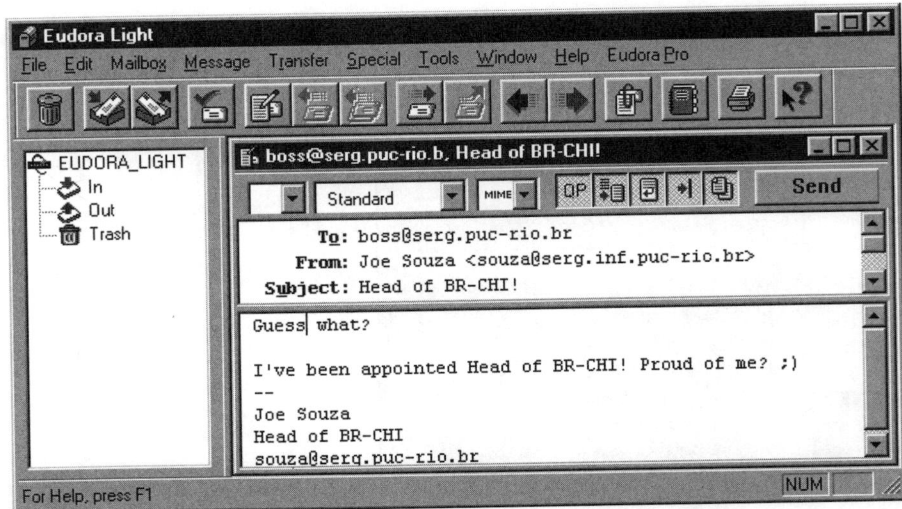

Figure 4.2e
Joe copies and pastes his alternate signature at the end of his message. Screen shot reprinted by courtesy of Qualcomm Incorporated.

> *Looks fine to me!*
>
> What Joe forgets, however, is that the standard signature is automatically appended at the end of every message marked to be signed with the standard signature. So he actually hasn't done what he first wanted to do.

The way to change signatures is very simple once you know it: It suffices to select the value alternate (instead of the default standard) in the pull-down list right above the message composition canvas (figure 4.2.f). But the communicability of the designer's deputy's discourse has some fundamental problems. First, it does not give the user a clue of what these values refer to. Second, it inexplicably switches the code type for communicating actions involving standard and alternate signatures. Whereas you create and edit them through menu selection, you can only switch them through selecting from a unique pull-down list in the interface. In terms of Umberto Eco's Theory of Sign Production, presented in chapter 2, this is clearly a case of what he calls *ratio difficilis*, or a difficult relation to establish between expression and content, given the existing codes where this relation is known to hold systematically.

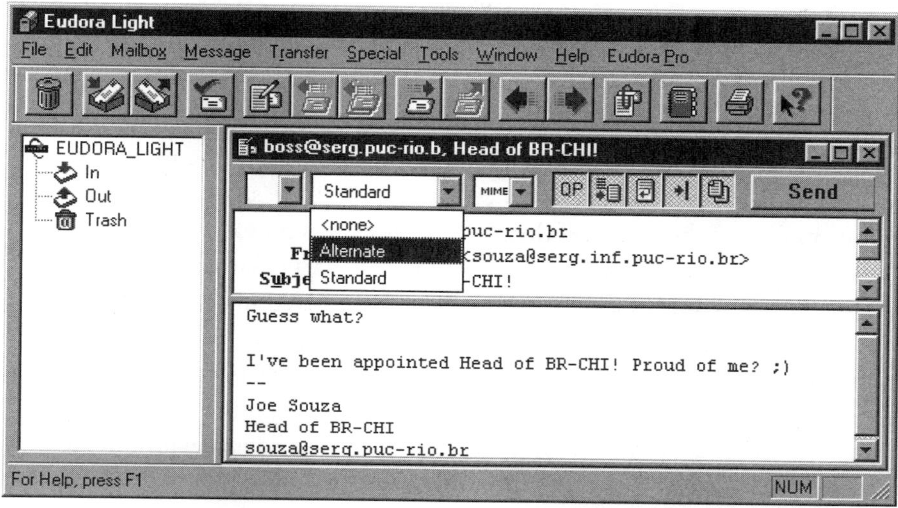

Figure 4.2f
How to switch signatures in Eudora®. Screen shot reprinted by courtesy of Qualcomm Incorporated.

Later versions of Eudora have a much more elaborate interface for signatures and *personas* that the user can create and choose from. Moreover, many usability checklists commonly used by designers would have spotted the problem in this interface. What semiotic engineering *adds* to the picture is a more perspicuous characterization of the problem, and hence a qualitative indication of potential solutions. First, it shows us the articulation between interpretive and expressive codes in interface languages. Joe's problem was that he could not *tell* the "system" that he wanted to switch signatures. This is an expressive problem. The designer's deputy, however, was *telling* Joe how he could switch signatures—by activating a particular pull-down list right above the message composition canvas. But Joe did not get it. This, in its turn, is an interpretive problem. So, when interpretation and expression don't come together in communication, there is actually no communication.

Second, in the face of this communicative breakdown, Joe reframes his problem from one of switching signatures to one of inserting a particular textual content at the end of a message he is about to send, which *tells* us his conception of what a signature is. But the message "as-sent" is not identical to the message "as-seen," and this indicates to the designer that his sign for the presence of the standard signature (the value "standard" selected in the pull-down list above the message) is much weaker than the user's sign for the alternative signature (the actual text in it, at the end of the message). This is a valuable contrast in the (mis)use of signs in the encoded interface signification system. It gives the designer an indication of preferential sign types with which to encode the system's feedback to the user. The more closely the types adhere to the user's conception of what the signs mean, the better. A semiotic analysis of this sort will then tell the designers not only that better feedback must be given, but also what is "better" in this particular case.

Third, the fact that Joe mistakenly thought he had solved his problem (when he actually hadn't, or at least had not solved it as he first meant to) points to yet another problem in communication. Joe doesn't fully master the expressive code he is using to communicate with the system. He is prone to interpreting the system's signs in such a way that he finds evidence that his semiosis is in accordance with the encoded signification system, when it isn't. And in this case, the mismatch is affecting him (even if he is not aware of it). So the signification system is giving him the opportunity to strengthen wrong beliefs—a dangerous path in HCI. The ability to capture the problem and to analyze it in detail will give the application's designer the capacity to trigger his own semiosis and think more globally about his design. For example, the most obvious solution to all of these problems would be what more recent versions of Eudora actually do: adopt a WYSIWYG (what you see is what you get) strategy and automatically include the current signature text at the bottom of the text area where users can compose new messages. In Joe's situation, different problem-framing and problem-solving strategies could emerge if Eudora followed the WYSIWYG pattern. We might see some of the following alternatives:

- Joe would wish to create the new alternative signature *before* he started composing the message to his boss. In this case, he would create it with the same kind of interactive discourse he used in the original scenario, but the designer would have to help him tell the system that his new message to his boss should be signed with the alternate signature. A number of possibilities would arise, among them a more elaborate interaction to start message composition or a default unsigned composition mode that would always require a specification of which signature to use.
- Joe would wish to create the new alternative signature *after* he started composing the message to his boss. This would lead the designer to consider more carefully interactive discourse regarding message composition. If, for example, the

editing task started with a default unsigned message, the user would *always* have to specify explicitly which signature should be used. This is totally impractical if the vast majority of one's messages uses the same signature (the standard signature, according to this application's signification system). The very idea of a standard signature would not make much sense if the effort to use it were the same as that of using any other signature. But if the editing task started with the standard signature automatically inserted at the bottom of the text, Joe's problem could come up again. What should he do to replace that text with another? Probably, having the standard signature in the same text area as the message would lead to complicated problems: Would it always be possible to automatically delete just the portion of the text in that area corresponding to the message body? Or should the signature be in a different text area? Depending on the designer's solution, the shortest path to solving the problem would actually be Joe's copy-and-paste strategy, no matter how clumsy it looked to us in the previous story.

These considerations show that communicability evaluation deals with the user's and the designer's semiosis, and also—as will be seen in the following sections—with the evaluator's. It is a prime instrument for reflection in action, with the advantage that the categories of objects and phenomena to which it is explicitly related can guide the designer's reflection through the design space. These categories emerge from the semiotic engineering ontology for HCI and are centered around perlocution or perlocutionary acts (see chapter 2) associated with both the user's and the designer's deputy's illocution, or illocutionary acts. Major and minor failures in getting the listener to do exactly what the speaker expects can be distinguished and analyzed, helping the designers understand and resolve communicative breakdowns in HCI.

HCI encompasses speech acts performed by the user and the designer's deputy. Both produce illocutions where expression, content, and intent bring about some effect on the state of affairs—perlocution. When perlocution is completely consistent with illocution—that is, when the effects achieved by what is said fully coincide with what was meant to be the case—communication is totally successful. Otherwise, there are various types of problems, implying various degrees of severity, which can be distinguished according to the discrimination principle presented here. Global illocution and perlocution refer to the top-level intent of communication. Local illocution and perlocution refer to lower-level goals, produced on the way to achieving the original top-level goal.

If global illocution is not consistent with global perlocution, then this categorizes complete failures (I) of which

- the user may be aware (Ia)
- the user may not be aware (Ib)

If global illocution is consistent with global perlocution *but* local illocution is not consistent with local perlocution, then this categorizes temporary failures (II) where

- the user's semiosis may be momentarily halted because (IIa)

1. he cannot find the expression to convey the content and intent of his illocution
2. he cannot understand the designer's deputy illocution
3. he cannot find an appropriate intent to compose his own illocution

- the user realizes that he must reformulate illocution because (IIb)

1. the context of his illocution was wrong, although his intent was right
2. the expression of his illocution was wrong, although context and intent were right
3. the intent of his illocutions along a many-step abductive path was wrong

- the user studies the designer's deputy's illocution by (IIc)

1. engaging in implicit metacommunication
2. engaging in explicit metacommunication
3. engaging in autonomous sense making

If local illocution is consistent with local perlocution, then this categorizes partial failures (III) with

- potential residual problems for the user because he does not understand the designer's deputy's illocution, and thus somehow fails to do exactly what is expected (IIIa)
- no residual problems for the user because he fully understands the designer's deputy illocution, but somehow fails to do exactly what is expected (IIIb)

What this principle tells us is that there are three main communicative categories in communicability evaluation: complete failures (I); temporary failures (II); and partial failures (III). Other important factors notwithstanding, such as the frequency of breakdowns and the effort required to recover from them, these categories may correspond to different levels of severity. Complete failures are typically the most severe ones, whereas partial failures are usually less severe, especially if there are no residual problems in the user's interpretation. Temporary failures fall in between the two. Subsequent subcategorizations address more specific problems related to the origin or cause of the breakdown. Ranging from problems with the user's finding the right form to convey valid contents and intents to her being totally unable to think of a valid intent given the situation, breakdown subcategories can draw the evaluator's attention to some important semiotic characteristics, desirable or undesirable, that the designers should take into account.

Misunderstandings and disruptions may be related to different aspects of goal-directed (purposeful) activities. The user's semiosis may be mistaken with respect to the establishment of goals themselves, to the plans she has devised to achieve her goals, or else to the operations that are needed to carry out plans and achieve goals. These levels can be characterized, respectively, as strategic, tactical, and operational. It is interesting to see that some problems at a relatively lower level, such as faulty operations, can propagate to higher levels. For instance, if the user's goal is to create and edit HTML pages for a small Web site she is about to set up for herself, her inability to understand how to insert tags or create lists and tables using a particular HTML editor may lead to different outcomes. The user may give up using that editor and begin looking for some other tool (e.g., another HTML editor or a generic text editor that can save text in HTML format). She may also give up her entire plan (e.g., she may ask somebody else to do the job for her). Yet another possibility is that the user gets to *simulate* lists, tables, and other formats. She may, for example, use indentations and tab spaces, which replicate the same visual effects in a number of contexts, but bring up problems in others (like when HTML pages are resized with a browser). Thus, difficulties in taking the right actions to perform a task—or, in our semiotic framing of the problem, difficulties in finding an expression for the illocution to convey valid contents and intents—is a breakdown at the operational level that may lead to complete failures at the strategic level (the user discards the alternative to use the editor to produce the desired HTML pages), or to partial failures at the strategic level (simulated list and table formats are lost if pages are resized with a browser) derived from the user's adoption of the wrong tactics (*simulating* formats instead of specifying them correctly). In the latter case, the residual communicative problem is clear—the user will not realize that she has misinterpreted the tool until she sees a messy visualization of the pages she created. And until then, she may have repeated the wrong tactics in a number of other situations.

Such finesse in the analysis of communicative problems is particularly important for a semiotic approach. By exploring the traces of abductive paths followed by designers at design time (captured in the designer's deputy's discourse) and by users at interaction time (captured in tests and experiments), an evaluator may uncover crucial qualitative aspects of the signification system constructed by the designer in view of the one(s) that users actually master and prefer to use. In the next sections the categorization of communicative breakdowns, as well as their significance for HCI evaluation and design, are explained in detail.

4.3 Evaluating Communicability in HCI

The semiotic engineering method for evaluating communicability is based on observing a number of users' purposeful experiences with an application. It concentrates on analyzing certain (critical) parts of the application. The users' behavior during interaction is analyzed and interpreted with respect to the communicative breakdown categories mentioned earlier. The interpretation can be enriched by specific mappings and relations between these categories and any number of usability principles or guidelines, as well as categories or classes of problems dealt with in other theories. Evaluation is completed at the semiotic profiling stage, with an in-depth account of the designer-to-user metacommunication. An analysis of interface signification codes, and of how they are used by the designer's deputy and the user to produce discourse at interaction time, provides the elements that can trigger the designer's semiosis about various possibilities for the current application's (re)design or for the design of other applications. The communicative potential of certain interactive design patterns can be used to organize a knowledge base with valuable practical cases and to encode design culture.

4.3.1 Tagging User-System Communication

The first step in communicability evaluation is tagging a user's interaction with communicability utterances. It consists of "putting words in the user's mouth," in a kind of reverse protocol analysis. The evaluator watches a playback (or any equivalent reconstruction) of the user's interaction and searches patterns of behavior that correspond to the categories and subcategories mentioned in section 4.2. Such communication problems as the user's being unable to interpret some interface element, not finding where an expected element is, misinterpreting the meaning of perceived elements, and so on, are paired with one or more communicability utterances, according to the evaluator's semiosis and professional skill. For example, in the previous Eudora scenario, Joe was mistaken about what the option Alternate in the Tools menu meant, once an alternate signature was created. He thought that in a post-creation situation it could mean "activate your alternate signature." But it only meant "create or edit alternate signature." The evaluator then puts the utterance "Oops!" in Joe's mouth when she watches the playback and sees that he realizes his mistake and backtracks. She tags that particular span of interaction with "Oops!" Further along in the scenario, Joe is searching for an option that will allow him to switch his signature from standard to alternate. Following the same procedure, the evaluator tags this other span of interaction with the utterance "Where is it?" The set of basic communicability utterances that can be tagged to interaction spans is fixed and will be presented in detail in section 4.4. Some of them have been used in the Eudora example, such as "I can't do it this way," "I can do otherwise," and "Looks fine to me." The outcome of the tagging step is a set of associative pairs aligning spans of recorded HCI phenomena with communicative utterances (see figure 4.3).

Tagging is only applicable to goal-directed activities. Therefore, it must be preceded by a preparation step where the following occurs:

- The evaluator studies the application in order to form a preliminary assessment of the designer's metacommunication message.
- The evaluator selects crucial portions of the applications that will be used in communicability evaluation tests. Crucial portions are typically those where the evaluator senses the possibility of communicability problems. Occasionally the designers themselves may want to evaluate certain portions of the design in order to gain deeper understanding about the effects of their choices. Alternatively, such portions

Figure 4.3
An association of recorded interaction phenomena and communicability evaluation utterances.

may also be selected because they have been analyzed using other evaluation methods, for purposes of comparison or confirmation of various results.

- The evaluator prepares use scenarios that will maximally elicit communicative aspects of HCI in the context of the selected portions of the application, and recruits a number of participants (usually 3 to 10) that fairly represent the application's "typical user."
- The evaluator elaborates questionnaires and/or interview scripts that participants will be requested to answer before and/or after the test.
- The evaluator procures the means to (a) register the participants' interaction (e.g., using input/output capture software, video cameras, or any other equivalent means); (b) annotate interaction while she watches the participant's activity using a clone-display, a mirrored window, or plain over-the-shoulder observation; and (c) to archive the collected data in appropriate *medium* for multiple reviews and examinations.

Depending on whether the evaluation is made at early formative stages of design or later, the nature of communicability breakdowns that can be identified, as well as the way in which data is collected and interpreted, will vary. For example, using input/output capture software is impossible if a computational representation of the application is not available. Again, taking the Eudora example as a basis, if only a sketch of the various screens were available, then the scenario would have to be run differently. Instead of clicking and activating the interface as Joe did, he would probably just indicate to the evaluator what his next step would be. Therefore, instead of pulling down the Special and Message menus in search of an option to switch signatures, he would probably just tell the evaluator something like "Then I click here" or "Then I open this menu." The evaluator would subsequently show Joe all the signs that he would successively obtain with each menu. Joe's successive attempts to interpret and use the sketched signs would reproduce the symptom of a "Where is it?" utterance, regardless of any actual implementation of the interface. An interesting aspect of the method when used at this stage is that, since interaction is reported in words, the test is likely to give the evaluator a much richer set of signs to work with than what she gets from instrumented laboratory experiments with an actual implemented prototype. Through words, the user is likely to express certain important signs that are part of his semiosic processes by saying, for instance, "Where do I switch signatures?" His utterance in this case not only explicitly indicates an opportunity to use the "Where is it?" tag, but also names the function that the user is looking for "switch," but not "change" or "swap," signatures.

The idea of using utterances such as "Where is it?" or "Looks fine to me" expresses a radical commitment to exploring the facets of communication through communication. This mechanism advances certain opportunities not only for improving firsthand exchanges between users and the designer's deputy, but also—and just as important—for using online help resources to improve exchanges about the problems with firsthand communication. To facilitate this connection, the current set of communicability utterances has been inspired by research on online help (e.g., Sellen and Nicol 1990) and on explanation systems (Moore 1995; Cawsey 1993).

Thirteen basic communicability utterances characterize breakdowns in user-system communication, more appropriately framed as communication between the user and the designer's deputy: "What's this?"; "Why doesn't it?"; "Help!"; "Where is it?"; "What now?"; "What happened?"; "Oops!"; "Where am I?"; "I can't do it this way"; "Thanks, but no, thanks"; "I can do otherwise"; "Looks fine to me"; and "I give up." Basic communicability utterances apply to virtually all kinds of computer-based technologies. Special technologies like groupware, artificial intelligence, and virtual reality, for instance, involve specific types of breakdowns that can be tagged with "Who are you?," "Do you know this?," and "Let me out," respectively. Such specialized tags have not yet been extensively investigated in semiotic engineering.

"What's this?"

This utterance is used to tag interaction where the user expects to see an explanatory tip or any other cue about what a particular interface sign means. The typical symptom of "What's this?" is when the user positions the mouse pointer on an interface sign, waiting for a short explanation to appear on screen (right beneath the mouse pointer, in a message area, or anywhere else). It may also involve "opening" pull-down lists, menus, or dialog boxes to see what they *say*. The user is probing the designer's deputy's illocution (category IIc1). If the user is looking for a specific sign with which to express his own illocution, it is not a case of "What's this?" but rather of "Where is it?" Also, if the user explicitly calls a help function, pressing F1 (as in most Windows applications) or dragging a question mark onto the interface element he is trying to make sense of, the appropriate communicability tagging is not "What's this?" but "Help!"

"Why doesn't it?"

This utterance is used to tag interaction where the user is trying to make sense of the designer's deputy's message by repeating the steps of previous unsuccessful communication in order to find out what went wrong. The user is probing the designer's deputy's illocution by engaging in experimental sense making of his own (category IIc3). That is, he does not know how to express his intent but suspects that the sign he is currently examining is the one to be used in a somehow related illocution. Because of previous unsuccessful experience with the sign he is probing, the user tries to correct his understanding through repeating the same steps and checking for potential mistakes. If the user is repeating an operation because he did not perceive the outcome of the previous iteration and is clueless about what is going on, the tag to be used is not "Why doesn't it?" but "What happened?"

"Help!"

This utterance is used to tag interaction where the user explicitly resorts to full-fledged metacommunication in order to restore productive interaction. The typical symptom of "Help" is when the user deliberately calls a help function by pressing F1 (as in most Windows applications), dragging the question mark onto the widgets he is trying to make sense of, or asking somebody for help (e.g., the observer or a colleague). Reading documentation material offline also characterizes "Help!" The user is probing the designer's deputy's illocution by directly asking for help (category IIc2). As seen previously, if the user is only trying to activate tool tips, without explicitly invoking the online help function, it is a case of "What's this?" not "Help!" The motivation for singling out tool tip reading from other patterns of interaction that yield the same effect (like dragging the question mark icon onto a specific widget whose meaning one is trying to understand) is twofold. First, an explicit invocation of help is a different kind of illocution (a direct speech act) than eliciting information in passing while exploring interactive opportunities (an indirect speech act, considering that a moment of hesitation over the widget is enough to elicit the information). Second, from a discourse point of view, resorting to help is the hallmark of metacommunication in HCI. Even if users are not aware of the designer's presence and influence in interaction while they are involved in performing tasks and achieving their goals, they are much more aware of the designer's discourse when reading online help information. This difference in the users' degree of awareness is an important distinction that must be studied and explored if more sophisticated metacommunication is to be designed. Although used less frequently than one might expect, online help is a privileged communicative resource for designers. Later in this chapter I show how communicability and online help design can be brought together to offer users novel communicative experiences.

"Where is it?"

This utterance is used to tag interaction where the user expects to see a certain sign that corresponds to a particular element of his current semiosic process but cannot find it among the signs expressed by the designer's deputy. His semiosis is temporarily halted, because the user misses the form to convey valid content and intent (category IIa1). The user must be convinced that the sign he is looking for is the one he needs to express his current communicative goal. The typical symptom of "Where is it?" is when the user is continually browsing menus, pull-down lists, or any other structured signs. The user's search may be guided by his interpretation of the words or images associated with the structured sign he is currently exploring (which configures a *thematic search*) or not (which configures a *random search* or *exhaustive scanning*). If the user finds what he is looking for during short thematic searches, the breakdown is less severe than if he only finds it after long random searches or sequential scanning.

"What now?"

This utterance is used to tag interaction where the user is temporarily clueless about what to do next (category IIa3). His sense making is temporarily interrupted because none of the designer's deputy's signs mean anything to the user. The typical symptom of "What now?" is when the user is following a random path in interaction. If there is a search involved, it's a search for opportunity and chance. No goal-directed connection can be traced between one interactive step and the next. The "What now?" tag is subtly different from "Where is it?" especially if, in the latter, the user is engaged in a sequential search for content. The difference lies in the user's knowing the content he wants to express (the case of "Where is it?") or not having a clue (the case of "What now?").

"What happened?"

This utterance is used to tag interaction where the user repeats an operation because he cannot see its outcome. In the absence of evidence for the effect of his speech act (perlocution), the user cannot successfully achieve semiosis triggered by the interface sign he is using to express his intent (category IIa2). As in any sensible conversation, the user expects a sign of continuation from the designer's deputy. If the user's illocution is not followed by the designer's deputy's, communication is interrupted. The typical symptom of "What happened?" is the user's repeated activation of a function whose feedback is either absent or not perceived. Alternatively, the user may give evidence of noticing a signal (like a flicker), but not taking it as a sign (i.e., not taking it as a meaningful element in the situation). If the user takes as a mere signal what is meant as a sign by the designer, this is an important communicative disruption. If, however, the user is engaged in a fully connected abductive path (although potentially equivocal) and is fully aware of the signs emitted by the designer's deputy, the tag to be used is "Why doesn't it?" and not "What happened?"

"Oops!"

This utterance is used to tag interaction where the user momentarily makes a mistake and immediately realizes his slip. He sees that he used the wrong form in illocution (category IIb2). The typical symptom of "Oops!" is when the user is steadily engaged in a semiosic path and performs an operation that is clearly wrong or inadequate in that situation. He then immediately backtracks from that step with an "undo" function or, if the "undo" is not available, with any other operation that will immediately cancel the effects of his slip. The immediacy of the cancellation is an important factor in distinguishing "Oops!" from "I can't do it this way." Also, "Oops!" is an isolated breakdown, an important feature to distinguish it from the patterns of subsequent unproductive interactions that characterize "Where is it?" Typically, "Oops!" does not involve a search. If it develops into a search for a way to cancel the effects of a slip, then it indicates a very serious problem in the design. It means that an incidental mistake can disrupt the user's activity so radically that he has to suspend his original goal and engage all his communicative resources in restoring the productive path. The problem with the design is often one related to the designer's expression—mainly, its location or the physical representation of its content (an image or a word). However, the user's mistakes may also be fortuitous, in which case the evaluator must note that this particular tag occurrence is insignificant for communicability evaluation.

"Where am I?"

This utterance is used to tag interaction where the user is interpreting (and potentially using) signs in the wrong context of the application. The user's illocution would be a valid one in another context (category IIb1). This breakdown is not unusual in applications with different modes, such as text editors with distinctive editing and previewing modes. The typical symptom of "Where am I?" is when the user tries to execute operations or searches for the signs of one mode while in the other. The main problem in this breakdown is with the expression of context. The user is confused by the change in context. "Where am I?" should not be confused with "Where is it?," although during the user's search for an appropriate form of illocution (the case of "Where is it?") the user may occasionally enter a different mode to see if he finds the expression he is looking for. The evaluator's interpretation of the full interaction span is critically important in distinguishing one case from the other.

"I can't do it this way."

This utterance is used to tag interaction where the user abandons a path of interaction (composed of many steps) because he thinks it is not leading him toward his current goal. The typical symptom of "I can't do it this way" is when the user suddenly interrupts an activity he is engaged in and takes a totally different direction. It characterizes a realization that his semiosis was wrong and must be revised (category IIb3). "I can't do it this way" is different from "Oops!," because it implies a revision of a much longer semiosic path. Whereas in the case of "Oops!" the user immediately realizes his mistake and tries to correct it, in the case of "I can't do it this way" the user is abandoning (and consequently qualifying it as a revision of wrong assumptions) a whole line of reasoning and action that corresponds to a plan. This difference between the operational level of "Oops!" and the tactical level of "I can't do it this way" points to a difference in the severity of the breakdown. "I can't do it this way" indicates a breakdown where the user has invested much more time and cognitive effort in doing the wrong thing than does "Oops!" The rational connection between the interactive steps that characterize "I can't do it this way" is also crucial to differentiate this kind of breakdown from the one indicated by "What now?" Likewise, the subsequent changes of the system state, caused by the user's execution of actions along his path, are the distinguishing feature of "I can't do it this way" when compared to "Where is it?"

"Looks fine to me."

This utterance is used to tag interaction where the user is convinced he has achieved his goal, but in fact hasn't. It is a major communicative failure of which the user is not aware (category Ib). The typical symptom of "Looks fine to me" is when the user terminates interaction and the system is in a state that is not consistent with the user's overall intent and goal. On occasion, this phenomenon may occur locally, as part of a nonterminal interactive plan that the user abandons later. But, this is not its most relevant indication. In order to illustrate its relevance in terminating situations, I can mention applications that involve form-filling activities. Some automatically save the information provided by the user as he moves from one form field to the next. Others don't. When interacting with an application that requires an explicit saving operation, if the user thinks that he has successfully finished an information-providing activity without saving the form, it is a case of "Looks fine to me." There is a mismatch between the system's state (the outcome of the user's last operation before he terminates the activity) and the user's understanding of what this state should be in the case of successful interaction. The Eudora example in this chapter demonstrates another instance of "Looks fine to me." Joe was unaware of the side effect of his pasting the alternate signature text at the bottom of his message (the message was sent with two signatures: the pasted one and the standard one). So he thought the problem was solved (although with a lot of difficulty), when in fact the solution contained an important mistake. The problem is usually related to the expressions used in the designer's deputy's discourse. The user does not see what's wrong and interprets the signs expressing the system's state as an evidence of success. The actual failure may have different degrees of severity. For example, it may range from a relatively harmless problem, such as Joe's double signature in a message, to loss of data and other unrecoverable mistakes.

"I give up."

This utterance is used to tag interaction where the user explicitly admits his inability to achieve his goal (category Ia). It's a most severe problem of complete failure, whose typical symptom is the user's terminating interaction without achieving success. The distinguishing feature of "I give up" is the user's admitting that he has run out of some fundamental resource that would allow him to use the application successfully in a particular situation. Among such resources are knowledge, skill, time, patience, interest and motivation, and so on. The actual configuration of these resources is an important aspect for communicability evaluation tests. During the preparation steps, the evaluator must be careful to decide the quantity and quality of resources that participants will have for the experiment: how much time, how much information, the level of commitment with targeted results. All of these have a profound influence on human communication in general and consequently on communicability evaluation as well.

"Thanks, but no, thanks."

This utterance is used to tag interaction where the user is fully aware of the designer's deputy's discourse regarding the types of conversations that are expected to lead to a particular perlocution (which coincides with the user's intent), but he chooses to do something different than is expected (category IIIb). It points to one of the distinctive features of communicability evaluation, because it indicates a very subtle communicative mismatch that is not captured by other methods (e.g., usability evaluation). For example, assume that the designer of the application provides two ways for the user to terminate interaction: a "save and exit" and an "exit without saving" alternative. The user may be fully aware of the two, but he may have found out that the operating system's function to terminate tasks can be used as a substitute for the "exit without saving" termination dialog. The advantage may be that the user does not have to perform as many operations—a smaller number of clicks may be needed, for instance. So, with his own alternative, he saves time. From a communicative perspective, the designer's deputy is inviting the user to engage in a particular course of conversation, which the user declines because he has found a more convenient option. The symptom of "Thanks, but no, thanks" involves more than simply the use of operating system resources that can somehow override the application's functions. Some of the application's own functions may have side effects that lead the system to the same state the user wishes to achieve. For convenience, the user chooses to decline the conversation that the designer's deputy is expecting to have and follows another pattern of interaction (even if some risks are involved). This tag indicates an important phenomenon in communication—the user's preference for something other than what is proposed by the designer's deputy as ideal or, in other words, a mismatch between the speaker's model of the listener and who the listener actually is.

At times the designer's deputy may propose a number of alternative paths to the user. If there is an explicit indication of which alternative is ideal in which situation and the user chooses to do something else, the user is explicitly declining the designer's deputy's advice. If there isn't such explicit indication, but the salience of signs (which typically corresponds to the effectiveness of the affordances in the interface) suggests that the designer's effort to produce and communicate those signs has been considerable, the user is declining the benefits of the designer's efforts. Using the Gricean maxims presented in chapter 2, "Thanks, but no, thanks" indicates that most probably the maxims of quantity or relevance have been infringed by the designer with respect to that particular user.

"I can do otherwise."

This utterance is used to tag interaction where the user is not fully aware of the designer's deputy's discourse regarding the types of conversations that are expected to lead to a particular perlocution (which coincides with the user's intent). He then chooses to do something different than is expected but achieves the same perlocution (category IIIa). The crucial distinction between "I can do otherwise" and "Thanks, but no, thanks" is the user's awareness and understanding of design solutions. Whereas in the latter the user is fully aware of them, in the case of "I can do otherwise" he is not. The typical symptom of "I can do otherwise" is when the user achieves his goal (locally or globally) in a way that is not optimal (the most efficient and best fit for his situation), or that is unexpected in the presence of the designer's deputy's signs in a particular situation. "I can do otherwise" is usually (but not necessarily) tagged after some previous breakdowns have occurred. Because it is related to the user's inability to fully understand the design solution, it is likely that the nonstandard solution will be the outcome of the user's attempts to find the standard one. However, "I can do otherwise" may also indicate a residual misconception of the user with respect to how the application works (a more serious problem). For instance, the user may be systematically performing some task (e.g., "exit without saving") without knowing the potential problems that he may encounter if only minor changes in the situation apply. Suppose that the side effect of using the operating system's resources to interrupt processing, unlike that of the designer's deputy's suggestion to "exit without saving," is the automatic generation of a temporary backup copy. The copy may be stored in a temporary directory and be prompted for recovery the next time the application is used. The user may assume that the opening conversation asking him if he wants to recover the backup copy is some irrelevant interface babble, and he may get into the habit of just clicking on "no" without really bothering to understand what it means. This is an obvious opportunity for major problems in the future, when knowing what backup copies are, what they must be used for, and the resources required to generate and store them will be the difference between relief and disaster.

The value of paying attention to instances of "I can do otherwise" is to direct the designer's attention to residual meanings, especially when equivocal. These meanings become an active part of the user's semiosic processes whenever he is interacting with the application, and they can be used to explain a number of problems along the user's learning curve. Capturing this kind of breakdown, which may go unnoticed with evaluation methods that take success at face value (e.g., measuring only user satisfaction and mismatches between the meanings of expected and achieved goal states) is advantageous for designing computer-mediated communication. Among other things, it bypasses the troublesome concept of "a mistake" when the user achieves his intent in unexpected ways, but it retains the trace of a communicative mismatch. It also allows for fine distinctions between cognitive and communicative aspects. It will handle situations in which the user has enough cognitive skills about goals, plans, and operations, but engages in problematic communicative alternatives (e.g., ignoring the perlocutionary effects of suboptimal illocution).

The thirteen communicability utterances are in one-to-one correspondence with the communicative breakdown categories and subcategories presented earlier. This correspondence is shown in table 4.1.

4.3.2 Interpreting Tagged User-System Communication Logs

The interpretation of tagged interactions is directly dependent on the evaluator's semiotic awareness and skill. The categorization of utterances per se provides important input for her analysis of what is going wrong (and right) with the application under study. However, the greater her familiarity with the concepts presented in chapter 2, the more productive her analysis. Just as important as watching the interaction's playback is the examination of what the annotations made during the test and the pre- and post-interviews say. Post-test interviews are particularly important to disambiguate situations where more than one tag could be used, depending on what the user had in mind. For instance, the difference between a "Where is it?" and a "What now?" depends on the user's having established the content and intent of his next illocution or not. The evaluator cannot always tell this difference from just watching the interaction playback, and often not even from attentively following the user's illocutions at interaction time. She must identify such ambiguities during the test, and she must interview the user afterward to have the most exact picture possible of the user's semiosic states throughout the experiment.

Communicative success is marked by the absence (or insignificant amount) of communicative breakdowns. And communicability problems primarily depend on the following factors:

- the frequency and context of occurrence of each type of tag;
- the existence of patterned sequences of tag types;

Table 4.1
Categorization of communicability utterances for tagging observable interaction.

Category type	Subcategory	Distinctive feature	Utterance
(I) Complete Failures		(a) User is conscious of failure.	"I give up."
		(b) User is unconscious of failure.	"Looks fine to me."
(II) Temporary Failures	a. User's semiosis is temporarily halted	(1) because he cannot find the appropriate expression for his illocution	"Where is it?"
		(2) because he does not perceive or understand the designer's deputy's illocution	"What happened?"
		(3) because he cannot find an appropriate intent for illocution	"What now?"
	b. User realizes his illocution is wrong	(1) because it is uttered in the wrong context	"Where am I?"
		(2) because the expression in illocution is wrong	"Oops!"
		(3) because a many-step conversation has not caused the desired effects	"I can't do it this way."
	c. User seeks to clarify the designer's deputy's illocution	(1) through implicit metacommunication	"What's this?"
		(2) through explicit metacommunication	"Help!"
		(3) through autonomous sense making	"Why doesn't it?"
(III) Partial Failures		(a) User does not understand the design solution.	"I can do otherwise."
		(b) User understands the design solution.	"Thanks, but no, thanks."

- the level of goal-related problems signaled by the occurrence of tag types and sequences; and
- the subsidiary ontologies or classes of HCI problems from other theories, approaches, and techniques, with which the evaluator has enriched her interpretation.

The frequency of occurrence of each tag is obviously indicative of qualitative aspects of communicative breakdowns. For example, a high frequency of "Oops!" tags probably indicates ambiguities in the designer's deputy's illocution. A high frequency of "What's this?" indicates a mismatch between the signification systems with which the user is familiar and those used by the designer to express the designer's deputy's discourse. A high frequency of "Thanks, but no, thanks" indicates a mismatch in user modeling, if the participants have been carefully selected from among the targeted population of users. If not, it may indicate a problem with the test itself. A high frequency of "Thanks, but no, thanks" is nevertheless preferable to a high frequency of "I can do otherwise," which indicates that the user is not getting the designer's message or is getting it in the wrong way (with potential residual problems for future interaction).

The frequency of tag occurrence along the user's learning curve is likely to change (Prates, Barbosa, and de Souza 2000). As the user's familiarity with the application increases, tags like "Where is it?" or "What's this?" tend to become less frequent within the same range of perlocutions. An increase in the frequency of occurrence of "Thanks, but no, thanks" typically indicates the development of an interactive idiolect (i.e., a personal way to use the signification system to achieve communication). This may be used to help the designers explore alternatives for letting the user customize the application, or to elaborate different styles of interaction for specific classes of users. A persistent frequency of occurrence of "I can do otherwise" may, however, be troubling. It may mean that the user is repeatedly getting some aspect of the designer's deputy's message in the wrong way and potentially reinforcing his semiosis around an equivocal model of the application.

The context of occurrence of each tag is equally important. The iterated occurrence of "Where am I?" tags in the same context will certainly contain clues of a preferential type of abduction that has not been taken care of by the designer. For instance, in Pine®, a mail tool for Unix and Linux shells, the sign "I" is used to mean "show index for current mail folder." The perlocution of saying "I" as soon as Pine is launched, for most users, is the visualization of the user's Inbox contents. But if users frequently say "I" to view the attachments of a message (whose appropriate illocution is ">" or "V"), for instance, it is a noteworthy case of "Where am I?" An attentive analyst will spot in it an invariant problem in the user's semiosis. "I," for such users, means something like "show me the contents of [it]." But the designer's deputy interprets it as "show the index of the current folder." Therefore, although "I" is a perfectly valid utterance from the user's perspective, if he means to "see the contents of [the current message's attachment]," it is not so for the designer's deputy. The user is transferring an invariant meaning to a different context, something that the designer's deputy is not prepared to handle. But why not? "I" doesn't mean anything else when a message is open. And if it did, it would probably be the likely cause of many "Oops!" tags. So the tagging and its context, in this hypothetical case, would actually be telling the designers not only the cause of the problems, but also how to eliminate them.

At times, certain patterned sequences of breakdowns may occur repeatedly in the same experiment. Upon further examination, the pattern may tell the evaluator that the user's semiosis is not being appropriately cued. For instance, a patterned sequence of "Where is it?" followed by "I can do otherwise" suggests that the user tries to find the right thing to say, but, having failed, he adopts a suboptimal solution. The user misses this privileged solution, which must be frustrating for the designer. The "I can do otherwise" may be more a way out of the problem than a proper a solution. And, if so, the user may be also very frustrated with the experience. The importance of the pattern is that this situation most probably means something different than an "I can do otherwise" that occurs independent of previous breakdowns. In this other pattern, the user may think that his illocution is the right thing to say given the situation. And although this may be just as frustrating to the designer (because the user missed what he was telling him), the user may be satisfied and convinced that he understands the application well.

Likewise, patterns of long versus short sequences of such tags as "Where is it?," "What's this?," "Oops!," and others mean different things. Typically, a sequence of breakdowns of the same type means that the user is having great trouble not only restoring productive communication, but also finding signs that will change the direction of his semiosis and take him out of the problematic loop.

The level of goal-related breakdowns is also highly informative. In particular, it may indicate the case of some usability problems such as low productivity and user satisfaction (which belong to categories of HCI problems that are foreign to the semiotic engineering ontology). For example, the designer of an application may have designed solution paths that facilitate the user's tasks and considerably shorten the time for completing an activity. This may be one of the advantages marketed by the application's vendors (or something strongly related to it). If the users get the designer's message and adopt the suggested tactics to meet their typical goal(s), the benefit of using the application will be clear (and commercial success probably near). However, if they don't get the designer's message at this tactical level, all the pluses will be potentially compromised. Conveying such messages depends on successfully conveying operational-level messages. The added value of a semiotic analysis is the realization that lower-level communicative breakdowns may cause upper-level breakdowns. An analysis of causes and patterns of lower-level breakdowns may indicate some alternatives. For example, users may be missing the tactical-level message because there is a step in it during which their semiosis is temporarily halted. And how they restore communication after this breakdown is typically a trace of how the main cue for the designer's privileged tactics was lost. That is, users find a way to reconstruct meaning around a less efficient tactical alternative. A reinforcement of this suboptimal solution (i.e., learning that the right thing to do is to follow the path that eventually led to success) characterizes a very important communicative problem for designers. The users may find that the application does not deliver the promised gains in productivity (which is not true, in fact). The advantage of communicability evaluation is the possibility of finding out the causes of halted semiosis. The solution may even be very simple. A change of signs in the designer's deputy's discourse, ranging from adopting a totally different signification system to adopting only a different rhetoric in discourse produced with the same signification system, may eliminate the problem. The traces of the users' semiosic processes, collected during communicability evaluation tests, will be a most valuable input to the designer's decision. Finding that users are missing tactical affordances because they can't make sense of the operations involved in it, or because they can't command these operations appropriately, is a distinguished result of semiotic engineering evaluations of HCI (de Souza, Prates, and Carey 2000).

The evaluator's analysis and interpretation may be considerably enriched if the semiotic phenomena derived directly from tagging and communicative breakdown categorizations are paired with factors and dimensions accounted for by other theories, approaches, and techniques. For example, the cognitive walkthrough method (Wharton et al. 1994) is, as its name suggests, strongly committed to cognitive theories of HCI. It can thoroughly characterize how easy (or difficult) it is to learn the application from interaction alone. This cognitive (learning) process is equivalent

Table 4.2
Pairing potential HCI problems dealt with in the cognitive walkthrough and communicability evaluation methods.

Cognitive walkthrough issues	Communicability breakdown categories corresponding to the following tags
Will the correct action be evident to the user? (Will the user know what to do?)	"What now?" "What's this?" "Help!"
Will the user notice that the correct action is available? (Will the users see the system's cue?)	"Where is it?" "What happened?" "What's this?" "Help!"
Will the user interpret the system's reaction correctly?	"What happened?" "What's this?" "Help!" "Why doesn't it?" "Looks fine to me."

to sense making (a semiotic process), which suggests that many of the findings resulting from a cognitive walkthrough probably have counterparts among the results of communicability evaluation. In table 4.2, an alignment of the main issues dealt with in cognitive walkthrough evaluation and those in communicability evaluation is presented.

It is noteworthy that some of the breakdown categories dealt with in communicability evaluation have no direct correspondence with the general classes of issues raised by the cognitive walkthrough method. The category corresponding to the "Thanks, but no, thanks" tag, for instance, poses an interesting challenge for cognitive approaches in general, and for cognitive walkthrough in particular. How will an evaluator predict that users will decline the designer's privileged solution and choose another alternative? This epistemic limitation, derived from the foundations of the method itself, suggests that evaluation methods guided by traditional task models (where alternative plans to achieve a fixed set of predicted goals are specified) are likely to produce larger-grain characterizations of the user's experience. Typically, they will concentrate on goal-related levels of problems and delegate the finesses that are explicitly dealt with in a semiotic engineering categorization of communicative breakdowns to the evaluator's ability to relate problems to uncategorized dimensions of the design. Practical instructions about how to use the cognitive walkthrough method give explicit indications of the evaluator's skill in gathering "critical information" for (re)design. Preece, Rogers, and Sharp (2002), for instance, say that:

> As the walkthrough is being done, a record of critical information is compiled in which:
>
> The assumptions about what could cause problems and why are recorded. This involves explaining why users would face difficulties.
>
> Notes about side issues and design changes are made.
>
> A summary of the results is compiled. (P. 421)

The cause of goal-related problems, as seen earlier, is often found in communication. Therefore, a categorization of communicative problems will leverage the evaluator's diagnostics. Likewise, "side issues" from a cognitive perspective, are often "central issues" from a semiotic one. The case of "Thanks, but no, thanks" tags is an example. The residual effects of problems tagged as "I can do otherwise" is another. The level of semiosic commitment to unproductive sense making—distinguished by "Oops!," "Where am I?," and "I can't do it this way"—is yet another example.

One of the major advantages of using input from other theories at the interpretation stage is that the evaluator's semiosis is boosted by the complementarity and articulation among various HCI theories, thus broadening the scope of her analysis. This can only be beneficial for the evaluation, especially if more than one theory or approach is related to the semiotic one. For example, in addition to pairing communicability breakdown categories with the cognitive issues raised in cognitive walkthroughs, the evaluator gains insights from pairing them with some popular usability issues examined in heuristic evaluation (Nielsen 2001) (see table 4.3).

This pairing is different from the previous one because, as its name says, heuristics are principles derived from practical experience and observation and are not typically committed to ontologies and categorizations that are used in theoretical accounts of the observed phenomena. Therefore, unlike the pairings supported by theoretical associations that can be established between cognitive and semiotic phenomena in table 4.2, the pairings in table 4.3 are both less obvious and weaker than the previous. At times, the tags associated with one heuristic principle may seem best fit for another association. For instance, the "Thanks, but no, thanks" tag suggests a stronger pairing with the "User control and freedom" principle than with the "Match between system and the real world" one. However, a high frequency of occurrence of "Thanks, but no, thanks" suggests that what users do or prefer "in the real world" is not what has been encoded in the system. This tag may also be

Table 4.3
Pairing potential HCI problems dealt with in heuristic evaluation and communicability evaluation.

Heuristic evaluation issues	Communicability breakdown categories
Visibility of system status	"Looks fine to me." "What happened?" "What now?" "Where am I?"
Match between system and the real world	"I give up." "Looks fine to me." "Thanks, but no, thanks." "I can do otherwise."
User control and freedom	"Thanks, but no, thanks." "I can do otherwise."
Consistency and standards	"Where is it?" "Where am I?" "Oops!"
Error recognition and recovery	"Looks fine to me." "I can do otherwise." "Where am I?" "Oops!" "I can't do it this way." "Help!" "Why doesn't it?"
Error prevention	"Looks fine to me." "I can do otherwise." "What now?" "Where am I?" "Oops!" "I can't do it this way." "Help!" "Why doesn't it?"
Recognition rather than recall	"Where is it?" "What now?" "Where am I?" "Oops!" "What's this?" "Help!"
Flexibility and efficiency of use	"Thanks, but no, thanks." "I can do otherwise."
Aesthetic and minimalist design	(none)

Table 4.3
(continued)

Heuristic evaluation issues	Communicability breakdown categories
Help and documentation	"I give up." "Looks fine to me." "Thanks, but no, thanks." "I can do otherwise." "What's this?" "Help!" "Why doesn't it?"

paired with the "Flexibility and efficiency of use" principle, denoting that the range of illocutions that can achieve the same desired perlocution is wide.

These many-to-many correspondences between heuristic principles and communicative breakdowns that can be brought about when they are not observed in design might be interpreted as an indication that this pairing is not productive at the interpretation stage of communicability evaluation. If the occurrence of tags suggests one of many breaches of a heuristic principle, and vice versa, what is the pairing actually telling the evaluator?

At least two lines of thought lead to interesting answers to this question. One is that the correspondence may in itself show some clusterings of heuristic principles. For example, "Error prevention" obviously goes with "Error recognition and recovery," and maybe less obviously with "Help and Documentation." The occurrence of one or more tags that can be associated with any of these principles will probably show how these principles can or should be articulated with each other to resolve a communicative problem. Conversely, it will probably show communicative problems that stem from inappropriate articulation of such heuristic principles in design. The same applies to other related principles such as "User control and freedom" and "Flexibility and efficiency of use," "Consistency and standards" and "Recognition rather than recall," and so on. The other line of thought that shows the benefit of pairing heuristic principles to communicative breakdown categories is to trace the various dimensions of design that contribute to good designer-to-user metacommunication. For instance, a "Looks fine to me" tag signals a single basic category of communicative breakdown—a complete communicative failure of which the user is not aware. Pairing this tag to such heuristic design principles as "Help and documentation," "Error prevention," "Error recognition," "Match between system and the real world," and "Visibility of system status" calls the designer's attention to the factors that contribute to efficient communication. Therefore, his awareness of the importance of using familiar signification systems, of enabling implicit and explicit metacommunication dialogs, and so on may be raised. This pairing also enriches the answer to a question posed frequently by designers after their products are evaluated: "And so what?" Sometimes usability testing and evaluation provides designers with a list of problems found in their design, classified according to one or another taxonomy preferred by the evaluator. But it may not be clear how to prevent the recurrence of the problem. Designers may have done their best to follow a particular principle, yet the results show that at least in the case of a particular piece of design, their intent did not come through. The association of some of these principles with parts of a theory of HCI will allow them to step ahead of ad hoc diagnostics and enable them to think more broadly about the very process of design.

Table 4.3 also shows that some elements of one approach may not be dealt with at all in communicability evaluation. Such is the case of "aesthetic and minimalist design." Although Mullet and Sano (1995) provide us with the means to explore the associations between aesthetic and minimalist design and communicability, the focus on the core ontology of semiotic engineering becomes blurred along these lines and the analysis becomes less productive. Again, this shows the complementarity of approaches and helps the adopter of semiotic engineering see the boundaries of this theory. Other types of items that are not easily associated with the categories accounted for in communicability evaluation can be found among ergonomic criteria, compiled by Bastien, Scapin, and Leulier (1999) in the form of guidance, workload, explicit control, adaptability, error management, consistency, significance of codes, and compatibility. Although "significance of codes" and "guidance" might suggest that the pairing would be promising, the ergonomic perspective is not so directly related to the semiotic one (except through the associations already discussed in relation to the cognitive walkthrough and heuristic evaluation). For instance, "conciseness," "minimal actions," decisions about "location" and "format" of signs, and "information density" may all have a semiotic stance, but semiotic engineering does not explore these dimensions in greater depth. Communicability evaluation can be stretched to cover these issues, but the results may not be particularly illuminating or better than using other more direct approaches.

4.3.3 Generating the Semiotic Profile of Designer-to-User Metacommunication

The semiotic profiling stage finalizes the whole process of communicability evaluation. In it an in-depth characterization of the designer-to-user metacommunication is achieved. The designer's message can be spelled out by the evaluator, who will be able to assume the first person in discourse and say the following:

Who do I think are (or will be) the users of the product of my design?

The answer to this question mainly reveals the cultural, psychological, and technical characteristics of the *listener* of the designer's metacommunication message. The full range of communicative breakdowns presented so far in this chapter will detect matches and mismatches between the designer's intended listener and the actual listeners that represent the constituency of users that the design product will reach.

What have I learned about these users' wants and needs?

The answer to this question covers the range of perlocutions achieved by the illocutions that the signification systems used in the design support. Complete communicative failures will distinctively indicate severe breakdowns that must be corrected for HCI to fulfill its ultimate goal. Moreover, the distinctions among different goal-related levels of problems will help spot fine-grained mismatches between the designer's illocution (i.e., what he intended to say with the design) and the perlocution it achieves (i.e., what users get from it and do with it).

Which do I think are these users' preferences with respect to their wants and needs, and why?

The answer to this question is mainly the designer's justification for the signification systems he has used and for the rhetoric that can or must be used for valid illocutions that these systems support in the process of communication. A significant incidence of "I can do otherwise" and "Thanks, but no, thanks" tags in the evaluation will probably mean that the designer's understanding and rational justification for the decisions he made are not consistent with "the real world."

What system have I therefore designed for these users, and how can or should they use it?

The answer to this question tells how well the expression and content of the designer's metacommunicative illocution is being transmitted to the user. The expression will be directly connected to the actual signs that are used in the interface and that emerge during interaction. As a result, problems with the user's perceiving and interpreting such signs (such as those indicated by, e.g., "What happened?," "What's this?," "Why doesn't it?," and "Help!") will direct the designer's attention to a more efficient use of the user's cultural background. Likewise, the content of the metacommunicative illocution will be directly connected to the user's ability to derive productive semiosis from the expressions in the signification system. The "I can do otherwise" tag tells the designer that users are not getting his message, even if they are able to achieve short-term goals with relatively little trouble. It calls the designer's attention to the "therefore" that is deliberately present in the formulation of this semiotic profiling question: What is the cause of the user's missing the content of the message? If the answers to the previous questions have already indicated sources of communicative problems, these sources are very likely the cause of the problem here as well. However, the preceding questions may have indicated relatively minor problems, in which case problems may stem from the complexity of communicating with the system itself. For instance, taggings dominated by "Oops!" and "I can't do it this way" are likely to mean that there are illocutionary obstacles in the design that the user is not able to overcome so easily. Such tags don't mean that the user's background, their wants and needs, or their preferences haven't been taken into account. They only mean that the engineered sign system is difficult to use.

What is my design vision?

The answer to this question indicates how well the design rationale has been understood (and accepted) by the user. The occurrence of "Thanks, but no, thanks" is likely to mean that it was understood, but with some restrictions. In other words, the perlocution achieved by the designer's message does not fully coincide with his intent. This fifth question asked at the beginning of the semiotic profiling stage is particularly discriminative if there haven't been significant problems spotted in the answers to the previous questions. Specifically, it may help the designers evaluate the return on their investment in design. For example, if the application enables and highlights the use of certain conversational paths whose design and/or implementation have consumed many resources, the user's refusal to follow them is a very bad sign. Another interesting aspect of this question is that it can handle some branding and marketing messages, which are part of the design but have little or nothing to do with usability and other popular "*-abilities*" handled by alternative evaluation methods.

The semiotic profiling also makes an extensive use of the concepts presented in chapter 2. Three of them stand out as particularly productive at this stage: the communicative functions derived from Jakobson's model for communication; the pragmatic principles proposed by Grice; and the parameters of Eco's TSP.

Jakobson's model, which has been the source of fundamental concepts in the semiotic engineering ontology, will help the evaluator walk through the communicative design space and inspect the rhetoric of the designer's deputy's discourse. By contrasting this rhetoric with her findings from the tagging and the interpretation stages of the communicability evaluation method, the evaluator will assess the efficiency of metacommunication. She may use the Gricean maxims and Eco's sign production parameters to explain inefficiencies and to suggest potential improvements. For example, she may find that the designer's deputy's discourse is lacking in metalinguistic functions. That is, the designer's metacommunication does not make an efficient use of communication about the designer's message itself. Online help functions, information, and explanations during error prevention and recovery—all of these may have been poorly explored by the designer. The Gricean maxims will help her indicate the appropriate locus and quantum of metalinguistic functions that the application can use to increase communicability. Eco's parameters will help her express the metalinguistic functions in more efficient ways.

Moreover, bringing together metaphors and metonymies, on the one hand, and abductive reasoning and semiosis, on the other, the evaluator may even be able to identify the design cues mentioned by Brown and Duguid (1992) that are enhancing or hindering the communicability of a particular application. For example, abductive reasoning and semiosis are based on the universe of hypothesis motivated by the signs present in a particular situation. So, in the Eudora scenario described at the beginning of this chapter, the frequency of successful menu options as a way to communicate his intent reinforces the user's hypothesis that the appropriate illocution to switch signatures is a menu option as well. The problem of encoding illocution as a list selection is that pull-down lists are far less salient in the interface than menus (see the screen dumps in the scenario and check that there are only three pull-down lists in the main window, against more than three times as many menus). So it is only reasonable that the user will engage in a long series of breakdowns stemming from menu option explorations. Some important metaphorical and metonymical expressions have been cued by the user along the way. For instance, his suspicion that the option Alternate might refer to creating and editing the alternate signature, but also to switching to it, points to metonymical interpretation of the sign as standing for anything related to (contiguous to) the literal meaning of "alternate signature." Another metonymical axis has emerged in interaction when the user has tried to find illocution in the Message menu. Again, the sign "message" might reasonably mean anything related to messages, especially in the presence of a "change" option embedded in this menu. Finally, a powerful metaphorical expression has been used by Joe when he copies and pastes the textual content of the alternate signature and finds he has solved the problem. It denotes his intuitive understanding of what the signature procedure does (internally) and foreshadows design enhancements achieved in subsequent releases of Eudora by Qualcomm.

All of these elements may be explored in the semiotic profiling and produce an in-depth characterization of the application's communicability along with suggestions for improving the designer's deputy discourse. Another valuable procedure in communicability evaluation is to contrast taggings made by the evaluator, the designer himself, and occasionally the user. The designer has a privileged perspective on metacommunication, since he is the one who has built the designer's deputy's discourse and, consequently, the one who knows exactly what was meant by each and every illocution. The user, however, has some interesting epistemological limitations for the tagging. For example, the user cannot be expected to tag interaction with "Looks fine to me" unless he suddenly becomes aware of the fact that what he thought was an acceptable end state for his activity is in fact not one. The same applies to "I can do otherwise" tags, unless the user senses that there is a better way to tell the system what to do, although he is not capable of finding it. The author's experience with teaching communicability evaluation in graduate and undergraduate courses is that tagging interaction is an enjoyable learning experience for future HCI designers and researchers. The suggestion is that the utterances are easy to learn, remember, and use effectively. For this reason, as will be seen in section 4.4, they have been used as part of an expressive code that users can resort to in order to engage in explicit metacommunication with the designer's deputy.

4.4 Improving the Designer's Deputy Discourse

Communication is virtually impossible when interlocutors lack the ability to negotiate meanings. And one of the keys to negotiating meanings is the interlocutors' ability to explain what they mean by what they are saying. When transposed to HCI, this requirement sheds light on some fundamental issues. First, natural languages and computer languages are structurally distinct when it comes to supporting what Jakobson calls the *metalinguistic* function in communication (see chapter 2). Whereas natural language allows us, humans, to produce as many levels of metadiscourse as we want to, computer languages are bounded by self-description limitations imposed on every formal language (Hopcropf and Ullman 1979). In brief, computable languages cannot be used to specify the full range of their own semantics, which means that a system can only provide complete explanations about what it means if another system (that can interpret and produce the metalanguage of the original system) can tell it so.[3] Therefore, unlike humans, who can always explain what they mean by what they say, technically speaking, computer systems often have to ask *other* computer systems for an answer to this question. This constitutes what Winograd and Flores (1986) refer to as "systems that cascade levels of representation one on top of another to great depth" (87). Even if what we call *the system* is often a collection of numerous programs, each one specializing in interpreting and generating a particular level of representations (or, strictly speaking, a particular signification system), there must always be some *other* system to explain what the topmost representation-processing program *means* by most of what it says.

It follows from the preceding logic that the explanatory power of the designer's deputy's discourse, and consequently its ability to negotiate meanings, is limited by formal properties of computable languages. Even if it is "very powerful" by some practical criteria, or "powerful enough" within the range of acceptable performance, it is never comparable to what humans can do with and because of language. So the encoding of the designer's meaning negotiation ability (which is performed by his deputy) is a key issue for successful communication with the user. This involves two different processes: that of detecting when the user's illocution is incomprehensible and must therefore be clarified, and that of explaining what the designer's deputy's own illocution means. Both tasks are particularly difficult and complex for computer programs, as efforts in natural language understanding have shown (Moore 1995). The semiotic engineering alternative in order to maximize the communicability of the designer's deputy's discourse is to enrich the form and content of online help.

4.4.1 The Problem with Online Help

In the 1980s, Carroll and Rosson (1987) spotted the "paradox of the active user." Although knowing more about the application one is using is certainly a factor that promotes much better HCI and much higher productivity, users don't read manuals, don't use online help systems, and prefer to jump right into the doing instead of first learning what can be done. Evidence from numerous empirical studies about users' behavior led to minimalism—an action-centered approach to instruction where the context of real activities is the key to learning (Carroll 1998). Minimalist techniques used in online help systems, such as layering (Farkas 1998), seek to provide just-in-time and just-as-much information for users, even at the risk of not giving enough information for the user to complete the task (a case of "I give up"), or consuming a lot more of the user's resources than is actually needed (a case of "I can do otherwise"), or facilitating the elaboration of equivocal mental models that will cause problems in interaction later on (a case of "I can do otherwise" or "Looks fine to me"). These three risks have been spelled by Farkas (1998), for whom "the degree of the risk depends on how radically information is cut and just what is cut and how" (249).

What is cut and how is a decision that we humans make all the time whenever others ask us for information. We intuitively follow the Gricean maxims for cooperative conversation (see chapter 2) and make extremely fine-grained contextual judgments about the quantity, the quality, the relevance, and the form of information that must be provided. Such judgments lie outside the scope of even the most sophisticated expert systems, and in part this is why online help systems have a bad reputation for not helping you much unless you know the kind of help you need and know exactly how to ask for it. Most of the information they contain is related to the goals, plans, and operations involved in bridging Norman's execution gulf (1986). It's mainly about tasks, and not so much about the design decisions that support and explain the way in which they can or must be carried out in order to make computational sense. Knowing that such decisions exist and the extent to which they determine the quality of a computer artifact is the essence of true computer literacy.

Help systems are not typically designed to enhance computer literacy. Be it because computer literacy is an elusive concept, and/or because users are known to be bothered by intrusive instructions on their way to getting things done, the fact is that help systems concentrate on telling them just how to get things done, preferably in a minimalist way. The problem is that the users' semiosis is permanent and unbounded. So users will wonder and guess many things—right and wrong. Many of their guesses will have to do with the "whys" and "for whats" that help systems don't usually account for. Communicability evaluation is an efficient method for studying interactive patterns that are related to the users' wondering and guessing. Therefore, communicability utterances can be used to provide access to minimalist information about other dimensions of the artifact, especially design rationale. This kind of information may improve meaning-negotiation processes between the user and the designer's deputy at interaction time, because it widens the scope of signs that can play a positive role in motivating productive semiosic paths. This is the semiotic engineering alternative to enhancing the designer's deputy's explanatory discourse without having to resort to AI techniques. By expanding the scope of information content to topics that are not exclusively related to goals, plans, and operations, this alternative takes its cue from ethnography (Suchman 1987) and activity theory (Bødker 1989). A larger part of the users' opportunistic semiosis may be positively influenced by traces of the designer's rationale appearing during interaction.

4.4.2 The Semiotic Engineering of Online Help Systems

The kinds of information that are necessary for enriching the designer's deputy's discourse can be derived from various design models, such as user models, domain models, task models, interface models, and others. Therefore, the semiotic engineering of HCI is intrinsically related to model-based design (Paternò 2000). Silveira (2002) proposes that six design models be used in the construction of explicit metacommunication messages: a domain model, a user model, an application model, a task model, an interaction model, and an interface model. Different modeling techniques may provide input models for each of Silveira's models. Puerta's user-task, domain, presentation, dialog, design, and user models, for instance, are an alternative (Puerta 1996). Nevertheless, special attention should be given to differences in perspectives that guide the modeling activity itself. For example, there is a fundamental difference between Silveira's and Puerta's approaches, which requires that Puerta's models be enriched to meet Silveira's requirements. Puerta's primary goal in working with HCI models is to solve "mapping problems" and "enable the design of a wide variety of user interfaces previously unattainable using model-based technologies" (Puerta and Eisenstein 1999, 177). In other words, the focus is on supporting developers with automated design tools and environments that will enhance the consistency of interface design. Silveira's primary goal, however, is to support the elaboration of online help systems (Silveira, de Souza, and Barbosa 2001a, 2001b). The purpose of the information in Silveira's and Puerta's models is very different. Consequently, the perspective of information content is also very different. Puerta's user-task model can be instantiated with a GOMS model (Card, Moran, and Newell 1983; Puerta 1996), which contains the hierarchical specification of plans and operations that are needed for the accomplishment of certain goals. In Silveira's approach, task models must be enriched with certain types of information that are usually not included in generic hierarchical models of tasks and activities. Semiotic engineering task models require the following top-level categories of information:

▪ the hierarchical structure of tasks, subtasks, and operations required for the achievement of top-level goals, with their respective

- preconditions (if any);
- relative ordering (or absence of ordering);
- possibilities of iteration (none or one, one or many, any number, some specific number);
- alternative patterns (which mean that two or more of them can be used to achieve the same effect);
- associated signs from the signification system (independent of their being explicitly or implicitly referred to during interaction); and
- error prevention or error handling mechanisms.

▪ the type of task, subtask, or operation with respect to its content, form, or illocution:

- standard structured and nonstructured types;
- stereotypes that recur in different parts of the hierarchy with specific parameter variations; and
- ubiquitous operations, tasks, or subtasks of the hierarchy, which can be performed at any moment (e.g., abandoning the activity, saving data, and so on).

The most important property of such extended task models in semiotic engineering is that they provide an index to interaction models. They point at the specific types of conversations where the user's and the designer's deputy's illocutions bring about the perlocution specified in the task model. This is certainly an instance of Puerta's mappings, except that its purpose is fundamentally committed to communicative dimensions of speech acts, such as illocution and perlocution. Notice that Puerta's dialog models express the designer's deputy's illocutions as a class of relation between commands issued by the user (in our terms, the user's illocution) and a certain state of affairs that follow it (the corresponding perlocution). An explicit emphasis on distinguishing between the perlocution of the user's illocutionary acts and the designer's deputy's illocution following the user's perlocution is precisely what will make a fundamental difference in terms of metacommunication.

For example, in the Eudora scenario that dominates this chapter, the perlocution of Joe's having "commanded" (in Puerta's terms) the creation of an alternate signature is that the created signature can now be part of other illocutions (like "Switch to the alternate signature" or "Edit the alternate signature"). And this is precisely the user's intent. The problem is that the designer's deputy's subsequent illocutions are all problematic. For instance, they do not clearly say that the alternate signature is there. Neither does it clearly say how to formulate an illocution meant to switch signatures when a message is composed. As communicability evaluation shows, perlocution and illocution breakdowns belong to different categories of problems and must therefore be treated differently if we really want to help the users find their way in interaction. This is why all semiotic engineering models must privilege categories of information that will directly affect communication between users and designer's deputies.

The kinds of interaction model used by Silveira require that the following types of information be identifiable (Barbosa and de Paula 2003; de Paula 2003):

- *interaction scenes*, which all have
  - a topic, which is indexed to a goal, task, or subtask in the task model;
  - a conversation, which is specified by a sequence of alternate illocutions performed by the designer's deputy and the user;
  - an associated set of system processes that determine the global perlocutions achieved in the scene; and
  - an associated set of transitions that determine the conversational paths that precede and succeed global perlocutions achieved in the scene.
- *illocutionary components*, which all have
  - an identification of the interlocutor;
  - a generic natural language representation of an illocution's content;
  - a generic representation of the illocution's context (expressed as preconditions); and
  - a generic representation of entailed perlocution (expressed as postconditions).

The formalisms that can be used to specify semiotic engineering task and interaction models in detail are not important, provided that they support the expression of the types of information that these models must contain. In figure 4.4 a mainly visual characterization of the task and interaction models for a typical login activity shows how the elements in them are related. The alternation of illocutions by the user ("u:") and the designer's deputy ("dd:") in the interaction model defines the illocutions and conversational patterns (at an abstract level) that achieve the

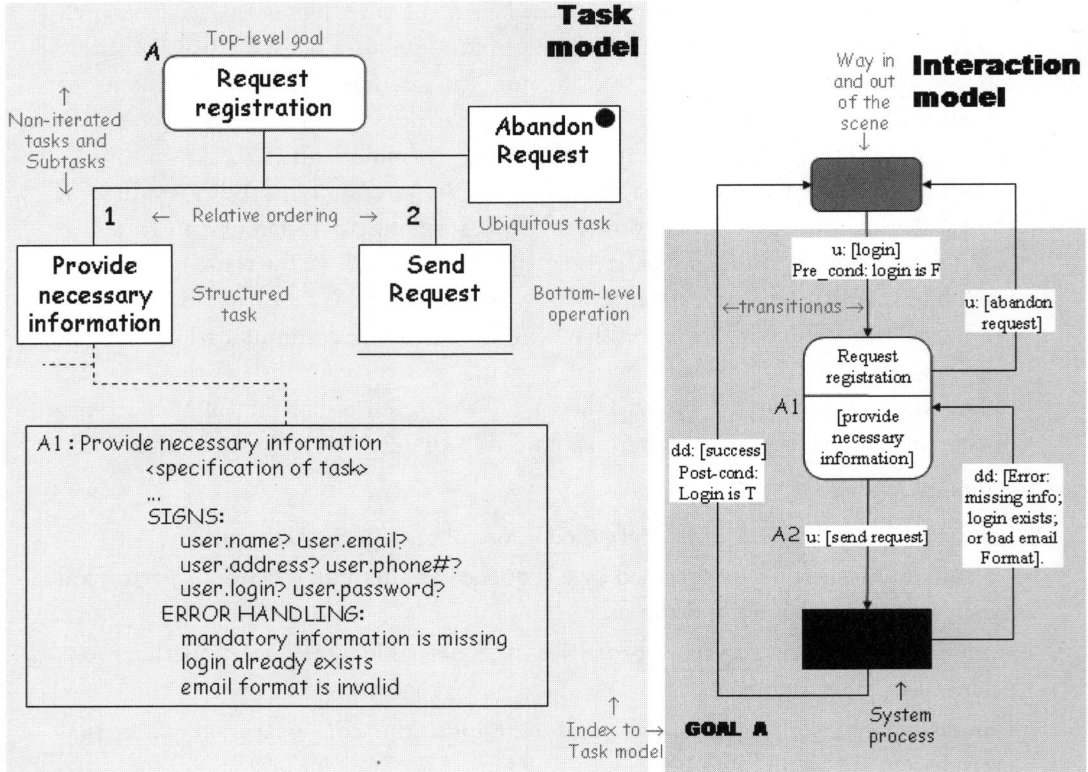

Figure 4.4
Types of information required in task and interaction models.

perlocution associated with the "Request registration" goal. Notice that conversations about errors, as well as conversations about abandoning the current goal, are explicitly defined in the interaction model based on specifications from the task model. The elements of these models will provide crucial information for resolving communicative breakdowns expressed by communicability utterances. For instance, "What happened?" requires information about the (form, content, intent of the) last illocution performed by the designer's deputy. "Where is it?" demands information about the range of illocutions that the user may perform given the designer's deputy's previous illocution and the perlocution achieved through it. "I can't do it this way" requires information about the scenes associated to the goals that users can achieve through the application.

Silveira proposes that help systems be prepared to use model information to address the following questions:

- Who are the application's users?
- What do they usually do in their domain of activity?
- What kind of intervention is the application's technology expected to achieve in the user's domain?
- Which domain objects are present in the application?
- What activities and tasks can be performed?
- Why are activities and tasks necessary? Whom do they affect? Whom or what do they depend on?
- What signs compose the interface signification system?
- How does interaction proceed?
- When and why is one kind of interaction better than another when they achieve the same effect?

She extracts the answers to these questions from the six models she uses to compose the designer's deputy's metacommunicative discourse (Silveira 2002). From the domain model, she derives domain signs that are implicit and explicit in the interface signification system. Each sign has an expression (or "name"), content (or "description"), and associated illocutions (or "utility"). From the application model, she derives the application signs that are implicit and explicit in the interface signification system. Like domain signs, each application sign also has an expression (or "name"), content (or "description"), and associated illocutions (or "utility"). From the user model, Silveira extracts users' roles and profiles. The profiles contain the user's identification and characterization (through relevant properties). User roles associate certain groups of users (or profiles) with certain tasks. From task and interaction models Silveira derives operational and tactical information. An important aspect of this information is the ability to distinguish between domain-related signs and application-related signs. While the former can be expected to be reasonably known by the users, and demand briefer explanations, if any at all, the latter result from a technological intervention in the domain, which is likely to require much more elaborate explanations and illustrations. Finally, from the interface model Silveira extracts sign types and tokens, as well as the kinds of illocutions in which they may appear.

Although the full spectrum of information in the designer's deputy's explanatory discourse might suggest that online help systems proposed by semiotic engineering are too complex (especially for the user), three strategies are used to simplify metacommunication and make it more attractive and useful. First, as already mentioned, the designer's deputy's discourse follows the minimalist approach and layering techniques proposed by Farkas (1998). This promotes more cooperative communication with the user, who ideally gets just-in-time and just-as-much information as he needs to proceed with semiosis. Second, metacommunication pervades all interaction and is not restricted to what is traditionally considered the online help function. It is presented in traditional form, but also through localized minimalist conversations. Moreover, the content of error messages and direct instructions is carefully designed to motivate productive semiosis, given their context of occurrence during interaction. Finally, the third strategy that facilitates explicit metacommunication between the user and the designer's deputy is the use of communicability utterances and typical phrases that express the need for help (Sellen and Nicol 1990). Table 4.4 illustrates utterances appearing in Silveira's localized

Table 4.4
Sources of metacommunication contents.

Element of localized interaction	Communicability utterances and help expressions
Domain and application signs	"What's this?" "What's this for?" "Where is it?"
Task structure (conversational intent and perlocutions)	"What's this?" "What's this for?" "How do I do this?" "Oops!" "What now?" "What happened?" "Who is affected by this?" "What does this depend on?" "Who can do this?" "Where was I?"
Sequence of actions (conversations)	"Why do I have to do this?" "Is there another way to do this?"
Actions (speech acts)	"How do I do this?" "Oops!" "What now?" "What happened?" "Where was I?"

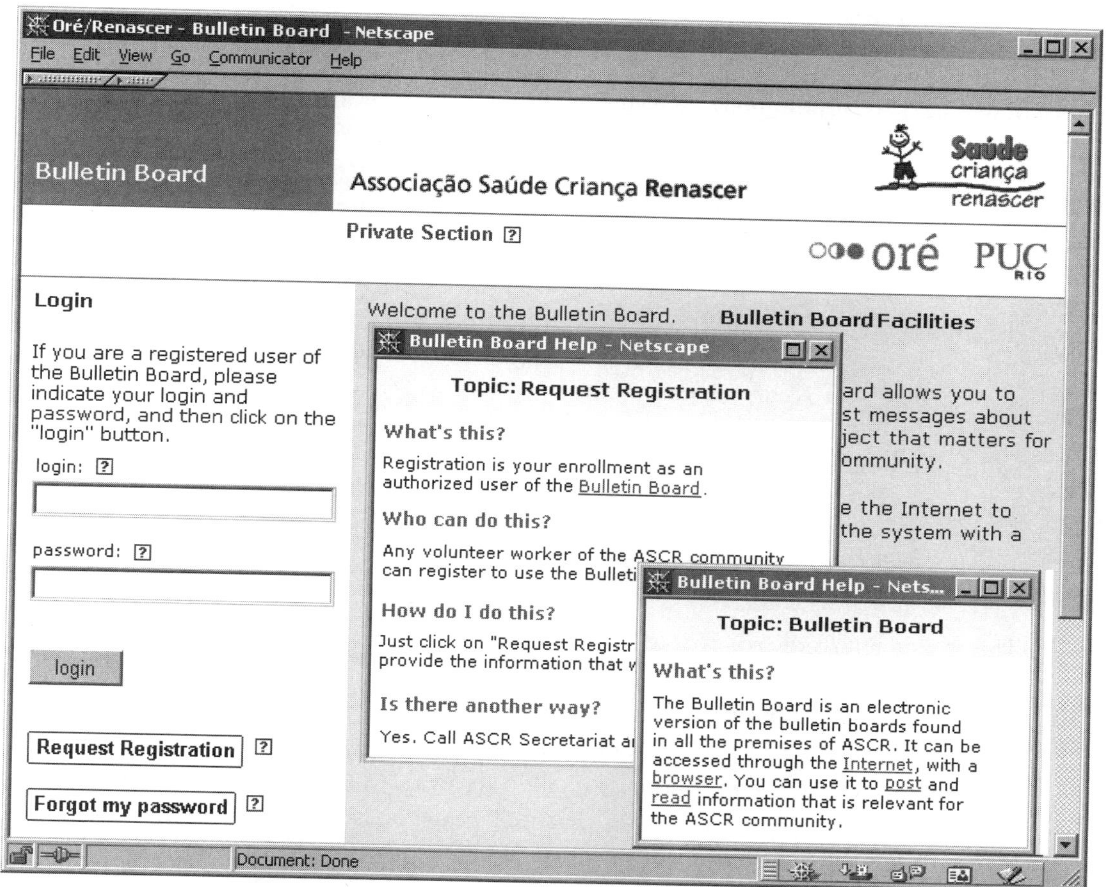

Figure 4.5
A screen shot from an implemented online help system that uses Silveira's model.

minimalist conversations and the corresponding source of metacommunication contents.

The effect of Silveira's model is illustrated in figure 4.5, where local metacommunication enabled during a request for registration to an online service is exemplified. The example is taken from an existing Bulletin Board application (de Souza, Prates, and Barbosa 2003) developed by the Semiotic Engineering Research Group for a Brazilian organization of social volunteers—Associação Saúde-Criança Renascer (ASCR). The textual content, all in Portuguese in the original application, has been translated into English by the author. The smaller browser Bulletin Board Help windows are opened when the users click on the blue question marks positioned next to certain interface elements, or when they click on a link that appears in the metacommunication message. The screen in figure 4.5 results from the user's first clicking on the question mark next to Request Registration, then clicking on the Bulletin Board link. Notice how the communicability utterances and help expressions are used to provide minimalist insights about the application. It is the HCI designer's task to define the kind of metacommunication associated with each element of the interface, and to select the utterances and expressions that will provide access to the designer's deputy's explanatory discourse. He must also identify the points of recurrent metacommunication, expressed as navigation links in the textual content of the designer's deputy's message. The complete method for building online help systems is presented in previous work by Silveira, de Souza, and Barbosa (2003).

4.5 Epistemic Tools for HCI Evaluation and Explanatory Discourse Design

This chapter introduced various epistemic tools that HCI designers can wield to reflect on the nature and the possibilities of metacommunication that can be achieved through computer artifacts. It started by extending the existing notion of *communicability* in order to account for all signs belonging to the application's signification system. It then proposed a method for evaluating the communicability of interactive computer artifacts, based on specific categories of communicative breakdowns. Such categories result from discriminatory principles centered on the two major dimensions of speech acts: illocution and perlocution.

The communicability utterances in themselves are a kind of epistemic tool in that they trigger the designer's semiosis in the direction of communicative breakdowns that must be prevented or circumvented in HCI. A more systematic use of this tool produces another set of tools presented in this chapter: the models and techniques that contribute to building the designer's deputy's discourse conveyed through online help. One is the use of communicability utterances and help expressions as a means to express the user's need for meaning negotiation, through explanations and clarifications. Another is the range of information that can be extracted from domain models, user models, application models, task models, interaction models, and interface models to compose the content of metacommunication messages sent through traditional online help, localized minimalist conversations about the artifact, error messages, and instructions. In particular the additional information included in hierarchical task models and the communication-oriented interaction models themselves widen the scope of metacommunication without requiring specific AI techniques used in explanatory dialogues (Moore 1995). Designers may simply use templates to generate the appropriate responses to the user's questions about the application. These templates can be generated based on a systematic correspondence between communicability utterances and help expressions, on the one hand, and information extracted from models, on the other.

5

The Semiotic Engineering of Customizable and Extensible Applications

In previous chapters we saw that the designer's deputy is a powerful abstraction in the achievement of successful metacommunication. It will convey to users the original design vision and have a range of conversations about it in order to clarify aspects of this vision and reinforce the users' semiosis toward interpretations that bring them closer to understanding the designer's intent. But we also saw that whereas humans interpret signs as part of an unlimited semiosic process, practical computer programs can only interpret them as part of algorithmic symbol processing.[4] This semiotic *gulf* between users and systems is of a different nature than the execution and evaluation gulfs characterized in cognitive engineering (Norman 1986). The semiotic gulf can only be bridged, although partially, if computer systems begin to accommodate expansions in the semantics of encoded signification systems that users are exposed to while interacting with computer applications. Only then can users experience something that somehow resembles human semiosis. Meaning expansions are regularly required for the success of human communication, both from a message sender's and a message receiver's point of view. Take the following dialog as an example:

Speaker 1: I see that some system components should not be accessible for changes. It's as if they were "impermeable" to customization and extension.

Speaker 2: Maybe. But what sort of "coating" would you use to help users identify permeable from impermeable components? It should not be a matter of trial and error, I guess. Nor of hiding these components, otherwise they would be "invisible" and not "impermeable."

Speaker 1 has expressed himself using a comparison (or *simile*). Speaker 2 has immediately expanded the semiotic space of the conversation and talked about "coating" (meaning an impermeable protection), adopting a metaphorical expression that leads naturally to other relevant aspects of the discussion—distinguishing between impermeable and invisible things. Speaker 2 is helping Speaker 1 elucidate his own meanings (see Jakobson's metalinguistic function in chapter 2) by using a rich form of expression that associates unusual (if not strictly incorrect) properties to systems' components.

Meaning expansions introduced by users have been the object of investigation of end-user programming (EUP) and more recently end-user development (EUD). Meaning adaptations of various sorts, not necessarily expanding the semantic base of encoded signification systems, have been the object of studies about customizable (and at times personalizable) interfaces. In this chapter I discuss the importance of EUP and customization from a semiotic engineering perspective.

Viewing interactive software as metacommunication artifacts highlights the fact that designers want to achieve a perlocutionary act when they send the metacommunication message to users. The message is encoded and communicated in an artificial signification system that is continuously processed by symbol-interpreting and symbol-generating computations triggered by interactive events. The range of symbol (or sign) combinations that can be interpreted and generated is technically infinite once the system is encoded as a true language. For instance, rules about the property "name" (that users can assign to files they create through various applications) typically characterize an infinite number of alphanumeric chains of characters. In other words, the set of all "names" can only be formally specified, but not exhaustively listed. This simple principle extends to much more elaborate and structured grammatical combinations that are systematically interpreted as system component properties, states, behavior, and so on.

When designers construct a *language* to convey their message to users, as well as subsequent user messages to the designer's deputy and vice versa, they are building semiotic infinities whose boundaries cannot be exhaustively known. Figure 5.1 identifies four different regions in the territory defined by linguistic specifications of significations codes. The central region in it is that corresponding to the designer's targeted perlocutions. Simple and compound signs and symbols in it refer to what the designer consciously meant to tell users (and consequently to get users to do with the system). Traditional online help usually depicts the range of utterances that belong to this region. The next surrounding region, in the ripple shape presented in figure 5.1, is that of simple and compound signs and symbols that are in accordance with the encoded system (i.e., they are grammatically correct) but that are not appropriate or useful in view of the designer's pragmatic goals. Utterances of this type

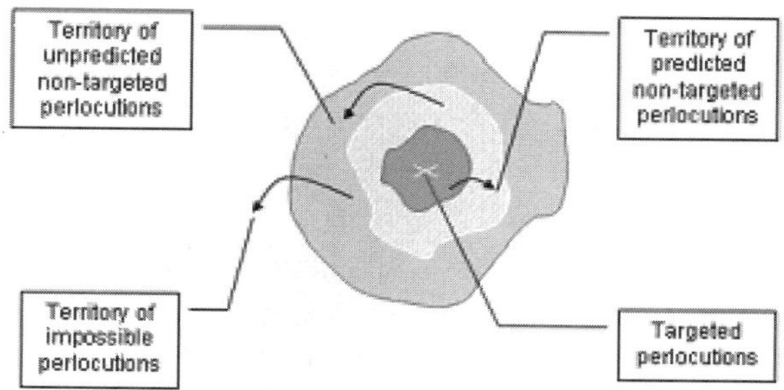

Figure 5.1
Different signification territories associated to interface signs.

typically result in warnings, error-preventing dialogs, error-handling instructions, and the like. Just like the previous type (targeted utterances), these are expected utterances, even if they do not lead to users' or designer's full communicative satisfaction. By predicting what users must and may say to express what they want to do, designers will provide the necessary mechanisms to effect what can be done and to prevent and explain mistakes when things cannot be done. However, there are other utterances that fall within the range of well-formed symbol or sign combinations, but that designers haven't really figured out at design time. These are the ones that cause the most disorienting interactive failures in HCI, stemming from messages like "A fatal error has occurred" or "Index out of bound." They are related to interactive contexts that the designer has not thought of, and has thus failed to prevent and explain appropriately, thereby not giving the user a chance to understand what happened and what must or can be done next. Finally, although there are technically infinite utterances falling within the encoded signification system, there are also infinite utterances falling without. The absence of a semantic type like "converted formats" in a text editor, for instance, may never enable expressions such as "Save as HTML." This combination of symbols (from a computer's perspective) or signs (from a human perspective) does not belong to the interface language that can and must be used by users and system. But this semantic type ("converted formats") and one of its instances, such as "HTML," is not a surprising sign in the semiosic processes of any contemporary user of text editors.

Figure 5.1 provides a background for understanding the complexity of communicating ideas, visions, principles, rules, and constraints through messages that can interpret and generate other messages. The fact that such communication is achieved through the use of an artificial code, or language, specifically designed for a particular metacommunication act, turns this language into a unique and arbitrary (in the Saussurean sense explained in chapter 2) signification system that users may wish or need to adapt to their evolving semiosic processes. This is the main motivation for developing customization and extension techniques that allow users to change the forms and/or meanings in the originally designed system. If all forms and meanings could be changed at leisure by users, however, this would allow users eventually to destroy the original designer's message and build another one of their own. This would be the equivalent of reprogramming the application through manipulating the signification system embedded in it. Reprogramming would not only be a difficult (and probably unattainable) goal for the vast majority of users, but it wouldn't actually make sense in the communicative perspective adopted by semiotic engineering. It would only make sense in a full-fledged programming and development environment where the designer's goal *is* that users create their own signification systems and messages encoded therein. So customizable and extensible applications must have signs and symbols whose form and/or meaning cannot be changed by users. They must be, so to speak, "impermeable" to changes in the signification system.

Impermeable signs and symbols constitute the identity of customizable and extensible applications. They are a permanent reference for symbol processing and semiosis and have the power to preserve the gist of the designer's metacommunication message. They must therefore be carefully designed and used in all communicative processes enabled by the application, including those that will introduce changes in communication itself. It is thus helpful to analyze the semiotic dimensions involved in changing signification systems from a system's and from a user's perspective.

5.1 Semiotic Aspects in Changing Signification Systems: The Computer Perspective

From a computer's perspective, a signification system is a *language*, or a system of related languages. And there are essentially three semiotic dimensions that computer systems can handle in processing languages: lexical, syntactic, and semantic. The lexical dimension accounts for the vocabulary that can be used to form meaningful sentences of the language. The syntactic dimension accounts for the kinds of combinations in which vocabulary items can be arranged and the structures, or higher-order symbols, that are created with such combinations. Finally the semantic dimension accounts for two fundamental operations in linguistic computations: It establishes the appropriate mappings between vocabulary items or higher-order symbols and representations or actions corresponding to what they mean; and it effects the operations associated with the computed meanings. The semantics of computer languages is often described in algebraic and procedural formalisms, or in natural language text (which handles both). The concepts introduced in chapter 2 help us see that computer languages merge the semantic and pragmatic dimensions of natural languages into the same linguistic component, understandably associated with computer language "interpreters" (i.e., sets of functions that can understand and effect what well-formed linguistic expressions *mean*).

A computer language can be altered in various ways. There may be lexical changes (followed or not followed by syntactic and/or semantic changes), syntactic changes (followed or not followed by lexical and/or semantic changes), and semantic changes (followed or not followed by lexical and/or syntactic changes). Figure 5.2 presents all the possibilities for manipulating, independently or jointly, the three dimensions specified in computer languages.

In the context of customizing and extending applications, it is important to notice the threshold between changes of types I, II and III, on the one hand, and those of types IV, V, VI and VII, on the other hand. The first three are meaning-preserving changes, whereas the others introduce meaning modifications in the encoded language. This helps us establish a formal distinction between "customization" (meaning-preserving alterations) and "extension" (meaning-changing alterations), which we will adopt throughout this chapter.

By preserving syntax and semantics intact, type I changes amount to renaming vocabulary items or introducing synonyms. This kind of customization can be done in many applications, although they usually have a number of items that cannot be renamed, for example. They are impermeable signs that constitute the application's

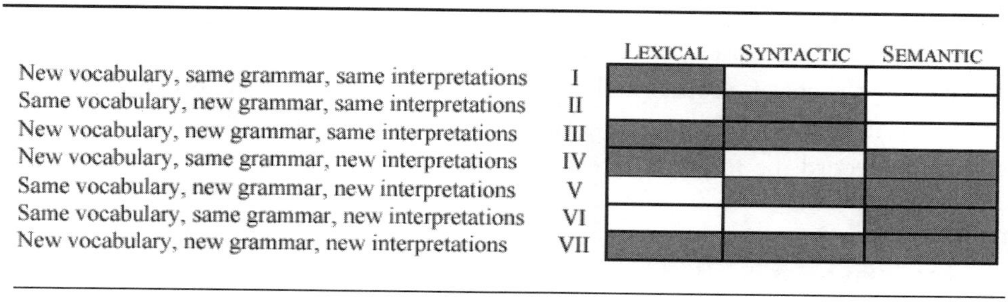

		Lexical	Syntactic	Semantic
New vocabulary, same grammar, same interpretations	I			
Same vocabulary, new grammar, same interpretations	II			
New vocabulary, new grammar, same interpretations	III			
New vocabulary, same grammar, new interpretations	IV			
Same vocabulary, new grammar, new interpretations	V			
Same vocabulary, same grammar, new interpretations	VI			
New vocabulary, new grammar, new interpretations	VII			

Figure 5.2
Possibilities for changing computer language dimensions.

identity (be it for HCI design or software implementation reasons, or both). The interest of associating impermeability to identity is to include the design of the application's identity as an explicit and fundamental step in the development of customizable and extensible applications.

By preserving vocabulary and semantics intact, type II changes essentially amount to changing the combinations prescribed by grammatical rules. It is not very useful to introduce new grammatical types if the vocabulary and semantic rules to interpret them remain the same. It also not very useful to introduce new higher-order symbols in the grammar if they do not advance any other interpretive aspect of the language. Thus, type II changes essentially enable the reordering of signs and symbols. This type of customization is supported by applications that allow users to change the order of options in menus and toolbars, for instance.

Some (lexical) changes in the vocabulary may require corresponding (syntactic) changes in the grammar, even if they do not introduce new meanings. For example, more elaborate paraphrases saying that "move file_F to directory_D" is the same as "file_F moved to directory_D" require that the lexical and the syntactic base be expanded, although no new meanings are introduced. These are type III changes, whose effect is to rephrase or paraphrase symbols and signs. An example of this kind of customization is macrorecording (not macro programming). Strict macro recording joins various lower-level sentences of the interactive language into a sequential structure that is associated with a "name." No new meanings are added to the interpretive component of the application. Because users perceive this differently (i.e., they see it as a new meaningful element that is being added to the signification system that can be used to express and interpret communicative acts), problems may follow. One of them is the encoding of constants and variables in macro recording. Since recorded macros are no more than a rephrasing or paraphrasing for existing interactive steps, important generalizations are not made (generalizations that users often expect). So, many macro recording mechanisms will encode the specific contextual values instantiated in the process being recorded as part of the macro *meaning*. As a result, if a user is editing "document1.txt" and decides to record the following steps:

```
Open File menu
Select Save as . . .
When dialog box shows up, select file type "HTML"
Press Save
```

she may be surprised to see that when she runs the newly created macro to save "document2.txt" in HTML format, the application will try to save the document as "document1.html," possibly in the same file directory in which "document1.html" was saved. This is an interesting evidence of how macro recording is meant by users and how it is handled by systems. By framing macro recording in terms of the types presented in figure 5.2, designers can see more clearly the trade-offs involved in using this type of technique.

Type IV changes, unlike the previous ones, explicitly introduce new meanings in the original language specification. However, the syntax remains intact. This is the case when new lexical items in the vocabulary are tokens of existing syntactic types, systematically mapped onto semantic categories and interpretive functions. In a way, this basic type of extension is present in all interactive applications that allow users to create objects (e.g., documents, images, projects, and the like). Every time a user saves a new document with any name he fancies giving it, the application's interactive code gains a new lexical item. Many applications explicitly incorporate such recently created items in the File menu to accelerate access, a powerful evidence of semantic expansion in the interactive code (even if transitory). Formally, type IV changes can only expand lexical semantics (i.e., directly related to the meaning of words, and independent of novel syntactic structures). Thus, in HCI this sort of change is typically associated to the creation of application objects and falls within the range of operations that the original application already does. Consequently, it does not represent a particularly challenging possibility to explore in isolation. The ability to introduce new lexical items expanding the syntactic and the semantic base concomitantly is a much more useful resource.

Type V changes represent a complex linguistic manipulation of formal codes. By using the same vocabulary, one can introduce meaning extensions signaled by different syntactic combinations and/or structures. An example of meaning expansions achieved with new syntactic combinations would be to allow reordering to mean different things. So if a particular interface can interpret the sequence "Select_object, select_tool, apply_tool_to_object," one can introduce a distinction by saying that the combination

```
Select_object, select_tool, apply_tool_to_object
```

means that the tool should not be kept selected for the next step of interaction, but the object should. The combination

```
Select_tool, select_object, apply_tool_to_object
```

would have the effect of preserving the tool selection and releasing the object selection for the next step. Notice that the actual dimension of meaning being manipulated in this case is the pragmatic one, and not really the semantic one. It is the contextual effect of using one phrasing or the other that is being changed, not the effect of the tool on the object. But because these two things are typically handled together in computer language specifications, the semantic component is the one affected.

Syntactic manipulations in type V changes do not have to be confined to reordering. The creation of new structures can also be associated with the introduction of new meanings. Keeping the context of the example we just gave for syntactic reordering, let us suppose that now one wants to introduce the possibility of applying tools to multiple objects—a possibility that does not exist in the original design. The application should handle structures like

```
Select_tool, select_list_of_objects,
apply_tool_to_list_of_objects.
```

This can be achieved by the introduction of list structures in the grammar, without necessarily expanding the lexicon.

However, in most practical situations, type V changes are accompanied by some kind of lexical change. If they aren't, some strange inefficiencies may arise. Let us examine the expansion that allows users to select lists of objects. Without any kind of lexical expansion in the vocabulary of the signification system, this new structuring requires that every object be individually named in the list. Therefore, if there are five objects that the user wants to operate upon, he will have to say, for example:

```
Select_tool, {select_obj1, select_obj2, select_obj3,
select_obj4,
select_obj5}, apply_tool_to_{obj1, obj2, obj3, obj4, obj5}.
```

In the context of direct manipulation, for example, some expressive facilities naturally accompany this possibility (e.g., using a bounding box to select multiple objects in the same region). In the context of linguistic manipulations, other facilities are used (e.g., using the combination Ctrl + A to select all objects, or combining Shift + ⟨arrow keys⟩ to express continuous multiple selections). The bounding box and the key chords are new lexical items that facilitate the codification of new structures.

When reordering introduces semantic distinctions, another sort of problem may be found: higher cognitive loads for retaining semantic distinctions that are not lexically marked. In the case of distinctive orderings causing the tool selection to persist across different interactive steps or not, although this design choice is easily encountered in some applications, users are often confused by which combination does what. To facilitate interpretation, accompanying vocabulary expansions such as a new sign or symbol to express each of the two modes of operation (e.g., cursor shapes assuming a form that refers to the selected tool when tool selections persist over various object selections) are good alternatives. So for practical reasons, type V changes usually give way to type VII changes in EUP or EUD circumstances.

Type VI changes introduce new semantics without affecting the grammar or the vocabulary. This represents a radical meaning modification of existing signs and symbols. If the modification is made directly in the semantic encoding of lexical entries and syntactic structures, it changes the original meanings of design and may thus potentially affect the application's identity. If it creates alternative interpretations, leaving the original ones intact, it introduces ambiguities in the interpretation of signs and symbols. So from a computer perspective, type VI changes are a potential source of problems for extending encoded signification systems in extensible applications, and should in principle be used very carefully, or not be used at all. The situation is different when we take a user's perspective, as will be seen shortly.

Finally, changes of type VII affect all dimensions of symbol processing. They require considerable linguistic intuition and encoding abilities not easily encountered in the population of typical users. Such intuition and abilities are not those applicable to the user's own language, but to artificial and formal languages, an even more restrictive requirement. The kinds of techniques that enable such manipulations on the originally encoded signification system are scripting and macro programming. However, the difficulty with these lies in controlling the preservation of meanings associated with the impermeable signs that constitute the application's identity. Suppose that the application we used to exemplify macro recording in the type III changes mentioned previously behaved differently. Suppose that after recording the Save as HTML macro, the user had the possibility of *editing* it, at leisure, to the extent that she would be able to modify the dialog that showed up in step (iii) and introduce in it the possibility of uploading the specified file to any FTP site on the Internet.

This seems like a plausible idea that a skilled programmer, as a user, might perhaps wish and be able to implement. The problem with this is that if the change is introduced only in the context of the Save as HTML function, the lexical entry Save suddenly becomes a confusing interface sign. The original Save cannot upload files, but the extended one, appearing only in combination with HTML files, can. A semiotic inspection will show that this represents a serious discontinuity in the signification "system" especially engineered for the application, in particular because the meanings associated with Upload to FTP sites suddenly enter the user's semiosic space. And there is no particular reason why these meanings would be unavailable for combination with other signs such as TXT files or PDF files, for instance (as the sign Save is). So, in their generalized form, type VII changes present a serious threat to the semiotic consistency of meaning extensions, which eventually may break the systematic nature of associations between form and meaning in the application's interface. One way to control semiotic consistency is to constrain the lexical and syntactic types that can be introduced by type VII changes. This is what is done, for example, in the case of agent-assisted extensions (e.g., AgentSheets® [Reppening and Sumner 1995]) or programming-by-demonstration techniques (e.g., KidSim [Cypher and Canfield-Smith 1995]).

After having inspected the seven types of changes that may be explored to customize and extend applications, we conclude the following from a computer's perspective:

- There are two different classes of modifications that users can introduce in applications: meaning-preserving and meaning-changing modifications. We propose that the former correspond to "customizing" applications and the latter to "extending" them.
- There is a type of extension (type IV) that is part of almost every computer application today. It allows users to introduce new "tokens" of prescribed grammatical "types" whose interpretation can be automatically derived from token-type systematic correspondences. So it is not particularly useful to include this type in a taxonomy of changes that can be made in the original signification system of customizable and extensible applications.
- There is a type of extension (type V) that may result in impractical expression requirements in HCI. In the absence of new lexical items that can express aspects of syntactic and semantic expansions to the original signification system, users may have to cope with inefficient structured expressions that use the same vocabulary or with particularly heavy cognitive loads to retain mappings of distinct semantic features onto syntactic structures that are not lexically marked.
- There is a type of extension (type VI) that, if made, may either destroy the application's identity (which we propose should never be the case in EUP or EUD) or

introduce undesirable lexical and syntactic ambiguities in the original signification system. So, it is also not appropriate to include this type in our proposed taxonomy.

- Finally, there is a type of extension (type VII) that, because of its complexity, requires further distinctions. Linguistic changes that affect the whole spectrum of components in the encoding of signification systems may be confined to the manipulation of only a subset of lexical, syntactic, and semantic types of items and rules (VIIa), or they may extend to all types (VIIb). The usefulness of linguistic expansions of type VIIa is directly proportional to the gains in expressive power enabled by the strict manipulation of a selected subset of the lexicon, grammar and interpretive rules. That of type VIIb expansions is directly proportional to the costs and benefits of checking that the desired modifications do not destroy the application's identity or introduce semiotic discontinuities into the expanded signification system (a very costly procedure).

In figure 5.3 we summarize our conclusions. The shaded rows correspond to the classes of changes that are either potentially problematic or semiotically impoverished. The implied suggestion is that the range of productive signification systems manipulations enabled by user-defined customizations and extensions includes only meaning-preserving lexical expansion or modification, meaning-preserving syntactic modification, meaning-preserving structural expansions, type-controlled linguistic expansions, and type-free linguistic expansions.

A frequently used adaptation that can generally be done at installation time deserves further attention at this point. We will call it *pruning*, since it consists

		LEXICAL	SYNTACTIC	SEMANTIC
Meaning-preserving lexical expansion or modification	I			
Meaning-preserving syntactic modification	II			
Meaning-preserving structural expansions	III			
Typically included in non-extensible applications	IV			
Meaning-changing structural expansions	V			
A threat to the application's identity in EUP / EUD	VI			
Type-controlled linguistic expansions	VIIa			
Type-free linguistic expansions	VIIb			

Figure 5.3
Semiotic aspects in changing computer language dimensions.

of selecting items that are to be "subtracted" (or not added, depending on our standpoint) from the complete application. For example, many text editors offer users the possibility of choosing whether they want to install spelling and grammar checkers. If users say yes, the signification system will handle all communication necessary to use the checkers as texts are edited. Otherwise, the signs supporting such communication will not (all) be part of the signification system, and probably the semantic base will not include the meanings associated with spelling and grammar checking. Because this kind of modification affects the semantic base, it should be classified as an *extension* according to the definition we propose. However, there are two problems with this classification. First, it is disturbing to have an "extension" whose result is actually a "retraction" of the semantic base. Second, and more important, because signs can be kept or taken out at installation time, usually, it is disturbing to decide whether they are part of the application's identity or not. In other words, are these retractable signs impermeable? If I say they are, by my own definition, taking them out of the semantic base affects the application's identity and amounts to letting users *destroy* the designer's vision. Nevertheless, it is the designer who is letting users retract the semantic base in this way. Therefore, the application's identity must somehow be unaffected by such changes. I thus suggest that impermeable signs come in two subclasses: essential and accidental. Both are signs that cannot be modified by users during EUD activities. However, accidental impermeable signs can be pruned (taken out) from the original signification system, whereas essential impermeable signs cannot. And it is the class of essential impermeable signs that constitute the application's identity.

Paying attention to pruning is important because the result of this type of modification should not introduce semiotic discontinuities in the signification system. So, for example, if users decide to keep the spell-checker but not to install the grammar checker of a particular text editor, they should not find themselves involved in communication about noun phrases or capitalization (signs that belong to the domain of grammar). One of the obvious design implications of this is that interface dialogs must be carefully segmented. Signs corresponding to meanings that have been subtracted from the semantic base at installation time should never arise in communication unless the purpose of communication is to add them back to the signification system.

The possibility of adding such signs back to the application suggests that the semantic base is in fact not affected by pruning. That is, users can plug such signs in and out as they wish, but the signs themselves are always part of the original signification system. Consequently, pruning can be viewed as a meaning-preserving operation in the sense that users are not definitively affecting the signification system, but only pruning the set of signs that they wish to talk about with the system. As a result, pruning comes closer to customization than extension, although it may deserve more attention from designers than do other kinds of customizations.

5.2 Semiotic Aspects in Changing Signification Systems: The Human Perspective

From a user's perspective, the relevant dimensions of codes are directly related to the kinds of communication they enable. Intent is the dominant dimension in a user-centered view of HCI. Semiotic engineering deals with intent in terms of illocutionary and perlocutionary acts (see chapters 2 and 4). Illocutionary acts (illocutions) characterize the speaker's intent with respect to what he wishes to achieve by expressing himself in one way or another (i.e., what he wants to [make] happen). Perlocutionary acts (perlocutions) characterize his intent with respect to the state of the world as a result of his expression (i.e., what actually happens in situated discourse). Expression is the second outstanding dimension in a user's perspective. It refers to the signifying code *forms* that can be used to achieve communicative goals (the user's intent). Finally, content appears as an important dimension in natural language communication. Expressions with different content are often used to achieve the same intent. Such is the case of direct and indirect speech act pairs like "Would you mind closing the windows, please?" and "It's really cold with the windows open, don't you think?" Likewise, expressions with the same content can achieve very different effects. Such is the case of ironic colloquial expressions like "It looks like you've been having a hard time," expressed in a context where "you" refers to somebody who is being asked a series of difficult questions during an examination, or alternatively to somebody who is sunbathing on a tropical beach.

In figure 5.4 we replicate the combinatorial possibilities that we used to analyze the specific semiotic dimensions from a computer system's perspective. This time, instead of having lexical, syntactic, and semantic dimensions, we have expression, content, and intent.

There are again two classes of modifications that a user may introduce in the application's signification system: those that conserve the same scope of intent accounted for by the original system and those that introduce new intentional elements. This subdivision should not, however, tempt us to replicate the customization versus extension distinction proposed in the computer perspective. From a

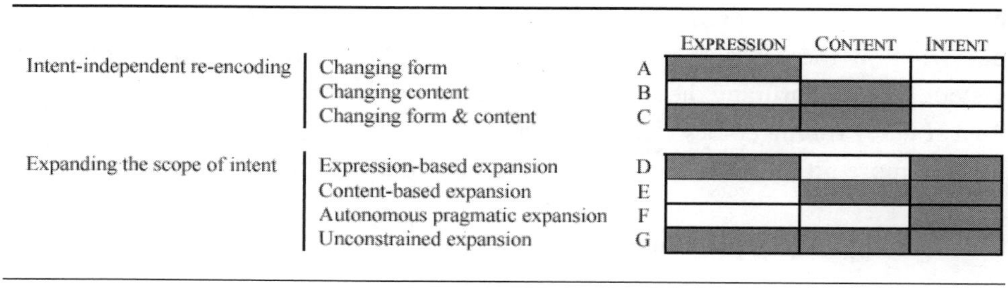

			Expression	Content	Intent
Intent-independent re-encoding	Changing form	A			
	Changing content	B			
	Changing form & content	C			
Expanding the scope of intent	Expression-based expansion	D			
	Content-based expansion	E			
	Autonomous pragmatic expansion	F			
	Unconstrained expansion	G			

Figure 5.4
Possibilities for changing communicative dimensions enabled by signification codes.

human perspective, "expression" encompasses lexical *and* syntactic aspects. Moreover, the "semantic" dimension in the computer perspective encompasses content *and* intent dimensions in a human perspective. In figure 5.4, the only trace of customization as previously defined is type A modifications, which are but one of seven potential modifications that users might wish or need to make in the encoded signification systems in order to suit their communicative purposes.

Intent-independent reencoding is an activity that adjusts the artificial code without explicitly aiming at introducing new intentional elements. Nevertheless, in the process of unlimited semiosis, as soon as there are new expressions and content there is automatically a chance to use them in order to achieve new intent. Let us suppose that a user records the following macro:

```
Find "Heading 2" format and replace it with "Heading 3" format
Find "Heading 1" format and replace it with "Heading 2" format
Go to beginning of document
Type 'Title'
Select previous word
Format selection as "Heading 1"
```

What this macro does is to add a new level on top of a two-tiered text structure. From the computer system's perspective, the macro does not introduce novel semantic elements. And, strictly speaking, from the user's perspective, his perlocutionary act can be achieved through the six steps he recorded as a macro named "Push_headings_down," for instance. So, we might argue that this constitutes an intent-independent reencoding of interface signs (one that introduces a new expressive alternative for preexisting content and intent elements). However, on the one hand, if the user introduces a new expression, presumably this operation satisfies some new dimension of the user's intent. In this case, we can say that the user's illocutionary act is that the system will do the six sequential steps one after the other, something that could only have been achieved through six individual illocutions before the macro was created. On the other hand, the user might wish to apply "Push_headings_down" two (or more) times in a row, in which case some nasty effects would begin to appear (see figure 5.5). All lower-level headings would eventually be flattened as Heading 3. So the introduction of new expressions in a signification system automatically magnifies the scope of communicative goals that can be achieved through the system, both from a strictly illocutionary perspective and from a broader perlocutionary perspective. This is what can be seen in the illustrative dialog at the beginning of this chapter, where Speaker 2 picked up Speaker 1's metaphoric line and built new expressions and meanings on top of it. Thus, type A, B, and C modifications in an encoded signification system are somewhat fictitious in HCI. Or, rather, viewing them in isolation from the user's ongoing semiosis may misinform some HCI design decisions relative to customizable and extensible applications.

The preceding example helps us illustrate the kinds of type D expansions that users might want to introduce in the encoded signification system of an extensible applica-

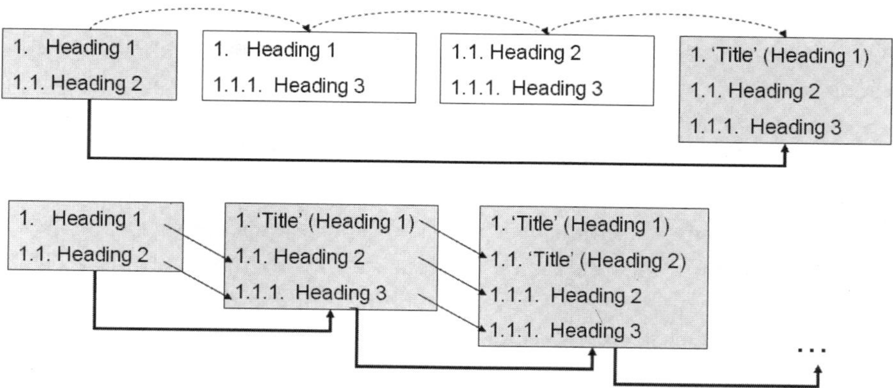

Figure 5.5
Effects of a recursive application of the Push_headings_down macro.

tion. The user's intent, of course, is not to lump lower levels of the text structure all together, but to extend the push-down operation to as many levels as there are in the text. Thus, for instance, headings at level 3 would be pushed down to level 4, headings at level 4 would be pushed down to level 5, and so on. The problem is that macro recording per se is not the appropriate mechanism to achieve the desired degree of generalization for the expression "Push_headings_down." A quite elaborate programming process would be required involving first identifying of the lowest-level headings, then pushing these down, and finally repeating the process until the topmost-level headings were reached. The usual extension mechanism for this is scripting or macro programming, which necessarily involves lexical, syntactic, and semantic manipulations of the encoded signification system. Therefore, type D and type G manipulations (where users are deliberately introducing new expressions, new content, and new intent) involve the same degree of semiotic complexity from a computer perspective. Although users may not have such a fine degree of semiotic awareness to explicitly classify what they want to do as type D or type G modifications, they know that recording macros is much easier than editing and programming them, and they know that introducing the "Push_headings_down" expression in the encoded system is different from introducing something totally new like "Upload_file_to_my_website" (assuming that this function is not supported by the application). Nevertheless, from the computer system's perspective, the difference may be no bigger than that between a type-controlled and a type-free extension.

The remaining two types of modifications in figure 5.4 are type E and type F. The invariant in these two cases is that the expression used in communication is the same, but the user *means* something else. Given the constraint we raised relative to preserving the application's (encoded) identity, when speaking about the semiotic dimensions in symbol processing, type E and type F modifications should not allow users to destroy the application's encoded identity. However, the user may well *repurpose* some of the application's encoded signs. And this is the gist of type F modifications. An example of such *repurposing* would be if the user said "Abort application," but meant "I am finished." Cast in typical interface signs, this is the difference between finishing the dialog in figure 5.6 with the appropriate DOS command, ⟨EXIT⟩, for quitting the session, and doing it by typing "Alt+F4" or clicking on the little "x" sign on the top right-hand corner of the window. Either one of the three alternatives (each one with a specific semantic interpretation encoded in the application) will result in finishing the conversation with DOS. However, "Alt+F4" is not the same as ⟨EXIT⟩, and if *meant* to be the same it is in fact a case

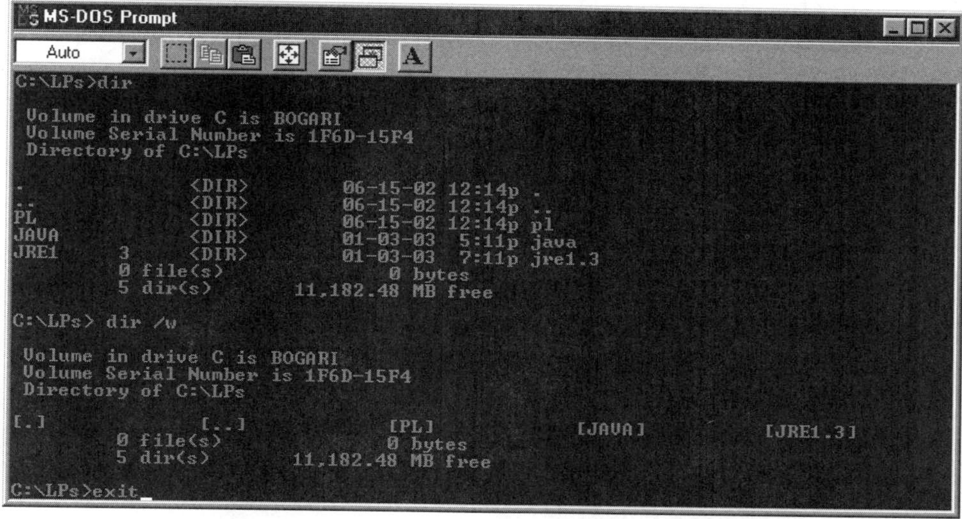
MS-DOS Prompt
Auto
C:\LPs>dir
Volume in drive C is BOGARI
Volume Serial Number is 1F6D-15F4
Directory of C:\LPs
. <DIR> 06-15-02 12:14p .
.. <DIR> 06-15-02 12:14p ..
PL <DIR> 06-15-02 12:14p pl
JAVA <DIR> 01-03-03 5:11p java
JRE1 3 <DIR> 01-03-03 7:11p jre1.3
0 file(s) 0 bytes
5 dir(s) 11,182.48 MB free
C:\LPs> dir /w
Volume in drive C is BOGARI
Volume Serial Number is 1F6D-15F4
Directory of C:\LPs
[.] [..] [PL] [JAVA] [JRE1.3]
0 file(s) 0 bytes
5 dir(s) 11,182.48 MB free
C:\LPs>exit_

Figure 5.6
A typical DOS® window and command. Screen shot reprinted by permission from Microsoft Corporation.

of repurposing "Alt+F4" to mean what "exit" means, a strategy that, as we know, will *not* always work well. An interesting aspect of type F modifications is that they are not modifications at all from a computer system's perspective on customization and extension. In this particular case, from the HCI designer's perspective, they may even constitute a "mistake" that will go unnoticed and be harmless in some cases, but not in others. In a communicability evaluation of the application, moreover, instances of such repurposing strategies are likely to be tagged "I can do otherwise." "Thanks, but no, thanks" would only signal extensions of this sort if the sign used by the user to *mean* what he wanted was never *deliberately* encoded by the designer as a sign to be used in association with the particular intent that the user is trying to achieve. If the designer intended the sign to be used in association with the user's intent, but in other conversational circumstances, this is not a case of repurposing the encoded meaning, but rather of disregarding the encoded rhetoric and creating one's own idiolect (an individual's language use pattern) to interact with the system.

Type E modifications are the last to receive our attention in this discussion. They innovate communication by allowing users to say something and mean something else (i.e., something other than the expression usually means). In the context of extensible applications, the idea is that users are exploring expressive types enabled by the existing forms associated to interface signs, but introducing innovation in terms of content and intent. This strategy is what we naturally do when using figurative speech, for instance. In natural language, if we say "That poem is a pearl" we of course don't mean to say that the poem can be mounted on a ring and used as an adornment. But we somehow mean "That poem is a jewel," and that it has a very special value. We are using a metaphor to express our opinion about the poem, and at the same time opening an avenue of signification possibilities along our metaphoric line. As has been shown in previous work (Barbosa and de Souza 2000, 2001), interpreting metaphors can be a useful mechanism for extending applications. Here is an example taken from Pine, a system that we used in chapter 4 to illustrate contexts for using the "Where am I?" tag in communicability evaluation.

In Pine, the sign $ is sometimes used to sort the index of messages in a folder. For instance, "$ F" has the effect of sorting the index of messages according to the "From" field; "$ A" sorts the index by "Arrival Date"; "$ S" sorts the index by "Subject"; and so on. Now, when the user is working with the address book, there are also fields in every address entry, namely, nickname, full name, Fcc, comment, and addresses. But, if the user chooses the sign $ to compose an illocution to achieve a sorting of address book entries, Pine tells him that command $ is not defined for this particular context. So, if the user doesn't know it, he will have only made a mistake. However, if the user knows that Pine originally cannot handle the sorting of address book entries, but wants to introduce this possibility in communication, "$ Nickname" becomes an intentionally innovative use of Pine's command language. The user's expression is metaphorical in that it does not make literal sense according to the interface code, but makes sense in an expanded scope of interpretation where analogies and resemblances are the key to sense making.

Metonymical expressions might also achieve interesting effects. Suppose that a novice Unix® user has a directory named "doc," in which there are files with extensions "txt" and "ps." Suppose, also, that this user for some reason wants to rename the "txt" files in the "doc" directory as "dat" files. In version 4.1 of the Unix command language, if from the hierarchical directory node immediately above "doc" the user says "mv doc/*.txt *.dat" (meaning "rename all 'txt' files in directory 'doc' as 'dat' files"), the system will issue an error message ("mv: missing file argument"). However, related commands where elements of the user's expression appear are executed without problem (e.g., "mv doc/file1.txt doc/file1.dat," "mv doc/*.txt .," and "mv doc/file1.txt file1.dat"). There are at least two important things that escape this novice user's understanding of how this operating system and its command language work. First, that the "mv" command actually manipulates a file's *address* in memory, and not its *name* (although the subtle difference between these concepts is often disregarded by nonnovice users). So, multiple files can only be manipulated through generalizing expressions such as "*.txt" if operations on each individual file's address have certain distributive properties (which "mv" happens not to have). Second, even if "mv *.txt *.dat" could be interpreted as a DOS "rename *.txt *.dat" (i.e., if the "mv" command could "change the names of all the *.txt files to *.dat files," as it seems to be able to do with individual files), the user's expression "mv doc/*.txt *.dat" would not necessarily mean (as intended) to rename "txt" files as "dat" files within the "doc" directory. It could also mean (and most probably would, in a Unix context) to move "txt" files from the "doc" directory to the "current directory" and rename *them* as "dat" files. The purpose of this example is to show that the user's meaning is expressed through a classical metonymic expression—"*.dat" is intended to mean "doc/*.dat" and that metonymic expressions may, just like metaphoric ones, be intentionally used to extend the range of illocutions (and perlocutions) that can be communicated over a particular signification system. So, in conclusion, type F modifications in a user's semiotic perspective allow us to explore the possibilities of extending applications through figurative speech.

The result of our semiotic analysis from a user's perspective is presented in figure 5.7, where shaded rows correspond again to cases that we are not considering in our classification. Strictly speaking, all user manipulations of the signification code are made to meet some kind of communicative goal (even if only as illocutionary

			EXPRESSION	CONTENT	INTENT
Intentindependent reencoding	Changing form	A			
	Changing content	B			
	Changing form and content	C			
Expanding the scope of intent	Rephrasing	D			
	Figurative speech	E			
	Re-purposing	F			
	Linguistic expansion	G			

Figure 5.7
Interesting semiotic dimensions for customization and extensions from a human perspective.

acts whose effect does not require any expansion in the system's semantic base). As a consequence, what we first called intent-independent reencodings does not constitute a useful class of possibilities in this perspective. The borderline between customization and extension, from a user's perspective, is also an artificiality, which reinforces some perspectives where both phenomena are treated in conjunction with each other (e.g., the end-user development perspective [Lieberman, Paternò, and Wulf, forthcoming]). However, from the user's point of view, there seems to be a scale of increasing semiotic complexity in the way that an existing signification system can be manipulated to introduce innovative communications. It ranges from type F modifications (repurposing of encoded expressions and contents), to type E modifications (figurative speech introducing new content and intent), to type D modifications (where users have to "create" new signs even if they will be reusing the original signification system's semantic base to achieve their intent), and finally to type G modifications (a full-fledged semiotic encoding, where the user has to introduce new expressions, with their corresponding content and intent).

The message for HCI designers working on customizable and extensible applications carries a wealth of points for consideration. As suggested in figure 5.8, the semiotic dimension and semiotic complexity correspondences between a computer

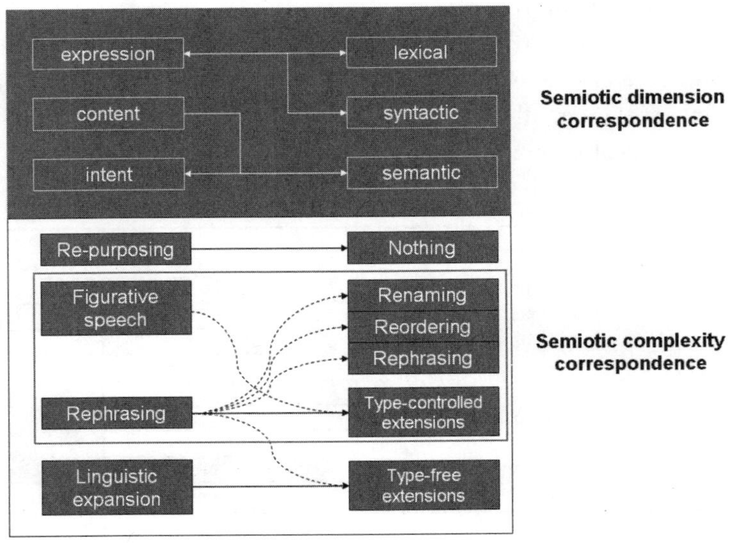

Figure 5.8
Correspondence between human and computer semiotic dimensions and complexity.

(system's) and a human (user's) perspective are somewhat disconcerting. What users view as a single semiotic dimension bifurcates into two semiotic dimensions in the computer system's perspective, and vice versa. Additionally, easy useful extensions from a user's point of view may be considerably difficult to achieve computationally. Likewise, easy computational modifications may require more elaborate semiotic operations from the user. Such mismatches in semiotic dimensions and complexity may well explain why good EUD applications are so difficult to encounter, and why many of the encountered ones are so difficult to use (and consequently not so good).

The benefit of spelling out the semiotic dimensions and complexity involved in customizable and extensible applications is to draw the designer's attention to meaningful design possibilities. The two levels of intermediary complexity from a user's point of view are the use of figurative speech and the rephrasing of expressions (to achieve some illocutionary goals). Although they are inversely proportional to the computational complexity of processing symbols in them, if the user had *some* intuition of symbol-processing operations, these could be leveraged to achieve interesting effects. In fact, that which we defined as customization activities from a computer system's perspective suggests alternative ways to introduce, gently, symbol processing. The very breakdowns that users so often encounter when trying to reuse recorded macros in different contexts may give them a very good and strong intuition of the difference between constants and variables in computation. Although they will typically not be able to name these programming concepts as such, they will certainly sense the difference between things that remain the same (although at times they shouldn't) and things that take on different values all the time. The same applies to breakdowns caused by underspecified contexts for recursion. They show to the user that some systematic (and inferable) changes every time the same computation is performed must be explicitly and thoroughly defined for a computer to work properly. These ideas have been explored for some time in the field of end-user programming (DiGiano and Eisenberg 1995; Cypher and Canfield-Smith 1995). Programming by demonstration (PbyD) is one of the techniques used for this purpose (Cypher 1993). But, as discussed in chapter 2, with respect to how different categories of signs bring out different epistemic categories in the user's mind, PbyD may emphasize secondness over thirdness, and thus never lead users into really understanding what programming is all about. The appropriate symbols, which will bring out thirdness in programming, must not be terribly complex (Nardi 1993). Some applications have been explicitly developed to help users build such

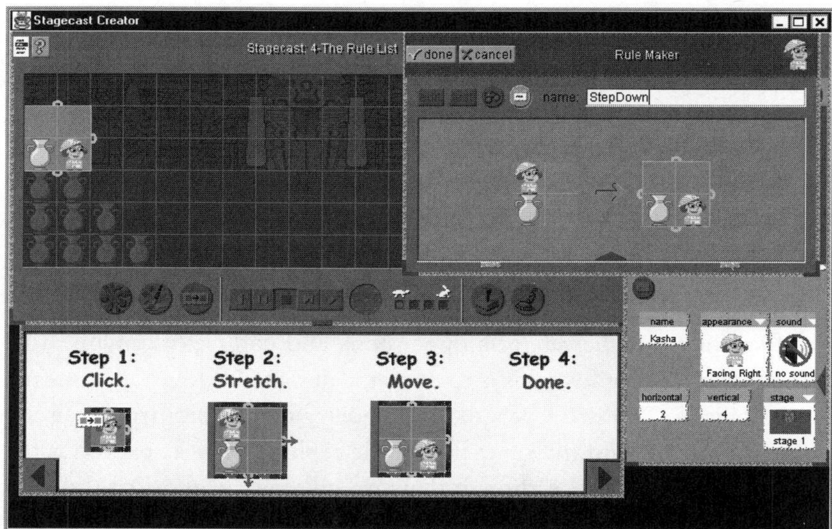

Figure 5.9
Screen shot from StageCast™ Creator 1.0. Screen shot reprinted by courtesy of StageCast Inc.

computing intuitions. This is the case of StageCast™ Creator, for instance, which uses a PbyD technique to help users specify very elaborate extensions to a series of visually encoded signification systems. In figure 5.9 we see a screen of StageCast Creator, showing how the new sign "StepDown" can be introduced in the original signification system, touching on lexical, syntactic, and semantic dimensions. The lexical dimension is dealt with by giving the new significant element a "name." The syntactic dimension and its corresponding semantics are controlled by graphically constrained representations of system states, before and after the desired operation. This kind of technique requires elaborate inferential machinery that generates new semantic elements from a combination of the lexical and syntactic manipulations that the user specifies.

The other benefit of spelling out the semiotic correspondences between a human and a computer perspective is that designers may evaluate more clearly the costs and benefits of exploring more elaborate interpretive mechanisms (e.g., those that can handle metaphoric and metonymic expressions). They can better understand the user's motivation or inclination to express himself in this or that way, or to expand the encoded signification system to include new expressions, content, and intent.

5.3 Interaction as Problem Solving and Design: The User's Conversation with Materials

Whereas traditional cognitive characterizations of HCI tend to cast interaction as problem solving, a semiotic engineering characterization leads us to view HCI not only as problem solving but also as design. Design is implicit (or explicit) in every act of communication, once communicators start to make decisions about how to use the available codes and modes of communication in order to compose a message with which they expect achieve their particular goals. Problem solving in HCI (i.e., finding the answer to questions like "How do I do this?") is preceded by problem setting (i.e., finding the answer to questions like "What is going on?" and "What kinds of problems and opportunities do I have here?"). The communicability evaluation method, presented in chapter 4, helps us see that problem setting is a crucial stage in HCI. If users set the problem differently from what the original designer expects, communication is more exposed to problems that can be characterized with such communicability tags as "I can't do it this way" or "I can do otherwise." Of course, once the problem is set and framed, the problem-solving stage begins.

The similarity between Schön's *reflection-in-action* perspective on design (Schön 1983) and the semiosic processes involved in signification and communication suggests that, like designers, users also have a kind of *conversation with (semiotic) materials*. They can express an infinite variety of intent (since every use situation is different from every other with respect to the physical and the semiosic context of its occurrence). If every intent were a different *problem*, then HCI would require solving an infinite variety of problems, with huge cognitive loads. But if every intent is a different *framing* of a finite variety of problems, then a few interesting consequences follow. First, human unlimited semiosis is accounted for by an infinite variety of interpretations that will determine "what is going on" and "what kinds of problems and opportunities" the user has in every particular HCI situation. Second, the limited interpretive capacity of computer programs is accounted for by a limited set of semiotic infinities, as we have put it in the beginning of this chapter. Although interface codes allow users to say an infinite set of things, there are other infinite sets of things that cannot be said (and/or interpreted). So, the users' task is to frame their intent *as* computable communication supported by the encoded signification system. Some framings will be successful, others will not. And the categories of unsuccessful framings will correspond to the categories of communicative breakdowns presented in chapter 4. Third, if users are involved with problem-setting (communication design) and problem-solving activities (decision making based on rational or fortuitous criteria), supporting the users' communicative design activities brings HCI designers closer to designing customizable and extensible applications.

As an example, an important piece of semiotic *material* that users can manipulate to design communication with systems is the set of interactive patterns encoded by the original designer. Direct manipulation patterns such as "dragging file icon 'f' onto application icon 'a' is equivalent to applying the function 'a(f)'" become a problem-solving *method* for every problem framed as function application. One of the advantages of this perspective is to account for communicative situations where function application is but one of the alternatives for framing the problem. The other may be, for example, to specify a procedure (like "open application 'a', create an object 'o_a', associate file 'f' with 'o_a', and terminate"). A practical instance of such different framings can be found in applications such as Winzip®. Users can achieve the effect of compressing a file in different ways. One is to drag the file icon onto the Winzip icon, usually placed on the user's desktop at installation time. Another is to open Winzip, create a new archive, and add the file to the archive. Both methods will result in a compressed version of the object file. Using the latter is like saying "Thanks, but no, thanks" or "I can do otherwise" to the designer's expressed *offer* to facilitate the user's interaction by allowing him or her to solve the problem with fewer steps. When the communication of methods are as successful as the communication of their relative advantage compared to each other (one of the key contents in the designer's deputy's interactive discourse), the designer is enhancing the communicative design environment that users will explore to frame and solve interactive problems. And the kinds of content required to support the users' design help them understand the expressive possibilities and limitations of the encoded signification system, which automatically advances some aspects of EUD activities.

The kind of communicative design most frequently performed by users during HCI is the design of interactive tokens. The encoded signification system enables various types of expressions (see figure 5.1). When users design tokens of such expressive types, they produce communication that falls into one of the three regions inside the perimeter of the signification territory covered by the encoded system. Some of the user's tokens will trigger predicted and targeted perlocutions; some will trigger predicted but not targeted ones; and yet others will lead to unpredicted and nontargeted effects. So, for instance, successful interactions will usually be the result of the user's designing the right tokens for targeted perlocutions. Likewise, interactions resulting in specific error messages or warnings (e.g., "Correct to: append/1?" in SWI Prolog), result from a faulty interactive token design (following with the SWI Prolog example, "listing(append/2)."). And yet other faulty token designs will trigger perlocutions that leave users rather clueless about what is going on (SWI Prolog's blinking cursor prompt following the sign "|" in response to the user entering the command "listing(append/1)", without the final ".", an example mentioned in chapter 2). Are users expected to understand why the SWI Prolog interpreter can guess that "append/2" should be corrected to "append/1" but not guess that "listing(append/1)" should be corrected to "listing(append/1)."? Users who do understand why the interpreter is prepared to handle one case but not the other have finer perceptions about the various interactive types handled by SWI Prolog's encoded signification system.

Modifications to the encoded signification system, from either a computer system's or a user's perspective, may involve the design of tokens and/or types. Types are conceptually defined by generative rules. Therefore we may have lexical, syntactic, and semantic types in computer codes. May we also have expression, content, and intent types? Yes, indeed. They capture the original designer's strategies for encoding signs from the application's domain, from the profiles of prospective users, from typical activities and task models, and so on. In chapter 4 we identified six basic models for which applications' designers encode that which they expect to be the users' expression, content, and intent to be communicated through interaction. The difference among lexical, syntactic, and semantic types is that expression, content, and intent types are not usually available for computation "as such," except in intelligent user interfaces that can collaborate with users to help them achieve their goals. In figure 5.10 we see how Microsoft® PowerPoint® 2002 captures a type of interaction and associates it with a possible user intent. The user is clicking on the crayons, but because they belong to another layer of graphics (the slide master, in PowerPoint jargon) the application does not allow him to select the image he sees. However, this pattern of interaction has been encoded by PowerPoint designers as a significant intent type encoded in the interface language—an attempt to select an image from in the background. So an interface agent pops up and asks the user if his intent is to manipulate images from the background layer.

The codification of intent types, as well as that of contents and expressions, is used extensively by interface agents who are trying to help users communicate their intent to the system. Making this codification more explicit would help users decide

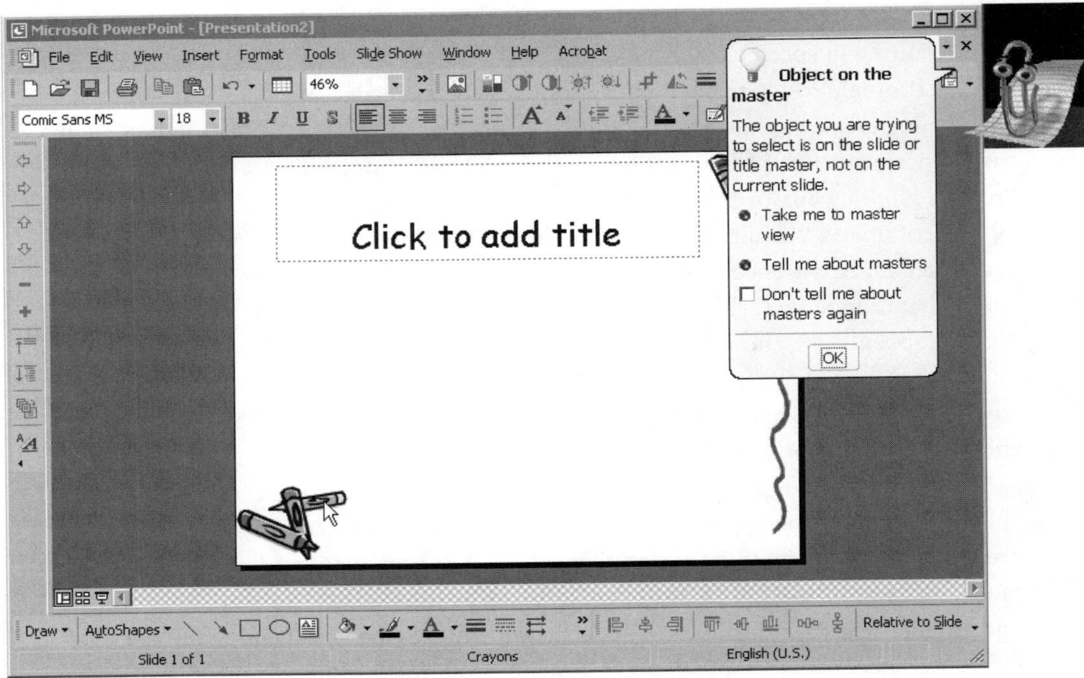

Figure 5.10
Microsoft®'s interface agent interprets an intent type—to select slide master graphics. Screen shot reprinted by permission from Microsoft Corporation.

if and how they want to extend or modify the range of communicative possibilities allowed by the system. For instance, if the user is insistently clicking inside a polygonal region from the top layer that corresponds to a polygonal region in the background layer where there is an object, the PowerPoint interface agent interprets that the continuous mouse clicks mean that the user "is trying to select an object from the background layer." However, this intent type does not extend to a similar interactive pattern that might mean something similar, too. If the user insistently clicks inside a region where there are no objects (in either the background or the top layer), the assistant can't make any sense of it. Surprisingly, for many users, the assistant does not suppose that the user is also trying to access the background layer in this case, too (e.g., to change the fill color of the slide master). Why not? "Why doesn't it?"

Because it doesn't, the user's expression is an innovative form of communication (with respect to the encoded signification system). Thus, here is a prime chance for EUD. The user has to encode this kind of intent and do the appropriate mappings from intent-content-expression to semantic-syntactic-lexical dimensions. This is legitimately an act of design, and the more semiotic materials are explicitly available to the user, the easier his encoding task.

One of the great difficulties for EUD in PowerPoint is that, although users can record, edit, and create macros, EUD is not conceived (designed) as a "semiotic design activity." For example, if the user decides to build a macro step-by-step, capturing the lexical and syntactic codification that corresponds to the expression he wants to use (e.g., clicking insistently on "nothing"), he will have lots of trouble. Recording insistent clicking yields no useful code in Visual Basic for Applications® (or VBA, Microsoft's macro programming language) as can be seen in the following transcription of the recorded "insistent clicking" macro:

```
Sub Insistent_Clicking()
'
' Macro recorded 9/17/2003 by Clarisse Sieckenius de Souza
'

End Sub
```

In fact, the user's strategy of using PowerPoint macro recording to gain access to the system's encoding of the expression he wishes to compose with others in order to communicate his new intent will fail altogether. Macro recording generates object-oriented code in VBA. That is, expressive types are mingled with content and intent types. For example, the code generated for clicking on the title text box in figure 5.10 and dragging it down to the bottom of the slide is

```
ActiveWindow.Selection.SlideRange.Shapes("Rectangle1").
SelectActiveWindow.Selection.ShapeRange.IncrementTop 0.25
With ActiveWindow.Selection.ShapeRange
.IncrementLeft 114#
.IncrementTop 314.12
End With
```

Notice that we see no "clicking" and no "dragging" in the code, which is exactly how the user expressed the action. But we see "select" and "rectangle 1," and can infer the semantic encoding of moving the text box as having to do with "IncrementLeft" and "IncrementTop" values. Moreover, clicking events, like all mouse-based interaction, must be associated with "an object." Therefore, there cannot be insistent clicking on "nothing," which defeats the whole communicative strategy conceived by the user.

This example reinforces the idea that EUP must not be such a big problem. The problem is the programming language that users must know in order to do EUP (Nardi 1993). The example illustrates one of the many kinds of mismatches between a user-centered and a system-centered (or application-centered) perspective on EUD. VBA is an incredibly powerful tool for programming extensions to a suite of Microsoft applications, once the user adopts an application-centered perspective. But it fails to deal with even the most basic semiotic intuitions that dominate a user-centered perspective. It does not portray the applications' signification systems in terms of expression, content, and intent types that the user might wish to modify and extend. Instead, it privileges the system's semantic dimension, even over the syntactic and lexical ones, starting from an ontology of application objects, then moving out toward certain types of behavior or states that encode syntactic and lexical information related to what users perceive as expressive types.

5.4 Some Epistemic Tools for Users and Designers of EUP Applications

By viewing users as designers, semiotic engineering places a great value on epistemic tools not only for HCI designers, but also for users. EUP applications are the best example of how and why such tools may help designers achieve good metacommunication and users achieve more resourceful communication with the designer's deputy. As mentioned previously, every application has a unique signification system, especially designed to convey the designer's message. Even if the signification system resembles others, used in other applications, each is still unique because its semantic base, where the application's *identity* resides, is unique. Therefore, although Microsoft®'s Office applications have similar and interrelated codes, for example, the signification systems used in Word, PowerPoint, and Excel are not the same. The same applies to Lotus® SmartSuite®. The signification system used in Lotus® Freelance® Graphics resembles that of Lotus® WordPro®, Lotus® 1-2-3®, and other applications in the suite, but they are not the same. We would never think that Freelance belongs to Office, or that Excel is part of SmartSuite, even if each individual application has its unique signs.

Resemblance among signification systems is of course a very powerful resource when users must *learn* a unique system for every unique application they wish to use. Having general design patterns instantiated (with the necessary adaptations) across classes of applications helps users infer and memorize what significant expressions mean or may mean in various contexts of use. But the first step toward patterned design is to decide (a) what to design and (b) why. In semiotic engineering, the answers are, respectively, (a) to design a signification system for communicating the designer's vision effectively, because (b) productive use of the designed artifact depends on the success of the designer's communication. Thus the selected design patterns must meet communicative needs encountered by designers at design time and by users at interaction time.

The gist of the designer's metacommunication message in customizable and extensible applications should let users understand or infer the scope and effects of possible changes. The paraphrasing of the message, with specific reference to how customizations and extensions must be expressed, is thus the following:

> Here is my understanding of who you are, what I've learned you want or need to do, in which preferred ways, and why. This is the system that I have therefore designed for you, and this is the way you can or should use it in order to fulfill a range of purposes that fall within this vision. *But, I know you may want to modify my vision in order to do things (in a way) that I haven't thought of. I can handle the changes you may wish to do, provided that you can say what you want in this particular code.*

In chapter 4, we proposed that the designer's deputy's discourse is composed of elements selected from six different models of the application: the domain model, the user model, the application model, the task model, the interaction model, and, finally, the interface model. The designer's deputy's discourse is then encoded in the application's unique signification system, which means that the semantic base of the system refers to the elements of these six models and to the relations among them. So we can expect to see semantic types in the semantic base. For example, an application's functions constitute a type, just as an application's objects, objects' attributes, and so on do. Such types help users internalize unique signification systems faster and more effectively. Likewise, interaction types like multiple and single selection of objects, activation of functions and procedures, naming and discriminating elements linguistically, all help users grasp the design vision and anticipate how the signification system can and must be used in communication with the system (i.e., the designer's deputy). Interface types (which are not the same as interactive types) also help users communicate more efficiently. Representing interactive types with constant interface types like the same kind of menu entries, or spatial relations, or font, reinforces the user's learning and facilitate recall and abduction. For instance, an interactive type like "this, that, or forget," three-way mutually exclusive choices where the first two are complementary alternatives and the third is a deferral, can be conveyed through different interface types. In figure 5.11 we see three of them. On the left-hand side, types are instantiated to different sets of values. On the right-hand side, types are depicted without values but with the significant meaning features that determine the order of choices.

Typed design, with respect to each and every model involved in building the designer's deputy's discourse, will not only facilitate learning and productive interaction, but considerably help frame and solve customization and extension problems. One of the most difficult issues in EUP, from a semiotic engineering perspective, is to motivate extensions that will not introduce semiotic discontinuities into the original system. For example, if the application's designer has encoded "this, that, or forget" interactive types as interface types like (c) in figure 5.11, allowing the user to encode an instance of "this, that, or forget" with interface type (b) will introduce a discontinuity in the original system. Although the discontinuity may be harmless in most situations, it may gain importance if (b) has been used originally by the designer to convey mutually inclusive choices among as many alternatives as there are. In this case, after the user's extension, interface type (b) (a list of items) will *mean* two different things. In some cases, it will mean "choose as many as you like from these," and in other cases it will mean "choose the most likely or the less likely alternative, or defer to make a choice."

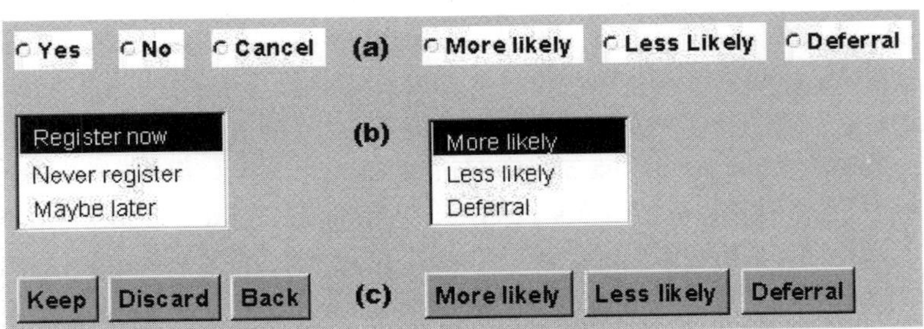

Figure 5.11
Alternative interface patterns for expressing the same interactive pattern.

Typed design is a by-product of model-based design, but software models are widely believed to be too time-consuming and to offer few rewards in professional use situations. So design types are usually those derived from professional practice and organizational standards. But they are not necessarily the ones that will allow designers to establish explicit semiotic connections between software model components and lexical, syntactic, and semantic dimensions of the original signification system. A natural resistance to spending lots of resources when benefits are unclear has been perpetuating HCI beliefs and solutions that may, and perhaps must, be replaced. And there are already signs of a growing awareness that unless there are radical changes in the way we think about computers and systems, users are not likely to experience any significant improvement when interacting with computers (Dourish 2001). The semiotic engineering contribution to the ongoing debate is to connect some points about model-based design that are usually considered in isolation or in a narrower scope (and therefore weakened). Design models, enriched by semiotic connections, can

- improve metacommunication (through an enriched designer's deputy's discourse, as seen in chapter 4); and
- facilitate EUD by supporting signification system extensions through
  - communication using (certain kinds of) figurative speech;
  - communication expressing explicit type-controlled metalinguistic operations; and
  - communication with fellow users or developers about (expected or effective) extensions.

5.4.1 Extending Software through Metaphors and Metonymies

Extending software through metaphors and metonymies is an EUP technique that operates on explicit semantic models of an application's signification system (Barbosa 1999). As designers encode elements of various underlying models, they must explicitly encode metaphoric and metonymic relations that they see among the elements of the signification system. For example, an examination of Pine's signification system may lead designers to see some analogies between fields appearing in a listing of inbox messages and fields appearing in a listing of the address book. Saying that both types of fields are alike will enable metaphoric interpretations of incorrect sort commands in Pine, such as "$ nickname." The command may then be interpreted to mean "do with ⟨nickname⟩ in the address book context what you would do with ⟨a field⟩ in the inbox context" (i.e., sort addresses by nickname).

This kind of interpretation depends on the implementation of abductive reasoning algorithms that will compute upon metaphoric (and metonymic) relations explicitly encoded by designers (Barbosa and de Souza 2000, 2001). Metonymic relations typically establish connections between part and whole, container and contained, product and producer, and so on.

When abductive reasoning leads to more than one plausible interpretation, communication with the user helps disambiguate them. An explicit encoding that fields in the inbox and fields in the address book are alike (metaphor) and that items in a folder are contiguous to the folder itself (metonymy) can yield interesting results. If the user is viewing the details of an address entry and says "I" ("I" is the command to view the index of messages in the inbox), the interpreter may conclude one of two things. That "I" means "Do in the address item view context what you would do in the inbox item view context" (i.e., show the index of other entries in the parent folder, the address book in this context), or that 'I' means "Do in the address item view context what you would do in the whole address book view context" (i.e., show the index of messages in the inbox). The overall effect of processing metaphors and metonymies is to enlarge the communicative possibilities over the same signification system and to achieve more forgiving HCI (where the notion of "error" is considerably relaxed). Moreover, some of the metaphoric and metonymic encodings may be permanently added to the signification system, if the user so wishes. For example, "$ nickname" may become what we call in communication a dead metaphor. It becomes a regular grammatical sentence whose interpretation is systematically associated with it every time it is used in communication. This is precisely how EUP may be achieved through interpreting certain types of figurative speech. The additional components are the abductive reasoner and the metaphoric and metonymic relations in the semantic base.

5.4.2 Extending Software through Explicit Type-Controlled Metalinguistic Operations

Extending software through explicit metalinguistic operations is usually achieved by macro programming or scripting. The border between extensions and full-fledged programming is not clear, since users can produce programs and scripts that introduce arbitrary modifications in the original applications signification code. In our first approach to controlling the types of modifications that users should be allowed to make, we proposed two principles applicable to the original system's signification code and to the metalanguage (the scripting or programming language) through which extensions are specified: the interpretive abstraction principle and the semiotic continuum principle (de Souza, Barbosa, and da Silva 2001). The principles were proposed for evaluating EUP. The interpretive abstraction principle aims at assessing how well the signification system abstracts and encapsulates the application's semantic base (original or extended), whereas the semiotic continuum principle assesses the obstacles in communicating extensions through an extensible signification system. In other words, the former takes an interactive perspective and asks "What do (new) interactive signs mean?," and the latter takes an extension perspective and asks "How can or should these extensions be signified for interaction?" The principles will help users find the answers to these questions more easily than they do in most commercially available extensible applications.

Given a signification system S, whose semantic dimension is specified in one or more languages L, S signs (simple or compound) are interpretive abstractions of L signs (simple or compound) if users can make sense of all S signs by resorting only to

- other signs encountered while interacting with the application where S is encoded (this includes the designer's deputy's discourse about the application); and
- their own cultural background (including knowledge of the application's domain, computer literacy, and common sense).

The interpretive abstraction principle is expressing general HCI knowledge—that interface signs should not require from users other knowledge than that introduced by the application itself and the knowledge the user already has about his world. However, it explicitly says that the ingredients in the user's semiosis are the signification system's signs (in particular, the signs of the designer's metacommunication, unfolded by the designer's deputy's communication about the application) and the cultural signs with which the user is familiar. In other words, both types of signs will merge to contribute to the user's sense making while communicating with the system. This principle also states that if signs from the semantic base languages (signs of L) inadvertently surface in communication (e.g., in error messages like "index out of bound"), the signification system is breaching the principle. As a result, the designers' attention is turned to the importance of framing the whole system as the object of design, and not only parts of it—a practice encouraged by some compositional design techniques that place a high value on reuse.

The semiotic continuum principle states that any two languages, L1 and L2, are semiotically continuous if

- L1 is an interpretive abstraction of L2;
- L2 is an interpretive abstraction of one or more languages;
- L2 has a specific syntactic structure equivalent to text—a compound sign with illocutionary and perlocutionary dimensions whose values are established according to users' goals and systems' functions, respectively; and
- any user who knows L1 and L2 can always translate L2 texts into actual or potential signs in L1.

An actual sign in any language (or signification system) is an encoded sign in the language. A potential sign is a nonencoded sign of the same (lexical, syntactic, or semantic) type as other existing types in the language (or signification system). For example, a potential interface sign is one that is designed according to existing design types. Thus, "wod" is a potential sign in English, but "wrsit" is not. Likewise, "Save as DAT . . ." is a potential sign in most commercial text editors' file menus, whereas "Save as 50%" is not. So what the semiotic continuum principle states is that the underlying model of signification systems (and types therein) should be known to users (intuitively or as a result of learning, with or without the help of assistants) if users are expected to manipulate one system to generate symbols in the other. Moreover, the semiotic continuum principle accounts for some of the innovative uses of signs in communication, according to Eco's TSP (Eco 1976). It is a clear case of users communicating signs that are not present in the signification system itself, but considering the existence and the logic of the signification system.

Because it deals with the pragmatic notion of *text*, the semiotic continuum principle can also prevent some common mistakes in EUP. For instance, if the scripting language and the interface language are semiotically continuous, scripts that do nothing (i.e., that don't achieve any kind of perlocution) or that have no corresponding interface sign to trigger their execution (i.e., they cannot be accessed by the user during interaction) may be syntactically diagnosed as faulty (because the text structure is absent from the script). Likewise, existing semantic types (to account for the user's content and intent), as well as syntactic and lexical types (to account for the user's expression) in the signification system, may be made available to users through various techniques. There may be templates in a database of scripts, which users may query by types of content, intent, and/or expression. There may also be scripting assistants to guide users engaged in building extensions. Even figurative speech interpreters may be used to infer the user's text from a literally incomplete or incorrect text in the script. For all of them, there are two important components in the application's architecture, from which semiotic continuity can be evaluated: a design rationale knowledge base and an intelligent extension interpreter (that can check extensions against the knowledge base, answer questions about the application's design rationale, and include knowledge about users' extensions in the base) (da Silva 2001). The knowledge base must, of course, have explicit representations for all design types, as well as the semiotic connections between such types and the range of actual or potential expressions, content, and intent that users can communicate. This kind of component is very similar to the ones that are used in programming by demonstration, for example. But in explicit metalinguistic operations, the kinds of extensions achieved by users may be different from the ones achieved by programming by demonstration (where the connection between interface language and scripting language is much tighter than in linguistic translation).

5.4.3 Supporting Users' Communication about Extensions

Another advantage of model-based design where connections between the user's and the system's semiotic dimensions are explicitly marked is that users can begin to communicate with each other and with developers about extensions (and customizations) to the existing signification system. Andersen (2001) has used the term "compulsive talkers" to characterize the fact that we continuously incorporate our experiences in communicative discourse. As a consequence, one of the desirable qualities of application's interfaces (and HCI as a whole) is that they must be "verbalizable" (Andersen's term). In other words, users must be able to talk about them. Semiotic engineering has a strict interpretation of this position and proposes that the designer's deputy must be able to talk about the application with users, in order to convey the designer's metacommunication message. That is, the signification system itself must incorporate verbalizations of the user's experience, which will appear in the designer's deputy's discourse. The semantics of such verbalized expressions is to be found, again, in the various design models generated by the designer in the process of producing an artifact that expresses his complete design vision.

One of the benefits of this is that users can more easily communicate with each other (user groups) and with developers and designers about their doubts and suggestions for modifications in the product. Thus, positive impacts on the software development cycle are likely to be felt. Moreover, as users begin to talk with each other about the application they share, they can begin to produce collaborative customizations and extensions, a highly desirable possibility in the context of groupware applications that must be flexible enough to support group dynamics in ever-changing contexts (Dourish et al. 1996; Jørgensen 2001). Experience with specific signification systems encoding different models involved in the design of workflow system (Cunha 2001) has shown that users find interesting ways to express their vision of applications extensions. Manipulations of signs appearing in interface layouts, networked representations of system's processes, and information structure diagrams have all been used to communicate the user's intent. Cunha's point is that if all such representations are explicitly articulated in a metalanguage, some types of extensions can be achieved by users themselves without intervention of developers. This is an important step in toward adaptable multi-user applications in general, where meaning negotiations are more complex than in single-user environments, and may therefore lead to more complex design problems, as we will see in the next chapter.

5.5 Epistemic Tools for the Design of Customizable and Extensible Applications

This chapter introduced epistemic tools that can help designers build customizable and extensible signification systems. It began by portraying software customization and extension as a means to approximate human semiosis, and thus to enable a more natural kind of communication between users and systems. This conceptualization led to an analysis of semiotic dimensions involved in symbol-processing activities performed by computer systems and in human communication performed by users. Two important epistemic tools were then proposed. First, a taxonomy of modifications that can be made to an engineered signification system, both from a system's and a user's perspective, allowed us to make some important distinctions. The taxonomy is not the same for systems and users, and technical distinctions between concepts such as customization and extension, although practical from a designer's point of view, have been shown to have no parallel in the user's experience. The taxonomy also suggested that different classes of modifications correspond to different degrees of semiotic complexity for the computer or the human being. So the second epistemic tool in this chapter was a set of correspondences that we can try to establish between the semiotic dimensions proposed for computers and humans. The result of such attempt shows that there is no one-to-one correspondence between them. On the contrary, correspondences are disconcertingly irregular or ambiguous, which helps explain why applications supporting EUD are so difficult to design and/or use. Nevertheless, as difficulties and complexity are spelled out, some interesting possibilities arise.

This chapter has again emphasized the fundamental role of design models in enhancing communication between users and computers, and in arguing for such models it has taken a few steps forward in identifying some interesting consequences of model-based design when semiotic connections between computer and human dimensions are established. In particular, semiotically enriched model-based design can support two types of EUP—extensions through figurative speech and through collaborative extensions. These possibilities show that model-based design may not only appeal to developers (who hope to achieve faster and better software development, resorting to automation, reuse, consistency, and other qualities), but also open new interactive possibilities and enhance the user's experience in interesting qualitative ways.

Finally, this chapter presented two principles that can be used to analyze languages, or signification systems, when the meanings of one are defined or expressed in the other. The interpretive abstraction and the semiotic continuum principles can be used to explain (and in certain circumstances to anticipate) difficulties encountered by users when building linguistic specifications of extensions to an existing signification system. The explanatory power of these principles can help designers understand semiotic aspects of EUP and thus frame and solve problems in such a way as to improve the user's experience while trying to tailor applications to their specific needs and wishes.

The taxonomies, relations, and principles presented in this chapter may be used to analyze existing customization and extension techniques and to explore novel ones. They help designers view EUD in various ways and thus organize the design space according to this view. An example what novel space organizations can do, as I suggested, is to view sign *repurposing* (or individual nonstandard use of interface signs in communication) as a kind of customization, and not just as a mistake. In connection with communicability evaluation, this kind of phenomenon is *telling* designers that software artifacts are indeed semiotic material for users to design communication as they can or wish. And it places a special value on encoding task models, user models, domain models, and so on, not as a prescriptive instrument for what users must do, for what they are, or for what they know, but very much as a meaning-negotiation instrument for letting them know what designers were thinking about all of this. Having this perspective on software design may even help users become codesigners of software, because they can begin to talk to developers about such meanings and their encoding. So the implications of semiotically enriched design may be far-reaching, which is my main motivation in organizing semiotic engineering as a theory that can be studied and critiqued before the knowledge it generates can take the form of design methods and techniques or computer-aided design tools.

6

The Semiotic Engineering of Multi-User Computer Applications

Advances in technology have popularized computer applications where users interact not only with a system but also, and more important, with other users. The purpose of interaction is widely varied—from collaborative work to entertainment, from socializing to professional or emotional support—and can be expected to follow human imagination wherever technological possibilities may lead. Terminology such as CSCW, computer-supported collaborative learning, CMC, online communities, virtual communities, communities of practice, e-groups, multi-user dungeons, and groupware illustrates some of the many different perspectives taken by researchers and technologists to explore computers as a *medium* for human activity.

We refer broadly to all kinds of software that aim at supporting or enabling human interaction online as *multi-user applications* (MUApps). Whether interaction is achieved through synchronous or asynchronous communication, with heavyweight (e.g., virtual reality) or lightweight (e.g., discussion forum) technology, in stationary or mobile equipment, the semiotic engineering of MUApps benefits from epistemic tools presented in this chapter.

6.1 Three Conceptual Metaphors for Computer-Mediated Communication

The design of MUApps has been extensively inspired by three conceptual metaphors: the communication center metaphor, the virtual environment metaphor, and the telecommunications device metaphor (see figures 6.1a,b,c). Two decades ago, Halasz and Moran (1982) warned designers about the harmful effects of teaching users the "analogy" instead of the application's conceptual model. Analogy, the authors said, should be used "as literary metaphor" (385)—a means for expressing new content, not a content in itself. However, as Lakoff's research (1987) in cognitive semantics

Figure 6.1.a
The system as a communication center.

Figure 6.1.b
The system as a virtual environment for interaction.

Figure 6.1.c
The system as a telecommunications device.

has shown, the boundaries between expression and meaning are not as clear as Halasz and Moran would wish. The use of metaphors motivates certain semiosic paths rather than others and thus affects cognition in important ways. The function of metaphors is not only to "simply illustrate individual properties" of objects (Halasz and Moran 1982, 385). Rather, "human conceptual categories have properties that are a result of imaginative processes (metaphor, metonymy, mental imagery) that do not mirror nature" (Lakoff 1987, 371) and things *as they are*. The users' learning of conceptual models is always affected by "mental imagery" springing from various sources: individual experience in the world, culture, the history of situated interaction with the application, the signs present in the application's interface, and so on. Hence the interest of exploring expression and meaning involved in these conceptual metaphors for computer-mediated communication.

The fact that these basic metaphors are present in most existing MUApps contributes to the formation of a microculture that plays an important role in how users categorize and understand concepts involved in computer technology to support group activities. A single application may incorporate more than one metaphor, and one of the important design decisions to be made in this case is how to articulate metaphors with one another so that users are not disoriented in categorizing meaningful elements of a conceptual model as it takes shape.

6.1.1 The Communication Center Metaphor

The communication center metaphor consists of an interpretive and expressive schema in which the MUApp is cast as a central service provider attending to the users' requests for communication. Various services are presented to the users in specific forms, which determine how requests are made. Figure 6.2 depicts a screen

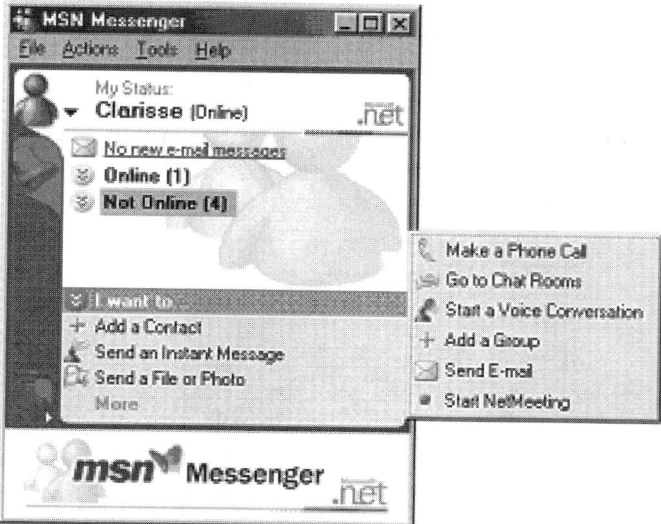

Figure 6.2
An instance of the communication center metaphor in MSN Messenger® 5.0. Screen shot reprinted by permission from Microsoft Corporation.

shot of MSN Messenger®, where users' requests are expressed in natural language sentences starting with "I want to . . ." This feature underlines the communication center metaphor, since the system acts as an attendant. The implicit conversational style (where the attendant is supposedly asking "What do you want to do?") carries important anthropomorphic (and social) ingredients compared to the one adopted by other MUApps, where services are expressed simply as "chat," "email," "teleconferencing," "file transfer," "discussion forum," and so on.

The metaphor may be expressed more weakly, as a mere evocation of the concept(s) it carries, or more strongly. Characterizing the system as an attendant that users talk to in order to achieve various communicative goals may go as far as incorporating human-like interface agents. Figure 6.3 shows a screen shot of

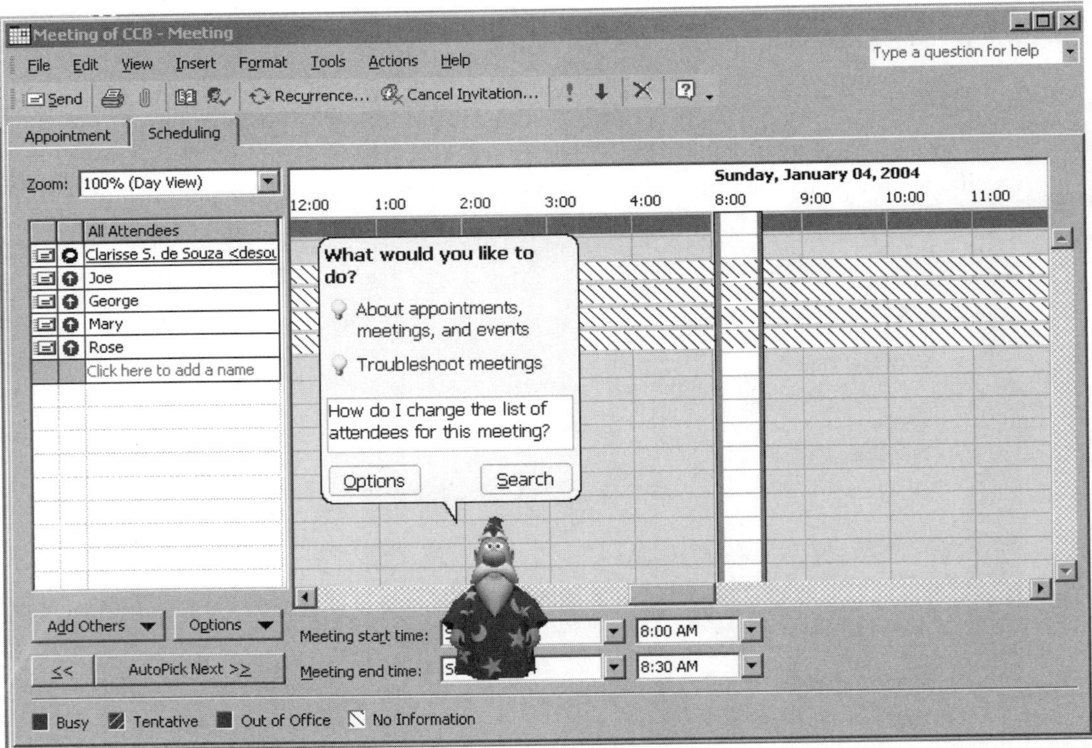

Figure 6.3
Microsoft® Assistant helps Outlook user change meeting attendants list. Screen shot reprinted by permission from Microsoft Corporation.

Microsoft® Outlook, where Merlin (the interface agent) is trying to help the user change the list of attendants for a particular meeting. The interface metaphor leads one to suppose that the agent can understand natural language and take intelligent action. Inasmuch as agents like Merlin are in fact able to help the users directly achieve their mutual communication goals, the communication center metaphor is strongly enforced.

6.1.2 The Virtual Environment Metaphor

The virtual environment metaphor is an interpretive and expressive schema where designers seek to promote immersive or semi-immersive experiences. The possibilities for interaction and activity are enabled by the structure of the virtual space where users are projected. The structure enables and suggests certain types of interaction, while inhibiting others. The designer's goal is to promote (semi-)immersive experiences that will help users learn certain conventions embedded in the application *and* develop their own conventions for interacting with other users. The role of the virtual environment metaphor is to stimulate users "to imaginatively project from certain well-structured aspects of bodily and interactional experience to abstract conceptual structures" (Lakoff 1988, 121), to cast their knowledge and practice of face-to-face contacts with individuals and groups in the MUApp environment. A good illustration of this type of design metaphor is Active Worlds®. Figure 6.4 features the welcome page of this 3-D chat. In the center of the page is the virtual environment where various users are chatting. Each user has his or her own representation (i.e., each user *is a sign*). The user moves around the world, meeting and talking with people (a projection of physical and social experience). The frame on the right-hand side of the screen tells the newcomer "how to move around," thereby emphasizing the designer's intent—that users will experience Active Worlds as a virtual environment where they can project noncomputational reality.

Anticipating the contextualized meaning and effect of direct manipulation signs (well-known to the computer literate) in semi-immersive MUApps may be an important initial barrier. For instance, what happens if a user clicks on the representations of others? What if he or she tries to drag and drop them around the virtual space? The environment itself usually contains other manipulable objects. For instance, in the context of a virtual 3-D bookstore, clicking on a book may mean "Let me see this book." Dropping the book in a shopping basket may mean "This is a book I intend to buy." If the book is taken to a checkout counter, this may

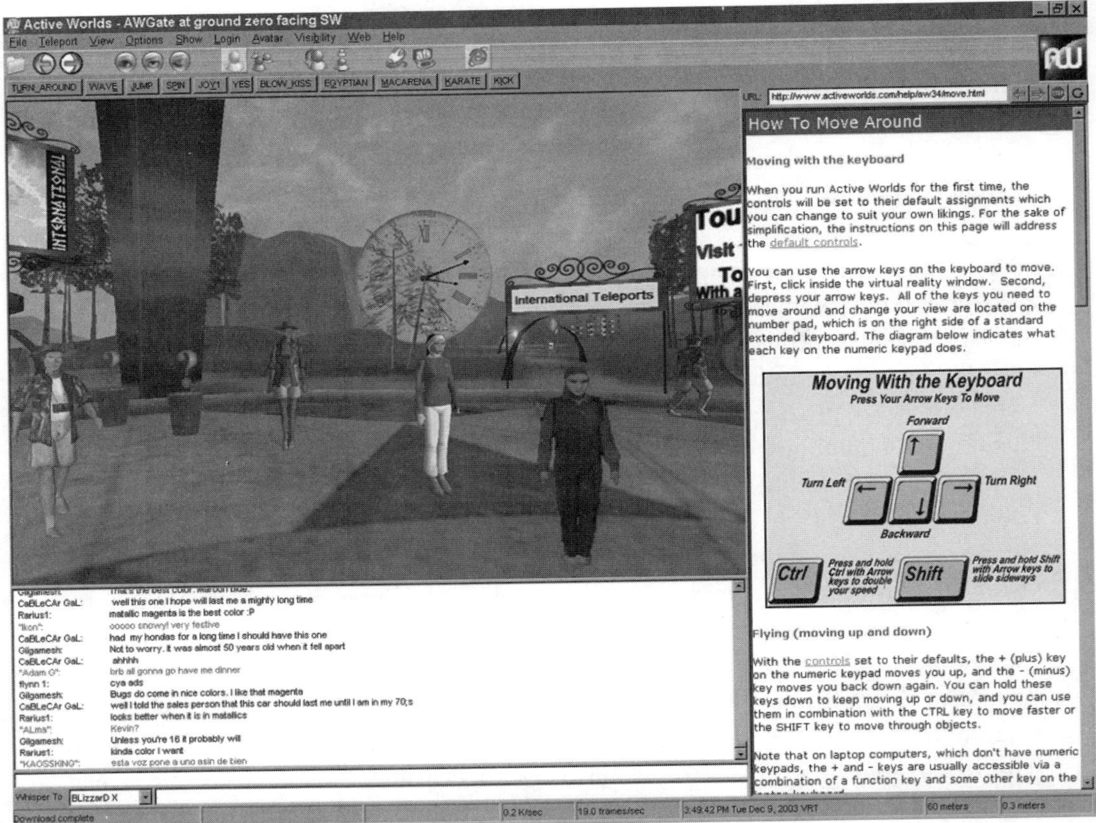

Figure 6.4
An instance of the virtual environment metaphor in Active Worlds®. Screen shot reprinted by courtesy of Activeworlds Inc.

mean "I am buying this book." The difference between manipulating representations of objects and representations of people is, however, considerable.

People have full-fledged cognitive and semiotic capacity. Their interpretation of computer-mediated interaction with others may bring up feelings of joy and pleasure, as well as discomfort and offence. So, the inherent challenge of designing MUApps that follow the virtual environment metaphor closely is to provide users with enriched signification and communication systems that will allow them to project their knowledge of the world onto computer representations in order to tell and do to others exactly what they mean (or as nearly so as possible).

As already mentioned, MUApps seldom match a single metaphor. Active Worlds combines the virtual environment and the communication center metaphor, for example. It provides an advanced mode interface, and users are warned that this interface "can be confusing" to novices. One of the features in such advanced mode is that there are side tabs on the left-hand side of the screen representing telecommunication services (like "contacts" or "telegrams"). In general, applications that offer a wider variety of functions will tend to contain at least a portion that is designed according to communication center metaphor, because it explicitly interposes an intermediary (that can occasionally provide explanations, prompt for more details, and/or treat exceptions) between user and services. This intermediary corresponds exactly to the conversational representation of the designer's deputy. The virtual environment also speaks for the designer, by means of a reified discourse that is considerably constrained compared to conversational discourse.

6.1.3 The Telecommunications Device Metaphor

The telecommunications device metaphor consists of an interpretive and expressive schema where the MUApp is cast as a machine or mechanism, in an emphatically utilitarian perspective. Users can wield the MUApp as a physical tool in order to communicate with others. A good example of this perspective is provided by RingCentral® PhoneWorks® fax (see figure 6.5).

Whereas in Messenger (figure 6.1) users request access to email or voice conversation using a dialog style ('I want to . . . Send Email' or 'Start a Voice Conversation'), in PhoneWorks users directly manipulate the controls on the device. One of the major design challenges with the telecommunications device metaphor is to keep the design simple, intuitive, and efficient. As more functionality is added to the system, more information is needed, more parameters can or must be set, more additional devices and systems tend to be connected and integrated to a particular piece, and so on. Consequently, maintaining the metaphor throughout the whole range of interaction possibilities is very difficult. In figure 6.6 we see that PhoneWorks uses an integrated address book, which is not a telecommunications device itself, but a memory aid that is typically used with telephones and fax machines. The design metaphor holding for the machine naturally extends to connected objects, such as address books and video cameras, for example. But as the number of connected objects increases, one approximates the virtual environment metaphor. Nevertheless, there is a crucial distinction between the two metaphors: in

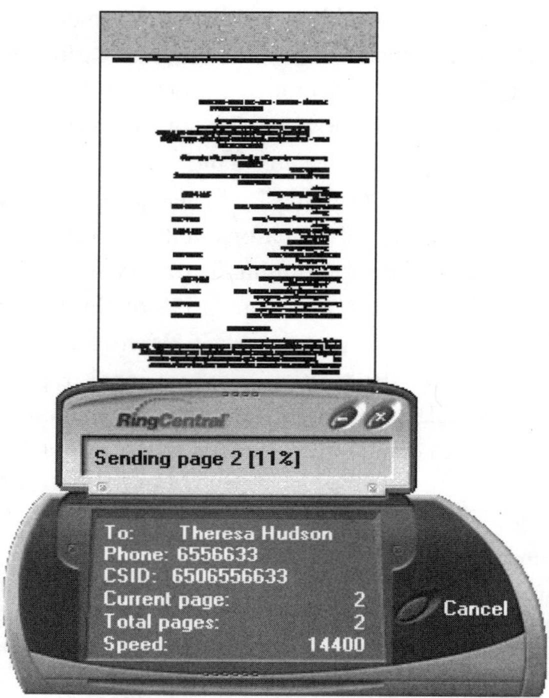

Sophisticated Fax Capabilities

The new PhoneWorks photo-realistic fax interface allows you to easily send, receive, and manage all your fax messages. It's a snap to fax directly out of any Windows' application by simply selecting the PhoneWorks printer driver when you "Print", or to broadcast a fax to multiple recipients. With PhoneWorks, you can even view your fax progress while it is sending or receiving.

Figure 6.5
PhoneWorks® photorealistic interface. Screen shot reprinted by courtesy of RingCentral Inc. (http://www.ringcentral.com).

telecommunications devices the self and others are represented only in linguistic form (e.g., by their names).

The physical and conceptual identity of address books and other virtual objects is substantially transformed and expanded in MUApps. Notice in figure 6.6 that RingCentral advertises PhoneWorks integration with other applications that can directly dial the numbers recorded in the address book. This possibility is not present in physical address books that contain only references, but not causal links, to phone

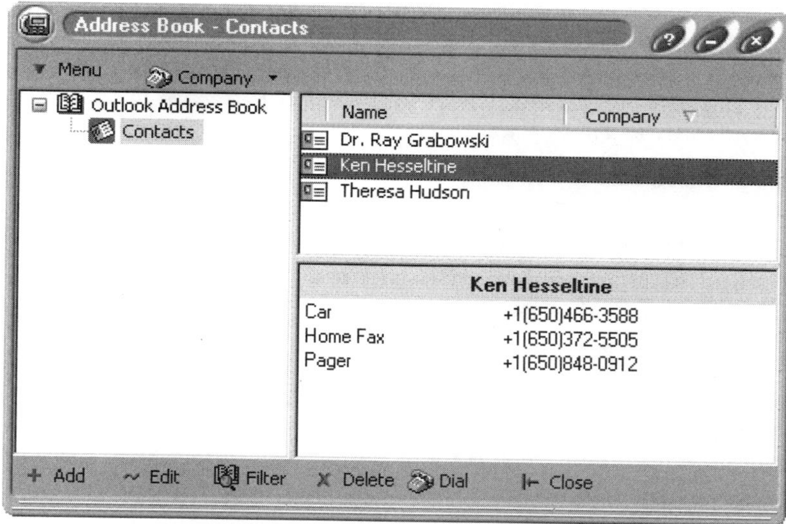

PhoneWorks Address Book

You can either use Microsoft Outlook or you can use PhoneWorks own powerful and easy-to-use address book to manage your personal contact information. It's easy to use the RingCentral address book to make phone calls. Simply double click on one of the phone numbers and PhoneWorks will dial the number and log the call. It's that simple!!!

Figure 6.6
Virtual address book integrated to PhoneWorks® extends the capabilities of its physical equivalent. Screen shot reprinted by courtesy of RingCentral Inc. (http://www.ringcentral.com).

numbers. Even street addresses may be linked to geographic positioning systems and online maps, which again transforms the nature of linguistic signs into something of an interactive experience. All these possibilities arise from intertwining the primary telecommunications device metaphor with other technological and cultural signs, some of them expressed as devices themselves.

6.2 Designer-to-Users Communication

The metacommunication message sent from designers to users in MUApps is the most elaborate case of all similar messages analyzed in this book. It contains the basic single-user message repeatedly invoked in previous chapters, but it also includes important additional elements. The gist of the metacommunication message for MUApps can be paraphrased as follows:

Here is my understanding of who you are, what I've learned you want or need to do, in which preferred ways, and why. And this is the system that I have therefore designed for you, and the way you can or should use it in order to fulfill a range of purposes that fall within this vision. *You can communicate and interact with other users through the system. During communication, the system will help you check:*

Who is speaking? To whom?

What is the speaker saying? Using which code and medium? Are code and medium appropriate for the situation? Are there alternatives?

Is (are) the listener(s) receiving the message? What if not?

How can the listener(s) respond to the speaker?

Is there recourse if the speaker realizes the listener(s) misunderstood the message? What is it?

The metacommunication message is highly nuanced. The MUApp designer is stating that users can find *answers* to the five groups of questions in the message. But *good answers* require good design. For example, some MUApps try to alleviate the communicative burdens of work group members by detecting certain communicative events and sending messages on behalf of users. In many situations these messages may be useful and help sustain the efficiency of collaboration. Let us suppose that one member is chatting with another member who suddenly loses connection. The "system" then automatically speaks for the member in trouble and replies to the sender's last message by saying "I am having trouble with my connection. Please, wait." The positive aspect of this message is that the user is immediately aware that chatting with this colleague is a problem at that moment. But, although the system intervention may apparently score high on usability and sociability scales, it prevents the user from finding the correct answer to the very first question in the designer-to-users metacommunication message. It has a lower score on communicability scales. Who is speaking? The system message is so misleadingly phrased that the sender of the first message may well go on and say "Maybe I can help you. What's the problem?" If his (presumed) interlocutor repeats "I am having trouble with my connection. Please, wait," he may well think the person is being rude (certain angry intonations of the sentence make this clear). The longer it takes to the sender to realize that the legitimate receiver is out of reach and that the system is intercepting communication, the greater the chances are that a breakdown will occur. When users eventually realize that the system *always* speaks in this way for members who are temporarily disconnected, they will probably start to wonder what other messages are being sent on the users' behalf (without their knowing it).

The communicability issue is not necessarily resolved by switching to third-person discourse. Suppose that the system detects the problem and responds to the original sender by saying "Your listener is experiencing connection problems. Please, wait." This is a better phrasing, and the user may even know that the message has been sent by "the system." However, on impulse the user may reply with "Thanks" (which would be a cute slip) or with "What are the chances that he will be back in less than three minutes? I don't have much time" (which would most probably lead to a major breakdown). The problem here is that the speaker (the system) is using a misleading code and *medium* (the same language and conversational space shared by humans for natural language communication) to engage in highly constrained, artificially generated communication.

The code and *medium* problem may be corrected by the use of more appropriate signs (e.g., a visual representation of the listener's state that tells other users that he is experiencing connection problems). Another important question whose answer the designers must help the users find is "What if the listener is not receiving the message?" For the sake of efficient communication, the MUApp should help users make useful decisions about what to do. For example, if the user can't wait long for the connection to be reestablished, it would be useful to leave a message wrapping up the interrupted conversation and proposing alternatives for what to do next. If the technology does not offer this kind of recourse in that same conversational context, the user may feel embarrassed to just leave or feel compelled to wait until the listener is back. Typically, some email message (referring to the context of their conversational breakdown) will be sent with an excuse and a proposal for the next steps. The notion of *appropriateness* thus extends to the realm of sociability and politeness, which technology may affect in surprising ways. And it helps one see that the mere effort of spelling out the contents of the metacommunication message proposed for MUApps can promote useful reflection-in-action during design.

The semiotic engineering of the designer's deputy's discourse explores very fine dimensions of human communication. The three conceptual metaphors presented in section 6.1 emphasize certain aspects of the design vision to detriment of others. The communication center metaphor usually incorporates attendants, implicit or explicit agents that can answer the users' requests for communication with others. Attendants can explicitly speak for the designer, not only achieving users' goals through the system, but also talking to them about the system in order to explain and illustrate features and possibilities, or to help them prevent or recover from breakdowns. They are the designer's deputies, and the greater their communicative competence, the greater the chances that users will get the wide spectrum of the designer's message.

In the virtual environment metaphor, the designer must speak through the environment itself, or be represented by a special character who inhabits the environment and may act as a host. If there is no helping agent in the environment, the complex design vision paraphrased earlier must be fully conveyed through the elements of the environment, their relations with each other, how they affect each other, and so on. Since other people's representations, usually referred to as avatars, are part of the virtual environment, all interaction with them is radically determined by interface signs. For instance, in 3-D chats the different positions and orientations of avatars (e.g., facing in one direction or another) will typically convey important meanings. When another user is facing in the opposite direction as you are, is he "turning his back on you"? If a user/avatar doesn't turn toward an approaching fellow (by commanding the new orientation of his avatar with a click or keystroke) what does this *mean*? How can a user/avatar *mean* that he is having an interesting conversation and others are welcome to *join in* but not to interrupt or disrupt the conversation? In face-to-face communication, physical signs clearly indicate when somebody wants or doesn't want to be taken away from a group conversation. Fully immersive environments, where sensory input is much more refined than in Active Worlds, may let users manifest their intent with natural bodily signs that have much higher immediacy than what we experience in the typical semi-immersive avatar situation. Still, the question is whether appropriate sign categories (with respect to expression, content, and intent) are available to users and, if not, how they can compensate for the absence.

In chapter 2 we introduced Peirce's phenomenological categories—firstness, secondness, and thirdness. The virtual environment metaphor for designing MUApps is an opportunity to use signs related to firstness, namely, the category of qualities that users can perceive (like other people's "presence" or "attitude," or certain conditions of the environment). It is also a prime opportunity to explore signs related to secondness, namely, the category of direct relations that users can perceive (like the "causality" between heavy traffic loads or narrow bandwidth and synchronous communication delays or failures), and thirdness, namely, the category of mediated (inferential or conventional) relations (like those present in culture, thought, and language). For instance, if the presence of self and others is represented by avatars, firstness gives way to secondness and thirdness with respect to representations themselves. In face-to-face communication, the presence of somebody is felt before it is interpreted. In a virtual environment, presence can be felt by signs of secondness (like the sound and image of the self and others) or thirdness (like the names and figures of avatars of the self and others). This phenomenon has important consequences for personal relations mediated by computers. Because users are deprived of firstness, although so many critical nuances of human communication are signs of firstness, they must resignify firstness as secondness or thirdness, and/or develop conventions to circumvent the loss of signification dimensions. One of the issues related to the losses of firstness has to do with trust and truth in chat rooms. For example, how can a young teenager know that someone she has just met in a chat room is indeed a friendly fourteen-year-old girl and not somebody else? In other words, how can we know when another user is being truthful and well-intended or not? Another is the need to express more explicitly (through secondness or thirdness) certain attitudes that are clear when firstness can be expressed and interpreted. For example, if we are not particularly interested in a conversation we are having, body language may subtly convey our availability to drop off the conversation and spare us from being rude and saying explicitly "I am not particularly interested in what you are saying." However, if attitude signs must be expressed by caricatured avatar looks, or explicit availability meters, than we are either necessarily rude to other people or deprived from experiencing more stimulating communication with others. Caricatures sometimes invite rude behavior. So, the big challenge for MUApps designed according to the virtual environment metaphor is that firstness (and to a considerable extent secondness, too) is nearly impossible to signify appropriately. And because such signs play a major role in cultural conventions related to appropriate interpersonal and public behavior, the quality of computer-mediated human interaction may be at risk.

Some of the points made here apply to MUApps designed according to the telecommunications device metaphor as well. When interacting with a virtual fax machine such as PhoneWorks (in figure 6.5), users also make important judgments based on signs of firstness, but relative to objects rather than people. The interesting factor in this metaphor is that, unlike the case of virtual environments, the user's activity is ostensively mediated by a tool—a computer tool, represented as an apparent replica of a physical tool with which the user is familiar. The tool explicitly creates a distance between the user and the person or people with whom he interacts. The sign of distance is inevitably present. A *tele*phone means (and is meant to compensate for) spatial separation in synchronous communication. The role of firstness in such MUApps interfaces is related to the role of *perceived affordances* (Norman 1988). The firstness of buttons in figure 6.5 means "press me." But firstness may be misleading. The fax page viewed on the fax machine does not behave exactly like a physical page. For instance, you cannot pull it out of the device and set it aside on your desktop. The extent of firstness in representing a system's objects and their behavior is one of the hard challenges in designing direct manipulation interfaces (Shneiderman 1983; Hutchins, Hollan, and Norman 1986). Direct manipulation deemphasizes the need and value of linguistic discourse, while emphasizing the value of intuitiveness and affordance. Users are expected to know what to do just by looking at and touching the artifact. Consequently, the designer's deputy's discourse becomes rather limited, because it is a radically reified discourse—a discourse about ideas and possibilities conveyed strictly through the representation and behavior of things.

HCI with MUApps designed according to the telecommunications device metaphor is an interesting opportunity for analysis based on activity theory. The focus of analysis when this theory is applied to studying HCI is on how human conscious behavior is acting through the mediation of various tools and sign systems (Kaptelinin 1996). In particular, activity theory is interested in how people's intent can be affected and shaped by the tools and technologies that they are using to act in the world. Thus, when using NetMeeting, for example, human communication is mediated by technology that allows users to employ audio, video, instant messaging, whiteboard, and even shared desktops for synchronous communication. Human experience is boosted by the technological possibilities opened by "co-interaction" with shared applications that are broadcast to the computers of all users connected in a synchronous communication session.

A semiotic engineering perspective complements activity theory by bringing the communication of design intent onto the stage of activity, as an explicitly engineered sign that is available and intentionally transmitted to enrich the spectrum of users' activities. Tool designers become participants in the activity (through the designer's deputy), even if they decline the opportunity to speak overtly about their intent and prefer to let their product be their spokespersons. Their underlying discourse, as a motif, permeates and shapes the users' experience, hopefully achieving the original design intent.

Although this metaphor may suggest that sociability issues are farther away than in the case of the other two metaphors, this isn't really so. In a classroom experiment where two groups of physically dispersed participants were observed while they used NetMeeting to discuss and decide about the best layout for their new computer lab, a number of sociability issues came up. Most prominently, users who had greater difficulty managing the whiteboard interface (where layout proposals could be drawn and edited by all participants) were left out of many important decisions. They were always behind the others in the discussion and could not make their points in time to get the others' attention. This caused a detrimental situation that, in real collaborative decision-making situations, might bring about undesirable effects. Also, since experiments lasted from fifteen to twenty minutes, some participants grew frustrated and irritable by the end of the experiment, causing the test to be interrupted before its conclusion.

What the three conceptual metaphors show is that the semiotic challenges of getting the metacommunication message to users are different in each case. The communications center metaphor facilitates conversation between the designer's deputy and the users. If the deputy has an explicit representation as an interface agent (like Office's assistant, for instance), it may even participate as a legitimate interlocutor in some kinds of interpersonal or group communication, to help facilitate the use of technology. The virtual environment metaphor is semiotically challenging because the regulating signs for face-to-face human communication, which designers strive to mimic, fundamentally refer to qualities and perceptions that existing virtual environments cannot handle appropriately. Such qualities and perceptions are evoked or represented by signs of secondness and thirdness that must be interpreted and learned by users, but cannot grant them the ability to enact the full spectrum of their social competence. Compensatory and remedial strategies are usually established by users through what Ellis refers to as "social protocols" as opposed to "technological protocols" (Ellis, Gibbs, and Rein 1991). Finally, the telecommunications device metaphor preserves the signs of mediation, and physical separation, in communication, and lets users choose which mediator provides the best match with their communicative needs and profile. Users don't communicate *with* the device, but *through* it. Hence the idea of *transparency* (Preece et al. 1994), of the system receding to the background and throwing the users directly into the "object" of their activity (Nardi 1996). The design challenges arise from firstness, once again, because design intent must be conveyed through qualities that can be directly perceived and interpreted by users, in a kind of primary semiosis (or intuition) that computer artifacts seldom sustain (being the product of intellectual work and unique human interpretations).

The articulation of metaphors with each other is not difficult—both devices and conversational interlocutors may inhabit virtual environments. Problems are likely to arise from short-circuiting metaphors, as is the case of anthropomorphized devices (talking telephones and fax machines) or mechanized communication centers (where there is no one users can talk to in order to request services, only machines). These design options will certainly bring about feelings of strangeness and oddity (which may ultimately be the designer's intent, as in games and entertainment applications) and require that users behave in unnatural ways. An appropriate choice of metaphors is critically important because MUApp designers determine the types and quality of communication and action that users will experience through the system's mediation. Design will determine if they can be cooperative, sociable, fair, and friendly toward each other. Design will determine if they can have fun, trust, privacy, and safety while they are together. It will determine the perceptions they have of each other, and consequently the individual and collective reactions to such perceptions. This shows the importance of an explicit reflection on the content of the metacommunication message in MUApps. The implications of each decision for the kinds of determinations exerted by design on the users' experience should become clearer as designers think through some of the questions they must answer with their product.

6.3 Problems and Challenges in Computer-Mediated Group Communication

From the very beginning of HCI studies there have been important calls for new perspectives on computer technologies for groups. Back in 1986, Winograd and Flores (1986) characterized computers as a "domain for linguistic action" (143), emphasizing the crucial role of human communication as the basis for coordinated group activity. Their view was opposed to the rationalistic problem-solving perspective then adopted by most researchers in AI, who pursued the opportunity to build intelligent decision-support systems to improve the efficiency of organizational processes. Calling the attention of computer systems designers to the enormous power they have in specifying the range of activities and values that gain or lose importance in an organization (a point made by others since the sixties), they proposed that computer technologies should concentrate on helping people establish and manage networks of commitments through linguistic action. Such was the gist of LAP, which has gained momentum again in recent years.

Some years later, Mark Ackerman (2000) proposed that the true intellectual challenge for CSCW applications was not of a technical order, but rather a social one. In his view, the most important issues in computer technologies for group action had to do with knowing more about the users' social competence and needs, and then building technologies that respond more appropriately to these than they now can. In his terms, this would help us bridge the "social-technical gap." At about the same time, Paul Dourish (2001) also voiced his conviction that more attention should be paid to what he called "social computing". Like Winograd and Flores in the mid-eighties, Dourish also stressed the social responsibility of systems designers, since "even the most isolated and individual interaction with a computer system is still fundamentally a social activity" (56). Design is necessarily interpreted and used based on social understandings shared by users and designers, and thus "another critical aspect . . . often overlooked is the interaction between the designer and the user through the system" (46).

The semiotic engineering of MUApps focuses precisely on the designer-to-user(s) communication and aims to help designers understand how their design may or will shape the interactions of people with tools and with other people (through tools). As designers elaborate on their intent and on how to convey it to users, they reach a clearer understanding of how users' life and work will be affected by technology. The common orientation emanating from the contributions of Ackerman, Dourish, and Winograd and Flores is that designers must carefully reflect on the social and ethical implications of the artifact they are about to produce. The semiotic engineering contribution in this picture is to give form to the materials and meanings that can trigger such reflection.

A walkthrough of the specific contents involved in the designers' metacommunication message can elicit reflection on important dimensions of CMC. In order to support this activity we propose a semiotic inspection of MUApps. The inspection procedure is guided by four sets of questions related to the metacommunication message contents. The questions focus on different components of communication, according to Jakobson's model presented in chapter 2 and briefly sketched in figure 6.7. Next to each set of questions are justifications and examples of how the inspection can be carried out (presented as "reflections").

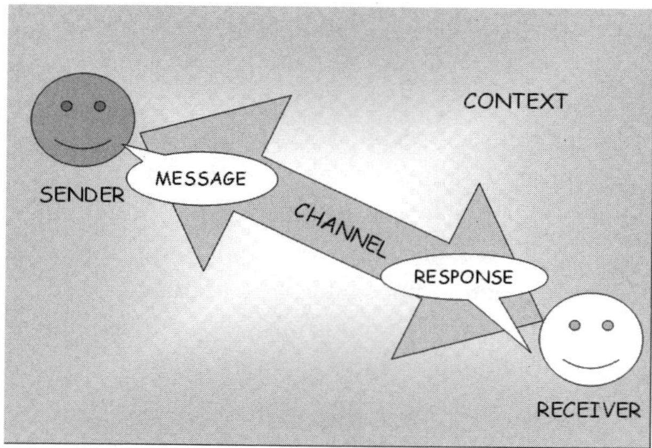

Figure 6.7
Focal points for a semiotic inspection of MUApps.

I Inspecting interlocutors: Who is speaking? To whom?

Questions:

1 Are the interlocutors represented?

Reflection In principle all CMC requires a representation of interlocutors (speaker and listeners). The only exception might be the implicit representation of *self* (the user) in MUApps that follow the telecommunications device metaphor. In this case, the user may be implicitly represented, as in interaction with any single-user application. All action and communication sent is sent-by-self, and all action effects and communication received are received-by-self. Implicit representations may become confusing in action and communication logs. For instance, in figure 6.5 there is not a representation of self.

2 Is the direction of interlocution represented?

Reflection The direction of interlocution is crucially important, since it determines the scope and nature of response. A clear identification of speaker and listener roles is always required in communication. Implicit representations may be problematic. Being a listener may be implicitly represented by the fact that the user is receiving/seeing the message. However, for every communication that immediately entails action, a clear representation of who is (are) the expected initiator(s) of the entailed action is necessary for efficiency and effectiveness.

Knowing who the other listeners are is important not only for coordination purposes but also for privacy and politeness. Unclear representation and control of the direction of interlocution may place participants in embarrassing situations. Blind-copied email messages, for instance, require very careful examination of the direction of interlocution. A blind-copied interlocutor has a very particular role to play in communication, and technology usually offers him or her very timid support against mistaken action. Blind-copied messages are a new breed of complex indirect speech acts introduced by computer technology. In bona fide situations, what is the listener of one such message supposed to do? The message is explicitly directed to somebody else, but at the same time it is intentionally sent to the blind-copied listener for a purpose that must not, by definition, be clearly stated in the speaker's message. The darker side of blind-copied messages (and of forwarded messages, to a considerable extent) is that they somehow facilitate and speed up the effects of questionable social behavior like gossip and deceit. Of course the technology was not made to encourage bad manners, but it creates the opportunity for new types of social conflicts that should be considered and discussed at design time.

3 Are representations indexical? Which are the dimensions of contiguity between representation and referent?

Reflection In the context of the representation of interlocutors and direction of interlocution, indexicality is an important issue. Indexicality is a contiguity relation (like causality and co-occurrence, for instance) binding representations to their referent. Genuine indexical signs cannot tell lies about their referent, precisely because they are not mediated by a third element. The relationship is more direct. For instance, in MSN Messenger® 5.0, if one of your contacts comes online, she cannot "not let you know" that she has logged in. This is because there is a causal relation (that she cannot mediate *as she logs in*) between the login event and a broadcast event that tells all of her contacts that she is online. So indexical representations of interlocutors and interlocutions give users less control in return for more fidelity.

The presence and activity of users in a MUApp is often represented with indexical signs. However, we should be aware that computer signs can rarely be *indexical* in a genuine sense. Except for signs of hardware activity (e.g., blinking LED lights, animated cursors, and so on) and very generic causal signs (e.g., response time for user and system action), indices of system, process, people, network status, and the like are all semiotically engineered signs that by convention represent contiguity between what they mean and what they refer to. In other words, a pop-up window saying “Clarisse has logged in” is a conventional natural language sentence (a genuine sign of thirdness) whose presence is contiguous (in this case, causally related) to Clarisse’s login in the system. The indexicality is thus established between the pop-up event (this particular sentence being part of it) and Clarisse’s current activity and status.

4 Are representations symbolic? What symbol systems are used? Who produces them? When and how?

Reflection Unlike indices, symbols are mediated representations. Because there is no contiguity between representation and referent, the relation between them may be mediated by various levels of semiosis (including inference, action, and other forms of sense making). As seen in the reflection on the importance of indexicality, we must establish precisely the level at which we want to examine mediation between representation and referent. In this case, we want to find out the kind(s) of mediation that can be used. For example, full-fledged linguistic mediation means that users can (or must) tell what they are doing for others to know it. By comparison, in a MUApp that adopts this kind of symbolic representation, online users can only know that Clarisse has logged in if she deliberately tells them so, or does something else that *means* she is online (like inviting others for a chat).

Linguistic mediation can, however, be more constrained and yet very effective. MSN Messenger itself has useful instances of linguistic mediation regarding users’ activity. As soon as she signs in, Clarisse may tell others that she is busy. She may even tell a lie and “appear offline.” This is a gain in control, and a loss in fidelity, but it has important sociability implications. Clarisse may want to appear offline because she is very busy and knows that one of her colleagues will come online only to discuss an urgent matter with her. So she wants to be available when that colleague signs in, but not until then. She prefers to do that instead of saying that she is “busy,” which others may read as “I’m here but please don’t talk to me unless you have something really important to say.” The linguistic control that she has in this MUApp goes as far as the ability to block some of her contacts temporarily, which amounts to disconnecting the channel for communication with them. With such tools in hand she can manage her work with greater discretion, making decisions about how not to expose herself and others to socially embarrassing situations online.

Questions about which signs are available, who can use them, when, and how should turn the designers' attention to the scope and nature of control that users have upon how they and their respective activities are represented.

5 Are representations iconic? Which are the qualitative dimensions privileged for iconicity? Are icons static or dynamic?

Reflection The importance of iconic signs cannot be underestimated in multi-user applications. First, as seen in chapter 2, icons are in theory the types of representations that are most appropriate for bringing out aspects of firstness that are present in their referent. In other words, icons are efficient ways to represent meaningful qualities about the referent. Second, as was seen at the beginning of this chapter, social relations are fundamentally dependent on significant firstness, like the presence and attitude of participants during social interaction. But again, computer signs are all engineered. Thus, iconicity (just like indexicality) must be established at the right level. Emoticons are perhaps the best example to illustrate how firstness can be represented in MUApps. The popular smileys, and the ever-growing variations on the original cartoon-like faces that simulate joy, sadness, surprise, complicity, and so on, show that they are an efficient sign system (originating in firstness) to communicate attitude. But, they are a *system*. In other words, although in many applications you can "make your own emoticon" and use it in creative ways, they follow some important rules and conventions. Graphically, for instance, they may have to fit in particular dimensions. Expressively, they may be (as most emoticons are) constrained to fixed representations of mood and attitude, which is an important restriction compared to face-to-face interaction (where mood transitions can be instantly expressed and sensed by participants).

Another important issue relative to iconicity (and to the previous types of representations, as well) is which set of qualitative dimensions in social interaction are accounted for by representations. Smileys are still a good example. Some attitudinal signs are not prominently conveyed by facial expressions. Relaxed and tense attitudes, for instance, are often more clearly conveyed by body movement and posture. The same is true for more or less respectful, more or less empathic attitudes. Therefore, if the domain of a given MUApp is one where these qualitative aspects of social relations are important, the designer should strive to let users communicate attitude in appropriate ways.

II Inspecting message and code: What is the speaker saying, and using which code and medium? Are code and medium appropriate for the situation? Are there alternatives?

Questions:

6 Are speaker and listeners supposed to share the same signification system?

Reflection The relevance of sharing the same signification system in communication is obvious. But this question is intended to go one step further to determine whether speakers and listeners can *use* the same signification system they share when communicating with each other. For example, before installing software or subscribing to online services, users are generally asked to manifest their agreement, consent, or acceptance with respect to the terms included in licenses and policies. Although speakers (software manufacturers and service providers, in this case) and listeners (users) are expected to share the same signification system (a natural language), they do not share the same *expressive* systems as far as technological protocols are concerned. Whereas speakers can say whatever they need to say in usually long texts, listeners are confined to press one of two or three buttons saying that they agree, don't agree, or (occasionally) need to know/think more about it.

The communicative power of speakers and listeners in such situation is very unbalanced, and not surprisingly users adopt an alienated attitude recognized by a number of service providers who beg their customers to pay attention to terms and conditions by saying: "Read these carefully. These are not the usual yada yada yada." Increased efficiency and speed (the alleged reason to facilitate the acceptance of terms in various sorts of formal agreements by allowing users to manifest consent in "one step") is a two-edged sword. Deborah Johnson raises interesting ethical issues involved in buying and selling software. Although she does not explicitly address communication (especially communication through software), what she says is a good illustration of the importance of *expressive democracy* in licensing and purchase agreements achieved almost exclusively through interaction with a system: "To force someone to do something is to use the person as a means to your ends and to disregard their ends. As with honesty, it is easy to understand and avoid extreme violations, but harder to understand the territory in between" (Johnson 2001, 179). Forcing users to say only yes or no to agreements, for instance, is a way to disregard the user's ends. What about questions he or she might want or need to ask? It is true that users can always call the company, send a fax or email, and so on. But in the specific communicative context where users are being asked to decide if they accept the proposed term or not, what if they say 'No', meaning "Not yet, because I have some questions to ask you" or "No, because I don't really understand what you mean." And what if, as is so often the case, they say 'Yes', meaning "Yes in principle, but I would like to ask you some other questions" or "Yes, but I don't really know what you mean" or "Yes, just because I trust or hope that you are honest people and would not cause me any harm if I used your products and services"? If the user's interlocutor doesn't want to hear about the actual user's intent behind a yes or no what sort of commitment is there?

One of the most important points of inspecting the extent to which speakers and listeners share the same signification code, both while interpreting each other's talk and while expressing their own intent, is to find out whether technology is not giving unbalanced power to interlocutors and, by so doing, being unethical or unfair.

7 Can or should the speaker encode or convey his communication differently (for sake of efficiency, effectiveness, cooperation, politeness, privacy, trust, etc.)?

Reflection This question is the expected follow-up to the previous one. Does expressive balance mean that all CMC (including all kinds of user interfaces) should avoid expressive shortcuts like push-button utterances? No. This is not what it means. It only reinforces the justification for the main tenet in semiotic engineering, which is to let the users know the designer's rationale and decide what they want to do.

At the beginning of this chapter, I illustrated a situation where the system sends a message on behalf of a user who is experiencing connection problems. The idea of letting a user know that his or her interlocutor is momentarily out of reach is excellent, of course. The problem is that expressing the message as if it had been sent by the user in trouble (who may not know about it) creates a problem with trust. Out of all messages that seem to have been generated by interlocutors, which ones actually have? The same example showed that choosing to say "Your listener is experiencing connection problems. Please, wait" is better, but still not good enough. The code used to communicate the problem suggests that the current interlocutor (the system) has the same communicative competence as the user and his former interlocutor. Therefore, it is not surprising if the user engages in conversation as if the system were able to handle the same spectrum of communication as any other user. And this will necessarily lead to breakdowns.

Cooperation and efficiency must be pursued in communication as well. If there is no follow-up conversation that the system (in fact, the designer's deputy) can handle after communicating a user's disconnection, the code and/or *medium* for this communication should be clearly distinct from the code and medium used for interpersonal synchronous communication. Many applications have efficient ways of doing this, like combining aural and visual signs that tell someone's interlocutor is out of reach.

But this is not the only situation where mistaken codes and *media* can interfere in the success of online communication. In NetMeeting, for example, there are certain configurations of videoconferencing sessions in which when one particular interlocutor opens the whiteboard to sketch his idea (even if he has no intention of sharing it immediately with others) the whiteboard window pops up in every other user's screen. What does the pop-up window mean in this situation? "Shall we use the whiteboard?" "Have a look at this." "Oops!"? The problem with NetMeeting in this situation is that if the user merely wanted to suggest that other users turn to the whiteboard too, barging into everybody else's screen is not the polite thing to do. Hopefully, the user will have asked others in the chat or videoconference window if they agree to use the whiteboard. But in order to do the socially appropriate thing, the user should know that the whiteboard is going to pop up in everybody else's window. Does he know it? If not, the situation can be truthfully characterized by an "Oops!" (see communicability utterances in chapter 4), socially accompanied by an utterance like "I'm sorry." The problem can be easily avoided by letting the users know what will happen, and giving them the ability to decide whether they want to invite others to use the whiteboard (before broadcasting the process to every other user in communication) or just use it privately for their own purposes.

In addition to these, design issues also strongly affect the network of commitments that communication typically starts in coordinated action. As Winograd and Flores (1986) have pointed out, the appropriate response to communication is often action that evolves over time and affects other people. If speakers and listeners don't have the appropriate communicative capacities to negotiate meanings before they turn them into action (or request action), an avalanche of misunderstandings and failures may follow. Ironically, The Coordinator has been criticized for *implementing* in technology fixed conversational structures as if speech acts could be predictably mapped onto rigid patterns of action and behavior (Bowers and Churcher 1988). This icon of LAP somehow failed to let users negotiate and control how each communication should affect others (and the self).

The importance of reflecting upon *appropriate* codes and media for interpersonal communication online is tied to McLuhan's ominous statement ([1964] 2002), "The *medium* is the message." So, design decisions about how messages are encoded in a particular *medium are* decisions about the effects of such messages as they are sent to their receivers.

8 If there are better alternative codes and *media* for communication, why isn't the speaker using them?

Reflection When the technology provides alternative codes and *media* for communication that are more appropriate in the situation than the ones being used, issues of intentionality can be raised. This is related to the differences captured in communicability evaluation when "I can do otherwise" and "Thanks, but no, thanks" tags are used to characterize a user's behavior. However, in the context of social relations established in MUApps, this may have important human consequences. If we generalize the enhanced NetMeeting example (assuming that users have control over whether various devices automatically pop up in everybody else's screen), sociability in the group may be negatively affected in two very distinct situations. Suppose that one member of the group *knows* that he can control automatic pop-ups, and decides to say "Thanks, but no, thanks" to the designer's polite overture and request that fellow users agree to use the devices first. Other members may grow justifiably annoyed with this person and segregate him from the group. But if this person doesn't get the designer's message and *means* to say "Shall we use this device?" when he, not knowing better, activates the device in everybody else's window, he may quite unfairly get the same kind of social response he would have had he meant to be inconsiderate. And this is obviously unfair. If the designer has failed to clearly tell this user about the consequences of interaction, then the designer has exposed the user to social conflict.

This situation calls the designer's attention to the effect of default values. These are normally chosen for protecting or facilitating the user's task from a data integrity point of view. That is, default values suggest the logical nondestructive choice that users should make in the context of task-oriented activities where objects and processes dictate the path that best preserve the integrity of their data. But when objects become subjects, or people, and processes become commitment, default values must be established according to different scales. Therefore design is very likely to involve very complex choices between protecting people's tasks and protecting people's relations.

Although choices are very difficult to make, when users *know* the constraints imposed by design, they are naturally more forgiving. And design choices themselves become important signs in group semiosis. If users cannot do otherwise, their interpretation of windows suddenly popping up in their screen, distracting them from what they were doing, is less likely to generate hostile feelings. It may lead them to consider that what the pop-ups are showing is potentially important to what they are trying to do. So, they are motivated to check the message that is, in itself, somebody's attempt to collaborate with them. Technology becomes part of the group's signification system, and it may require that certain social conventions be revised, replaced, or complemented by protocols that can hold the group together and sustain sociability in the computer environment.

III Inspecting the channel: Is (are) the listener(s) receiving the message? What if not?

Questions:

9 Is there a representation of channel and intended receiver(s) status?

Reflection The importance of representing context has been extensively emphasized in previous questions. Again, an investigation of the nature of signs used in representations of channel and receiver status is required. Aspects of firstness, secondness, and thirdness, aligned with timeliness for detecting problems, are important, but sociability issues arise here again. In one of the previous examples in this chapter I mentioned the importance of representing the user's status without exposing him or her to embarrassing situations. In a thought-provoking paper about manners in using contemporary telecommunications technology, Gary Marx (1994) provides numerous examples of why it has the potential to undermine the dignity of individuals: "In limiting and channeling response possibilities, the format of the new technologies may alter communication patterns by lessening reciprocal social skills and weakening the ability to express nuance and complexity" (541). Limitations in channeling response possibilities are to a large extent determined by design, during the semiotic engineering of signs for representing the various dimensions of social interaction enabled by MUApps. One of Marx's examples, although a decade old by now, hasn't lost its power:

> If [a] caller is left only with the answering machine message, is it rude to hang up without leaving a message after listening to the recorded message? If so, is it sufficient to simply report the fact that you called, or should the purpose of the call be revealed as well? (With unprotected caller-ID the question is moot since the time of the call and number of the caller are automatically recorded. So too with a service called "last call return", which permits you to automatically connect with the last person who called.) In such cases is it presumptuous and intrusive, or expected and thoughtful, for the person called to return your call on the assumption that you still wish to speak with them? (P. 544)

Notice that if, in a similar situation online, a MUApp designer opts for making communication more *efficient* by capturing the identification of everyone who calls you while you are away from your computer, manners may be at stake in the exact same way. What do you do if all you know is the name and email of 10 people who have called you? What do they do if they can't prevent your system from capturing their call, but can't leave a message telling you not to bother to call back? These issues hinge on others discussed in questions 7 and 8, and naturally lead us to questions 10 to 13.

10 If the communication channel is defective or the intended receivers are not available, can breakdowns be prevented or resolved? How?

Reflection At the very basic level of communication, this question refers to the user's ability to detect that the intended listener(s) cannot be reached and then decide what to do. If absence cannot be detected, the speaker may wrongly assume that his or her message is getting through and take premature follow-up action. What if the action is difficult or impossible to revoke later? For example, suppose that a group decides to play bingo together. The play is informal, much like in a face-to-face social meeting, where one person draws numbers and announces them to the players, who then check whether the numbers are on their cards. Unlike professional online bingo sites, where databases randomly generate cards and track the numbers on each individually purchased card, in this group's situation the person who is running the game simply uses a physical bingo card set and randomly assigns cards to every other group member. The game strongly depends on everybody having equivalent connection quality. If one of the players has a temporary problem, the other players and the person running the game should know what is happening and wait. Otherwise, the disconnected player may be wrongly penalized for technical problems that he usually cannot control. So, if the player does not get back online immediately, the group should decide what to do. Unless this group can easily check the status of communication channels and of other players, the game cannot be played fairly and, as is often the case with games, some players may get really upset if they think the others wronged them.

The important point about this question and the example I am using to illustrate it is not to say that playing bingo online in this way is not a good idea. Rather, we should examine the possibilities of preventing or circumventing this type of problem, which is likely to affect other instances of interaction online. The bingo situation shows that, assuming that this is a group of friends who trust each other and just want to have some fun together, the group should immediately know if one of the members experiences technical problems during the game and be able to decide what to do next. In a social face-to-face situation, if a player receives a phone call, usually others wait until the call is over to continue the game. And if for some reason the call is likely to be a long one, the player asks somebody else to check the numbers for him or her until the call is over. So the question is what the group can do online. Can somebody check the numbers for the player who is temporarily out? And when he or she is back, can the group know it immediately? Can somebody report what has gone on while the player was out? Can the person who is running the game start logging the announced numbers (which is trivial if the group is using chat to communicate) and send the log to the absent player as soon as he is back? These are rather simple things that depend on good design rather than heavyweight technology. If this game situation is transposed to an organizational environment, where coordination is needed for action involving liability issues, it is clear that designing for timely problem detection and, in particular, for taking agile remedial or preventive action before social consequences grow out of control is a major target.

The bingo example is paradigmatic of a wide spectrum of situations, especially considering LAP. The solution seems to center on tools that will support the (temporary) logging of group activity and the generation of reported speech (like narratives) from logged information. All of this could be accompanied by tools that facilitate catching up with an ongoing process after momentary absences. However, the typical unstructured chat log is of hardly any use in decision-making discussions. The kinds of tools that will generate the appropriate signs of temporal and logical relations in discourse are much more elaborate and depend strongly on semiotically enriched underlying models of discourse. In them, there are at least two very important structuring signs that are not present in most chat logs available to date. One is a useful referential structure saying not only who says what but also who says what with respect to what. Threaded chats seem to be an interesting alternative to explore. The other is the rhetorical relation between utterances. An efficient communication that a certain set of interventions are all explanations of a previous utterance, or that another set contains interventions that express opposition to the content of a previous one, helps returning discussants and latecomers gain a quick view of where and how the discussion is going. So a designer might consider tools to facilitate such abstract instant views of communication.

IV Inspecting the receiver's response and context: Is there recourse if the speaker realizes the listener(s) misunderstood the message? What is it?

Questions:

This is probably the most crucial set of questions for organizational systems, since they refer to the scope of control that users have upon the propagation of mistaken communication and action in computer-supported group activities.

11 Was the listener's response an equivocal action? Can the action be detected and revoked? How? By whom?

Reflection Equivocal action can lead to humorous reaction or to disaster. In between the two extremes are countless variations of consequences that designers must consider when building MUApps. Prevention and remedy depend critically on the timely and correct detection of the mistake. At times, the first person to detect it is the one who has taken the action. At other times it is one of the people affected by the action. And there are also times when only an outsider can detect that something has gone wrong in a process where action-takers and others affected are so immersed in the situation that they are blind to their own mistakes.

Technology easily creates specific kinds of blindness that have important ethical implications. It should not be expected to prevent unethical conduct that cannot be prevented in society in general. But it should certainly not facilitate or lead to unethical conduct, especially by obscuring the consequences of a user's action online, or by not giving him or her enough control to correct a mistake. MUApps are perhaps the kind of application where "designing for error" (Lewis and Norman 1986) is the most critical design imperative. Carefully elaborated metacommunication from designers to users plays a fundamental role in helping users themselves develop group practices and strategies that will use the technology wisely and productively.

Decisions about how to halt and revoke mistaken action must be followed by decisions about who can do it. This may lead to complex conflicts of accountability. For example, in principle it would be appropriate for the group member who takes action to be the only one able to change its course or stop it. In a hierarchical structure, it might be acceptable that other members who have enough authority be able to change and stop mistaken action of subordinate members. But if technology rigidly implements such hierarchical relations, in some domains the tendency to meet disastrous consequences when mistaken action occurs may be strongly increased. This may simply be because hierarchical action conflicts with timely action. Maybe the first person to see the mistake is a group member who is low in the hierarchy (probably because he is the one most immediately affected), and it may take a while before the news about the mistake percolates up the hierarchy to the first person who has enough authority and availability to take corrective measures.

The rigidity of rule-based action was one of the major points raised by Winograd and Flores (1986) two decades ago. Models of group action that are strictly focused on rationality (where mistakes have little place, if any, and rules take over opportunity) miss an important share of what may really be going on in human activity.

12 Was action accompanied by a communication? Can communication about action be revoked? How? By whom?

Reflection This question is an extension of the previous one, and it is purposefully included as a distinct item for reflection because when action is followed by communication, both (action and communication) must be corrected consistently in the case of mistakes. Saying that the correction has been done before the action itself is corrected, or saying that it will be done before really knowing if the action can be corrected, may introduce yet more mistakes and problems in the system.

So pairs of coordinated action and communication deserve even more careful design.

The interest in examining the relationship between action and communication (that usually reports the action) resides in the fact that communication may play a positive and timely role in remedial steps. Communication may traverse hierarchical structures faster than decisions and actions. And it may help groups manage critical situations with more agility.

It is important, however, that communication channels and codes support signification systems where there are distinct signs for communication conveying important alerts. They should be differentiated from casual communication, for instance. Because alerts sent along informal parallel channels of communication can be useful to control the effects of mistaken action, a careful semiotic engineering of distinctive signs of intent in this case may open useful opportunities for handling breakdowns online.

13 Does revoking the communication entail a new network of commitments? Should the network be facilitated by the system, and, if so, to what extent?

Reflection The purpose of this question is to call the designer's attention to the fact that the use of technology for correcting mistakes made through (or because of) technology itself may be problematic. In previous questions I discussed the potential value of providing informal means of communication in technology that can primarily control work processes more rigidly (e.g., workflow systems). However, as Dourish (2001) points out, users appropriate technology in surprising ways. Although design can substantially determine the range of possible appropriations, from the moment that collective semiosis takes place there are literally infinite possibilities that fall within this range.

In chapter 5 I discussed the notion of semiotic infinities and showed that such infinities may be considerably different from each other. MUApps are an interesting case where decisions must be made about which infinities are more important than others and why. Workflow systems introduce typed infinities that enable the automatic generation of various signs (including reports, newsletters, alerts, and even work processes and commitments). But these infinities are monotonous (in every sense of the word). They are predictable, uniform, hopefully unfailing, and for this very reason potentially alienating. So the availability of informal communication channels that will serve as safety nets in case of major breakdowns may end up absorbing some important portions of a workflow system simply because group members are more comfortable and satisfied when they are directly in touch with each other. And when this happens, the workflow system itself is likely to begin telling lies.

For example, suppose that in the workflow system there is a process requiring that a particular report be sent from User A to User B by a certain date. The report is expected to be sent through the system, an action that automatically generates various signs. First, the system reports that User A has done his task and that it's now User B's responsibility to make the next step in the process. Second, it informs the upper management that the state of the process is flowing as expected and that questions and requests about it should be sent to User B. But, what if User A sends the report to User B using the informal channel, and—even better—predicting the consequences of this decision, he also informs the upper management, through the same informal channels, that he has done so. In this situation, everybody but the system knows what they have to know. The group's understanding of the activity state is correct, but the system's understanding and representation of it is incorrect. This makes the system lose credibility and defeats the whole purpose of using workflow technology.

Design decisions about preventing and recovering from mistaken action and communication are very hard to make, and there is no recipe for successful designs. The ethical step to make is to let users know and decide as much as possible about design, both during the design process and later when the MUApp is in use. This naturally leads to customization and extension issues (see chapter 5), associated with the notion of system accountability (Dourish 1997). The use of efficient and effective self-representations of computer systems may attenuate the disparities between the technical and the social perspectives in CSCW. And this is at the very heart of semiotic engineering. The self-representation of "the system" can be explicitly elaborated in the designer's deputy's discourse. This allows designers and users to be in touch and to share the responsibility for the use of technology, coming closer to meeting a variety of ethical imperatives.

The semiotic inspection of MUApps can be a powerful design and evaluation tool. A systematic walkthrough of its questions can draw a professional's attention to the tight relations among various elements of design. Part of this inspection has been presented elsewhere in the form of a communicative adequacy test for online communities technology (de Souza and Preece 2004).

6.4 Pragmatic Principles, Speech acts, and Technological Protocols

As computer applications began to be used for social, emotional, cultural, and even political purposes, it became clear that HCI designers needed to know much more about the social sciences and humanities than they used to. At the same time, it was also clear that the complexity of issues involved in designing good MUApps requires knowledge that cannot be captured in teach-yourself formulas. Complexity cannot be reduced by following a series of steps or checking a number of properties if the background knowledge that gives meaning to procedures and checklists is not there. So the aim of semiotic engineering is only to help designers organize the design space, formulate relevant questions, search for answers (through research, experimentation, consulting with other experts, professional training, etc.) and develop their skills to communicate solutions in such a way that they can fairly share the responsibility for their design with those who will buy it and/or use it. Semiotic engineering provides *reading*, an interpretation of complex problems, and promotes a kind of reflection that is typically conducive to interdisciplinary regimes in research and professional practice. In this reading is the seed for contents that belong to the metacommunication message and for the communicative competence that the designer's deputy must have to support productive and pleasurable user experiences.

In this perspective, the role of specialized knowledge generated in the context of other disciplines is to inform design and promote reflection. Pragmatic principles, for example, can be used in the design of MUApps. If the cooperation maxims proposed by Grice (1975), or even the politeness maxims proposed by Leech (1983), are *implemented* in a MUApp, they are encoded in the application's signification system. In other words, they have an impact on the designer's deputy's behavior, on the interpretation that it generates for users' behavior, and on the types of communication (and their corresponding effect) that users can have with the deputy and with other users. If the Quantity Maxim is encoded in the MUApp signification system, for instance, then certain consequences may follow. The designer's deputy's discourse may have little or no redundancy when communicating with users, since redundancy (by definition) multiplies the occurrence of the same piece of information in discourse. Similarly, structured user-system and user-user communication is likely to contain little or no redundancies. This design decision has pros and cons, as some of the examples in this chapter have already suggested. The pros center around efficiency and speed in communication, whereas the cons center around difficulties in detecting mistakes. Redundancy is an important factor in communication, since it can help verify content validity continuously and speed correction if, in a particular context, content is found to be wrong.

The influence of the Quantity Maxim in design can reach far. For example, email addresses of online community members are critical for community managers. This information must always be up-to-date in order to ensure that members can be reached. In order to ensure that email addresses are up-to-date, MUApps designers may choose, among other possibilities, to have the system periodically ask everyone if they have changed their email address, to use banners to warn users about the importance of keeping their email addresses up-to-date, or to use the user's email address as his or her login. The first and second choice may be a nuisance for people who are not likely to change their email addresses. The two types of communication violate the Quantity Maxim for these users, since not only do they already know that it is important to keep their email addresses up-to-date (and don't need to be told about this all the time), but they are not likely to change their addresses to begin with. This makes the third choice seem very attractive, because users will realize that they must notify the community manager of a change of email address the next time they login using the old address. However, the effect of this strategy is that the user's identification is his or her email address. The designer must therefore be careful to reveal this identification to the community manager only. Otherwise, all email addresses of community members will be known to everyone. And this has negative privacy implications that designers want to avoid. As a result, users would probably end up with two identifications—one for the community manager, and one for community members (e.g., like a nickname). This example calls attention to causal relations between representation and referent and to indexical signs. A minimalist interpretation of the Quantity Maxim in design may augment the designer's tendency to choose indexical signs in user-system and user-user communication. Indexical signs may trigger very powerful semiosis (especially if the causal relations binding representation and referent are part of long causal chains that can be traced in the users' activities). But precisely because they can do it, they may expose more about the users than they are willing to expose.

A similar reasoning can be applied to how speech acts are encoded as part of signification systems designed for MUApps. The Coordinator is a good example of the possible problems generated by causal encodings of the primary structure of speech acts. Promises, or commissive speech acts, generate commitments. However, phrasing an utterance as a promise doesn't necessarily make it a promise. The listener, for example, must take it as a promise. And a listener can always decide not to take a promise as a promise. Besides, there are different degrees of commitments involved in promises—at times a promise is not kept and there are no consequences (social, psychological, or other) for any of the involved parties (promisor or promisee). At other times, quite contrarily, an utterance is barely phrased as a promise, and yet the consequences of not keeping it are disastrous. The nuances of meaning in each case are so subtle that even promisor and promisee may be mistaken about the strength of the commitments entailed by promises. Thus, it is not surprising that a causal encoding of speech acts into conversational structures that will track that promises are kept, that directives are met, and so on eventually brings about more tension or misunderstandings than expected.

Ellis, Gibbs, and Rein (1991) distinguish between technological and social protocols. Technological protocols are group interpersonal contact practices that are built into hardware or software (i.e., encoded into the MUApp signification system), whereas social protocols are mutually agreed-upon practices that the group formally or informally decides to follow when they are together online. The authors note that when design privileges social protocols over technological ones, processes become typically more adaptive, but this choice may also lead to distraction and inefficiency in group activities. On the other hand, technological protocols can be overly restrictive, preventing the group from developing their own idiosyncratic way of interacting with each other. Since designers of MUApps must eventually choose when to go for one over another kind of protocol, it is helpful to help them represent their vision and rationale, to let the signs present in design semiosis materialize somehow and talk back to designers during reflection in action.

Prates (1998; Prates and de Souza 1998) and Barbosa (2002) have developed a conceptual architecture model for MUApps design-support tools called MArq-G*. The model has been conceived to help designers materialize part of their vision and rationale about group communication processes. The interesting thing about MArq-G* is that it encodes certain communicative dimensions that designers must think about during design. As decisions about the values and signs associated with each of these dimensions are made and expressed in a design language, heuristic rules about the interaction among such values and signs can be used by the interpreter of MArq-G*, which then prompts the designer to think about potential inconsistencies and trade-offs. The MArq-G* architecture is presented in figure 6.8.

Although Prates and Barbosa initially conceived of MArq-G* for only a subset of the dimensions discussed in section 6.3, the value of the model is that it

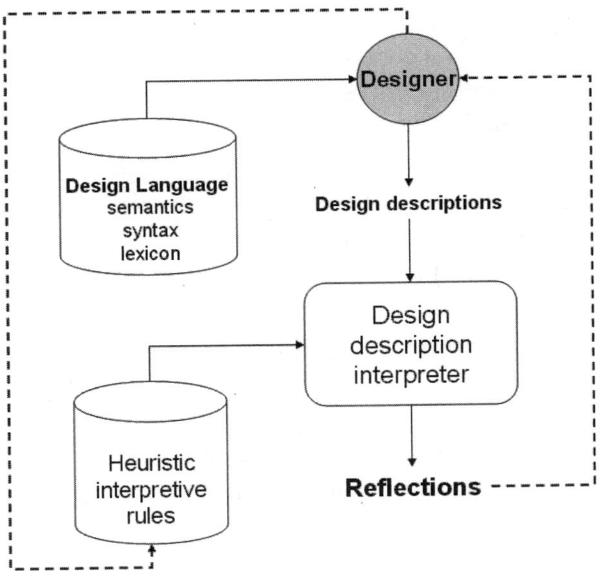

Figure 6.8
MArq-G* components.

accommodates expansions to account for as many dimensions as designers wish to consider at design time. For the sake of illustration, let us look at an instantiation of a specific set of dimensions and rules used by Barbosa to illustrate the types of reflections that MArq-G* can support during design. The instantiation refers to a description of NetMeeting and focuses on the way this MUApp works when the whiteboard is opened by one of the group members who are together online. In order to clarify the nature and consequence of decisions, let us recall how NetMeeting works in the context of a hypothetical scenario. It involves three participants—A, B, and C—who have different hierarchical roles in the social context where they are. A is B and C's superior. So these three are using the chat tool to talk about a conference A and B have been to, and C doesn't quite understand the physical layout of the exhibit area. So A and B have different ideas of how to tell C about it. Whereas B chooses to write a more detailed description of the area, A decides to make a drawing on the whiteboard and explain the spatial configuration with it. What happens is that as soon as A opens the whiteboard, it simultaneously pops up on B and C's screens. B interrupts his typing in the chat tool and momentarily wonders how the whiteboard appeared on his screen. A is not completely aware of the kinds of disruption she may be causing to B or C, because in her mind she is only drafting the exhibit area, which she will be talking about when she finishes.

Barbosa's illustration focuses on the illocutionary force taken up by certain speech acts when they are encoded in the technological protocol. The relevant portion of the design description, which we have translated and adapted from the original in Portuguese (Barbosa 2002) to fit the purposes of this chapter, is as follows:

Roles Supervisor is a role; Helper is a role.
Group Members A is a member; B is a member; C is a member.
Classes of Objects Tool is a class of objects.
Objects Chat is an object; Whiteboard is an object.
Role Attribution A is a supervisor; B is a helper; C is a helper.
Group Hierarchy Supervisors are superior to helpers.
Shared Objects Chat is shared by A, B, and C; Whiteboard is shared by A, B, and C.
Communicative Profile Any member can communicate directive speech acts to other members regarding objects that they share.

Now, in the heuristic interpretation rules of MArq-G* there is knowledge about the illocutionary force of directive speech acts. The illocutionary force is the combination of the speaker's intent and the contextual conditions that must be true so that the speech act can be accomplished (e.g., sincerity conditions, preparatory conditions). Two of these rules are:

Rule #N In a hierarchical group structure, directive speech acts sent from superiors to subordinates have force of order. If order is not the intended illocutionary force, there must be explicit signs to distinguish and verify illocutionary forces that can be associated to directive speech acts in this case.

Rule #N + 1 In a hierarchical group structure, directive speech acts sent from subordinates to superiors, or communicated among members at the same hierarchical level, have force of suggestion. If suggestion is not the intended illocutionary force, there must be explicit signs to distinguish and verify illocutionary forces that can be associated to directive speech acts in this case.

As the MArq-G* interpreter processes the descriptions for this group of three people, it detects that there are different illocutionary forces for directive speech acts: orders and suggestions. The MUApps signification system may explicitly encode these two meanings, by having differentiated lexical signs for one and the other, or ascribe these meanings to the signs occurring in the interlocutors' semiosic processes. Explicit markings give users much more control over illocutionary force. For example, if there are no markings, all directives sent from member A (see previous example) to B and C will be always interpreted as an order. But there may be times when A just wants to make a suggestion—not force her ideas on others just because she happens to be the others' superior. These reflections are triggered by the contents of rules N and N + 1.

Prates and Barbosa have implemented a design language and a knowledge base with nearly sixty heuristic rules written in Prolog. Their original design tool cuts across most of the questions presented in section 6.3, but only a few types of reflections have been included in the knowledge base. Nevertheless, the type of tool they have developed can be expanded to include not only a larger portion of the reflections in section 6.3 but, in fact, additional questions and their corresponding reflections. An important aspect of this tool is that the character of the rules in the knowledge base is merely descriptive. Building on the same NetMeeting example, and assuming that there are no signs in the MUApps signification system to differentiate between illocutionary forces (as is indeed the case in NetMeeting), an order and a suggestion from A to B and C are indistinguishably encoded as launching the tool in all the subordinate participants' desktops. However, subordinate participants may minimize (and ignore) the directive to use the tool, and just keep doing whatever they were doing before. This design feature in NetMeeting introduces an ambiguity that touches on questions 11, 12, and 13 in section 6.3: What if the listener misunderstands communication? The problem with NetMeeting is that the misunderstanding may take a while to be detected. How will the supervisor know if subordinates have minimized the whiteboard on their respective screens? NetMeeting's designers have decided to assign all these decisions to the social protocol. The technological protocol does not help participants control the status of shared applications to this level of detail. Thus the knowledge base may warn designers that certain breakdowns may follow from this decision. But it will not prevent designers from proceeding with their design decisions and overriding the rules relative to detecting misunderstandings.

The particular implementation of MArq-G* made by Prates and Barbosa is less important than the type of computer tool that can be developed to help designers express their rationale and reflect upon the potential consequences of their decisions. A valuable by-product of using such a tool is that final design decisions and trade-offs may be encoded in the designer's deputy's discourse about the technology and help users have a clear idea of the MUApps they are using for interacting with others online. It is particularly important for designers to share responsibilities with the users of the technology they produce, especially in the context of MUApps that can be used for social, emotional, cultural, and political purposes.

6.5 Technological Signs and Their Impact on Group Semiosis

Ellis, Gibbs, and Rein's early discussion (1991) about decisions on what to assign to social protocols and what to assign to technological protocols when talking about computer applications for groups might lead designers to suspect that social protocols may *always* override, modify, or control what is encoded in the technological protocol. For example, if NetMeeting's technological protocol appears rude to other group members, for barging onto their desktops with a new tool, the right thing to do it to negotiate the launching with other members through chat or videoconference. This strategy may work, although it leads to the sorts of consideration about manners that Gary Marx (1994) makes. Technological protocols, however, reach much farther than this.

In a study about the expectations that potential MUApps users have about this kind of technology (da Silva et al. 2003), we have found that a group of people who met regularly face-to-face for a weekly academic seminar had the following categories of expectations:

Regarding the presentation of the content of their discussions online, they expected that they would have
information filtering;
summaries and abstracts;
structuring and visualization of information.

Regarding the ability to reproduce or approximate the kinds of interaction that they had face-to-face, they expected that they would have
enriched representation and control of the context of communication;
the ability to use gestures and to express their feelings and attitudes.

Regarding privacy issues, they expected that they would have
privacy among members, in particular:
the ability to have private conversations,
the ability to organize individual and collective spaces;
privacy regarding visitors and new members:
the ability to decide which portions of group discussions and materials visitors would be able to see.

Regarding the style and exercise of leadership, they expected that they would have
encouragement to participate in group activities;
mutually agreed procedures for decision making;
coordination or moderation of discussion sessions.

Regarding their participation in group decisions, they expected that they would have
the ability to make group decisions about allowing or not allowing visitors to access group discussions;
the ability to make group decisions about what to do with members who do not contribute to discussions;
the ability to make group decisions about how to present collective information (to insiders and outsiders).

A semiotic inspection of three lightweight contemporary environments popular among online groups showed that what such potential users expect and what they get from such environments is considerably far apart in a number of cases. Part of the distance is due to questionable design decisions that, for example, prevent users from organizing their discussions and materials in effective ways, or make it difficult for them to control how much of their activities outsiders can have access to when they are visitors to the group. Another part of the distance is due to the technological restrictions of lightweight environments. The signs that express feelings and attitudes, for example, are not particularly refined in such environments. Body language and facial expressions are typically sacrificed in nonimmersive MUApps, causing nonverbal communication to suffer considerably from lack of expression. All the discussion about signs of firstness in section 6.3 is applicable in this case. However, the most interesting indication of this study has been the possibility that the rule-based nature of computer programs (which all MUApps ultimately are, no matter what the share of decisions that designers assign to social protocols emerging from interaction in the computer *medium*) is incompatible with the dynamics and flexibility of human interaction.

In part, this was the point made by Winograd and Flores (1986), when they called to the attention of organizational systems designers the fact that all computer programs necessarily affected the relationships and the achievements of people who used them. But it seems that the authors' new foundations for design, replacing goal-directed rational models of human activity with models of human coordination for action through communication, still dictates and imposes important constraints on social interaction. Our study suggested that the symbol-processing nature of computation requires that every group online must be represented and computationally interpreted and controlled according to a fixed set of rules. It is as if all groups, even the most ephemeral and informal ones, necessarily had to obey a certain number of unchanging rules. These basic rules determine the necessary conditions for the group to be created, for somebody to become a member, for any member to express whatever they want to express, for any other member to react to a member's expression, and so on. Unlike with natural groups, whose members typically have an unconscious knowledge (often a mere intuitive feeling) of the principles that hold the group together and give meaning to their activities, with online groups self-consciousness and observation of rules is an imperative. Thus, by necessity, an extensive share of human social competence is transformed online. The place and role of intuitions is shifted to other spheres of human interaction, and a number of familiar signs in face-to-face communication must be resignified within a technologically constrained semiotic space.

By examining the expectations of participants in our study, we concluded that the difficulty in designing MUApps is not only that there is so much to know about and that decisions are always so hard to make. It is also that the current model of computation that determines the implementations of computer applications for groups does not allow us to meet some cherished social values like *spontaneity*, *informality*, *flexibility*, and *freedom*. These signs were explicitly mentioned in the answers given by participants to questions asked in our study's interviews.

Paul Dourish (2001) has recently raised a related point. He writes, "HCI, from its very beginning, took on the trappings of the traditional computational model and set out its account of the world in terms of plans, procedures, tasks, and goals" (4). His critique is directed to the role that representations have had in this tradition. Representations have led to disembodiment in action—that is, to a separation between mind and body, between thought and action. And Dourish's point is precisely to reconcile the two, and to achieve embodied interaction, interaction "rooted in the ways in which people (and technologies) participate in the world" (189). However, the author concedes that software is a representational medium.

If representations are inevitably at the heart of software artifacts, then again it seems that although the kinds of rules processed by MUApps can be made more flexible, more adaptive, more embodied, the semiotic engineering of representations will always determine the types of rules that users will have to know and live with as they use computers to interact with other people and achieve a wide variety of goals and effects.

6.6 Epistemic Tools for the Design of Multi-User Computer Applications

In this chapter I have introduced epistemic tools that can help designers formulate and explore semiotic issues involved in the design of MUApps. First, I presented three basic conceptual metaphors that are used in isolation or in combination with each other in practically all contemporary MUApps: the communication center metaphor, the virtual environment metaphor, and the telecommunications device metaphor. I have shown that each metaphor motivates the use of different types of signs, and by so doing each favors certain aspects of communication to the detriment of others. I have also shown that these metaphors can be articulated with each other in coherent ways, but the discourse of the designer's deputy can only be explored to the degree of finesse introduced in previous chapters of this book if a linguistic system can be extensively used. Strictly visual signification systems are excessively confining to communicate the whole spectrum of meanings involved in group interaction online through the mediation of artifacts resulting from human interpretation and imagination.

Then I characterized the content of the metacommunication message from MUApps designers to MUApps users. From this characterization I derived a semiotic inspection procedure consisting of a set of questions about the structure of user-system and user-user communication. For every question I presented types of reflection that can be triggered by such attempts to find an appropriate answer. These types referred to channels and codes of communication, to the categories of signs in encoded signification systems, to the values (social and other) that provide a backdrop for interpretation of computer-mediated communication, to the possibilities of detecting and correcting communicative mistakes, to the roles and expectations held by interlocutors, and so on.

By aligning the concept of technological protocols to encoded signification systems in MUApps, I have analyzed the trade-offs of design when it comes to implementing meanings that are part of causal relations expected to hold when they are used in technological contexts. This led me to examine the fundamental effects of computation on group relations and activities. Computer programs are rule-based symbol processes that challenge many users' aspirations with respect to the nature and quality of their interaction online, such as spontaneity, informality, flexibility, and freedom. Computer programs require that users follow the rules encoded in them, something that naturally promotes a higher degree of self-consciousness and regulation than in many natural face-to-face social relations.

Although I have not and cannot give definitive answers to the issues raised in this chapter, the message repeatedly stated for designers is to improve the communication of their design vision to users. This will not only allow them to share more fairly with the users the responsibility for the technology they have designed, but it will also trigger the users' collective semiosis in potentially surprising directions and clever practices.

III

Questions

Use your light,
but dim your brightness.
—Lao Tzu

7
Reflection

I am now coming to the end of this book, when it would be time to present my conclusions. However, in the semiotic vein so strongly emphasized in the previous chapters, I deliberately choose to talk about reflections rather than conclusions. The book is a testimony to my own ongoing semiosis, and I hope that the signs I have used to express my perceptions will stimulate the readers' semiosis along a new path of exploration and discovery. There will be counterevidence to many of my abductions, new signs for continuing research, all very welcome as in any scientific endeavor.

The following sections are three notes meant to sound merely as a soft final chord. The first evokes the relationship between semiotics and computation; the second, the relationship between semiotics and design; and the third, the role of epistemic tools for HCI designers and users. Some signs on the road ahead resonate with this chord, and with them I finish this book.

7.1 Semiotics and Computation

There is a short story by Umberto Eco called "On Truth: A Fiction" (Eco 1988), which represents through fictional narrative a longstanding philosophical debate about the definition of meaning and where it resides. The short story is worth mentioning in this final reflection, because it touches deep on meaning and accountability, two issues seldom discussed in HCI despite the relevance of their implications.

The plot of the story is an insightful allegory. Sometime in the future, the members of an outer-space expedition all die on another planet, defeated by dysentery. Not knowing if this incident calls for retaliation, the leaders of the project on Earth decide to find out first what has really happened. A second expedition is then sent to the planet in order to investigate whether the members of the previous one have been poisoned by the natives. It is known that they drank as water what the natives call "water." This expedition tests the natives to find out which feelings or mental representations they have when they hear the word *water*. But the problem is that natives don't speak like humans. When a child approaches a hot stove, for instance, a mother says: "'*Oh my God, he will stimulate his C-fibers!*'" (Eco 1988, 41). Because this expedition fails to advance the investigation, a third expedition is sent to the planet. The mission is now to find out if, in the expeditioners' view, the natives can understand the meaning of any sentence at all. The method they use is to explore the meanings stored in this planet's computers. Why? Because computers necessarily have representations of whatever it is that *meaning* means to the people who build the programs that run on them. AI programs, in particular, have the additional capacity to make *meaningful computations* on representations. Therefore, their algorithms are themselves representations of what meaningful computations mean to the people who build them.

The story develops in a kind of reversed Turing test, where one of the expedition members steps into the carcass of an empty computer and talks to another computer *as if* he were a computer himself. As the human performs wonderfully in the reversed Turing test, the computer reveals all it knows about the representations and meanings it can compute upon. The computer lets the expedition member know that it defines itself as "only a semiotic machine," inexorably interpreting expressions in accordance with higher-order expressions. But it cannot, however, explain why or how its own interpretation process works. All the computer succeeds in saying about its masters is "I don't know if my memory is the same as that of my masters. According to my information, they are very uncertain about what they have inside them. . . . That is the reason why they set me up. They know what I have inside me, and when I speak in a way that they understand, they presume that they have the same software inside them" (Eco 1988, 59).

This allegory touches on philosophical issues that permeate everything we do in HCI. Positivist traditions have encouraged the view that computer users have in mind some achieved, unchanging, "objective" knowledge, purposes and perceptions that can be modeled and mirrored in various types of software artifacts. So there have been calls for technology that supports more embodiment, situatedness, and deeper social and context awareness, all of which are fundamentally right in denouncing reductionist attempts to squeeze the whole spectrum of users' understanding and experience into mechanical systems that follow strict logical procedures.

However, one of the hard problems in HCI and in computer science in general is precisely what program producers and program consumers take program representations to mean. As suggested in Eco's fiction, when they understand program representations they tend to presume that such representations are somehow "true." But they are only true to what programs have "inside." Why are program producers and consumers inclined to see truth in programs? And what does this truth mean?

In our daily lives, we are constantly exposed to things that are not true. Many of them are just plainly stated as such—they are formulated as conjectures, hopes, fears, jokes, possibilities, assumptions, ideas. And we are fully capable of dealing with things that are explicitly not true, or not even meant to be true. The hypothesis advanced in this book is that, to date, the main foundational theories in HCI have tacitly assumed that computer programs must contain true statements about the users' "inside"—about their mental behavior, their intent to act in the world, their way to perceive and relate to the environment, and so on. No theory has overtly questioned who is making such statements, or how far these statements can be carried when it comes to designing and engineering computer artifacts. Psychophysical laws, probabilistic principles, statistical evidence, and even minute observations of past and gone experiences have been often expected to spell out the truths to be modeled and encoded in computer programs. But the disorienting evidence of how such truths are not *true* in so many contexts of use has been taken as an indication that there is something wrong with the theories.

But there isn't necessarily anything wrong with the theories. What may be wrong is how we interpret them, and what we expect to be able to do with them. Semiotic engineering makes an important switch in this perspective, by claiming explicitly that computer programs represent what "a designer" takes to be true about the nature, the usefulness, and the impact of the artifact being designed. It frames software as a very particular kind of discourse, communicating ideas elaborated by people, to people, and about people—not ultimate truths. A designer should thus be radically honest, at design time and at interaction time, replacing the notion of truth with that of *beliefs*. The goal of HCI in semiotic engineering is to allow users to react to technology just as they react to communication that makes them an offer. What if they used the technology being offered? Do they want to use it? How do they want to use it? Would they wish to adapt it, to make changes? Users are naturally more inclined to relate to technology that wears its weaknesses and limitations on its sleeves, but much less inclined to be tolerant with technology that is built and expressed as a claim (rather than a belief) about who they are and what they want.

Theories, in my perspective, should not be used as the providers of truths and definitive answers to be encoded in computer programs. And this applies to semiotic engineering itself, of course. Most of the hard problems in HCI will never have a final answer. Designers must just learn to deal with them and share their efforts and responsibilities with users. Talk to them and let them talk back to them, at interaction time, right there "where the action is." This is not the kind of embodiment that Dourish (2001) has proposed pursuing, but it is a kind of semiotic embodiment, which leaves traces of the designer's sense making in the artifact's interface and allows users to relate explicitly to the designer's mediated rational presence in the artifacts that we build.

As Eco's short story shows, computers are a privileged medium for the deepest possible inspections of what is involved in communication because, unlike humans, they algorithmically produce all and only the meanings that have been explicitly selected to be part of the signification systems encoded in them. The relationship of computer meanings with each other can be inspected to exhaustion. A program is the full specification of how representations affect and are affected by others. A program is a unique sign of its creators' thought, a sign that tells a lot more about its origin, purpose, and behavior than any other sign in our culture. But, typically, neither program producers nor program consumers take programs to be such signs. Semiotic engineering is a theory oriented toward enabling designers to explore this possibility and to see which consequences follow from it.

7.2 Semiotics and Design

Semiotics and design have very strong relations. They have been previously explored with specific reference to visual design in HCI (Marcus 1992; Mullet and Sano 1995), to computer systems design in general (Nadin 1997), and also to architectural design (Broadbent 1980; Medway and Clark 2003) and design in principle (Newton 2004). In this book I have used Schön's reflection-in-action perspective on design (1983) as a background theme for presenting and discussing semiotic engineering.

The technical rationality perspective (Simon 1981) that Schön has so strongly criticized in the eighties covers a considerable portion of design in engineering. It supports designers' judgments about the constraints imposed upon artifacts by established laws, principles, norms and, values. The key in the technical rationality perspective is the word *established*. Once there is a fixed set of assumptions that cannot be questioned or changed by designers (for scientific or other reasons), a number of consequences follow from them. Enduring assumptions of this sort eventually constrain the portions of design affected by them in a limited number of problem-framing and problem-solving possibilities that become and are passed on as technical knowledge.

Technical knowledge carries certain self-accomplished prophecies in it. In civil engineering, for instance, the design of HVAC (heating, ventilation, and air conditioning) systems incorporates technical knowledge that can guide the patterns for distributing heat loads. The professional belief in such technical knowledge is so strong that AI systems have been built to find solutions and provide explanations for HVAC design (e.g., Garcia and de Souza 1997). This kind of sophisticated technological tool, praised by many in engineering, even allows designers to assign unpredicted values to certain design parameters. By so doing, HVAC designers introduce modifications in the system's knowledge base, strictly speaking, "novelties," "refinements," or "improvement" of previous technical knowledge. However, as I have shown in preceding chapters (especially in chapter 5), the system can indeed handle infinite possibilities, but they are all infinities of the same kind. Many expert systems demonstrate the value placed on technical knowledge by certain professions where design is involved. But not much attention is paid to the self-perpetuating beliefs that are passed on and tacitly accepted as "true practical knowledge" just because they can be expressed in computer-processible form and can generate representations of solutions to representations of practical professional problems.

As Winograd and Flores (1986) have shown, the assumption that software engineering can or should follow the same paradigm as other engineering disciplines is fundamentally flawed because the stuff of computer artifacts is language (representations), not matter. In other words, whereas physics predicts that certain heat loads will *cause* materials and fluids to behave in particular ways, cognitive psychology, social sciences, linguistics, or semiotics can not usually predict that certain representations will *cause* people to behave in this or that way. Nevertheless, computer science can, and does, predict that computer programs *cause* representations to generate and derive other representations. As I have suggested in section 7.1, the producers (including designers) of computer artifacts have sometimes taken computer programs for carriers of universal truths about users. And they have used pieces of knowledge from the humanities and social sciences for the same purposes that civil engineers pick knowledge from natural sciences, for example. Even HCI researchers have often mirrored themselves in this paradigm, using ontologies and methodologies that have worked for research in natural sciences as if they would by necessity work in the same way (if at all) for research in human and social aspects involved in software engineering. Results have not often been encouraging, of course, and doubts about the value of theoretical contributions of HCI as a field have been voiced (Landauer 1991; Rogers, Bannon, and Button 1994; Shneiderman et al. 2002).

Schön's reflection-in-action perspective is liberating in many ways. First, it rescues the freshness and creativity of our intuitive views about design from the confining territory of black art, where rationalistic views tend to place it. By defining design problems as *unique*, Schön is also saying that every solution is *unique*. And the uniqueness of design problems and solutions stems from the designer's inescapable freedom to interpret and frame the opportunity and purpose of design in totally contingent ways. Second, it recognizes the role of professional training and skills in design and places them at the same level as other professions generally taken to be more *technical*. The kind of professional knowledge that must be taught to designers is nevertheless a very particular one. Schön qualifies it as *epistemological* knowledge, that is, knowledge that will help designers come to know the nature of unique problems and decide how they can best be solved. Solutions may occasionally be a matter of selecting one or more problem-solving techniques that have worked in the past, but most of all they may also and more often be a matter of invention and experimentation, just as in scientific research. Hence the critical role of epistemic tools for design, and the need to equip professionals with the ability to construct design problems, use design research methods, hypothesize design solutions, decide how much they are worth, and express them as a design product. And third, Schön's perspective subtly changes the role of artifacts' consumers. Whereas consumers relate to concrete artifacts typically produced by traditional engineering disciplines as "utilities" or "appliances" (words that are particularly revealing in this context), when design begins to be viewed as intrinsically innovative the consumers' reaction must itself be innovative and judicious.

The representational nature of computer programs suggests that HCI design is a semiotic endeavor (Nadin 1988). But expecting that a direct "application" of semiotic methods (most of which are essentially analytic) will lead to the "solution" for preconceived classes of HCI design problems throws us right into the pitfall that Schön is talking about. Semiotic engineering is not meant to be a predictive or explanatory theory in the sense alluded to by Shneiderman et al. (2002). It is neither a theory that will "give quantitative estimates of human performance with input devices (e. g., Fitt's Law), menu traversal, or visual scanning," nor one that will "guide future designs, such as Don Norman's seven stages, Clark's common ground, or . . . direct manipulation" (688). Predictions about human performance and informed design guidelines may, however, be the result of a designer's reflection while using some of the epistemic tools presented in this book.

Some may hope that it will be a kind of generative theory, in Shneiderman et al.'s sense (2002), assuming that it "will open up new knowledge domains and guide us to innovative applications" (688). But this is not my own vision of semiotic engineering, if the kind of guidance expected is *generative* in a technical sense. Generation, in mathematical and linguistic domains for example, is a rule-based causal process by which new symbols are derived from root symbols (like theorems from axioms, sentences from a vocabulary, and so on). This is exactly the antithesis of this theory's goals, since it is totally incompatible with Schön's perspective on design, which I have chosen to adopt.

However, a loose interpretation of *generative* theories as *trigger* theories, theories that will initiate associative (semiosic) processes, rather than derivational (rule-based) processes, might allow me to say that semiotic engineering is in fact a likely *generative* theory of HCI. The epistemic tools presented in this book should trigger the designer's semiosis, which will eventually produce signs that will be encoded in a computer application's signification system. Then these signs will become part of the users' semiosis, both when interpreting the designer's message and when producing their own and unique interactive discourse. So the theory binds design signs and user experience signs in a continuum that hopefully will spark designers' and users' imagination and open some paths for innovation.

7.3 Epistemic Support for Designers and Users

Semiotic engineering, like other semiotic accounts of HCI, views computers as a *medium* for communicative exchanges. It is a unique medium in that interlocutors do not all belong to the same phenomenological category. Through programs, users communicate with other users, designers communicate with users, and programs themselves communicate with other programs. In other words, programs are also media, even though they are primarily messages, representations of meanings produced by designers and programmers.

A reversed formulation of McLuhan's principle—as *the message is the medium*—achieves more than a rhetorical effect. It suggests that the purpose of meanings (the message) encoded in computer programs is to support the exchange of other meanings (to be a medium). This book has shown that the semiotic engineering interpretation of what Reeves and Nass (1996) call "the *media* equation" (italics, mine) is slanted toward this particular reading of the relationship between message and medium. The aim of the theory is to support design—that is, to help designers get their message across to users. It is not an explanatory theory of how users make sense of computer artifacts. Semiotics, for example, would be an appropriate theory for this end. The reversed formulation of McLuhan's principle opens the avenue for designing different media in the computer medium. It is a more detailed articulation of the semiotic possibilities enabled by computers, one in which the role and purpose of design stand out more obviously.

Once the message in the computer medium carries the design intention, it is important that both designers and users get support for achieving metacommunication. The success of HCI design can be measured not only by the user's complete acceptance of the designer's message as such, but also by the user's interventions to adapt and repurpose the message for unanticipated goals and contexts. The contact between designers and users is established through the metacommunication message. Consequently, all the epistemic tools presented in this book center around the construction of this message. In chapter 4 I explored various types of breakdowns that may happen in communication between users and the designer's deputy. These breakdowns offer insights into the construction of online help systems, where the designer's deputy's discourse can be more elaborately presented to users. In chapter 5 I explored the conditions for encoding the metacommunication message into computable signification systems, and the limits of customizations and extensions with which users can adapt and repurpose this message. Chapter 6 presented a more sophisticated exploration of the metacommunication message as medium, identifying the particular contents in it that can affect the mutual relations and perceptions of users who are brought together within the domains of multi-user applications. The metacommunication paraphrase also broadly characterizes the contents that users are expected to detect in the designer's deputy's discourse. Such contents are important epistemic sources for the users' sense-making processes. As users deepen and refine their interpretations about the possibilities of the medium, their own semiosis is impregnated by the explicit signs expressed by designers in the designer's deputy's discourse.

Communicating knowledge is the central focus of semiotic engineering. HCI design produces artifacts that must come to be known through communication. Certain signs occurring in the designer's semiosis at design time will crystallize as signs encoded in the artifact's signification system. And this signification system is the same through which and with which users will express whatever their semiosis produces. And no one can predict the exact shape and length of users' semiosic paths.

In semiotic engineering designers figure as participants in (and not just builders of) the users' experience. They may choose to appear in disguise, letting the object of design speak for them, or to tell users explicitly what their vision and intent is. The choice of how they will participate in HCI is itself a semiotic choice. The theory aims at investigating computer-mediated and computer-encoded semiosis, in an attempt to raise both the designers' and the users' awareness of the medium created by the metacommunication message. Verbal communication is of course a prime means for expressing the variety of representations contained in computer programs. And the more users know about such variety, the greater the scope of possibilities for them to innovate and evolve. But verbal communication may step back and make way for other types of communication, whose limitations may be an important part of the designer's message. In computer games, for example, the designer's goal (and the users' delight) may be precisely to exercise imagination and play according to highly constraining rules that stimulate and challenge one's intellect and emotions. So designers can themselves play with signs and experience novel forms of communication, novel codes, novel channels, novel messages, and novel contexts.

The intended effect of a semiotic engineering of HCI is that computer artifacts themselves will be like epistemic tools for their users. If through interaction users gain new knowledge about their world (not only about the artifact!), and if this knowledge gives them the same level of satisfaction and achievement envisioned by designers, the engineered product is successful. The most important metrics of semiotic engineering success is not a measure of how much of the designer's meanings "coincide" with the users', but rather a measure of how much of the designer's meanings are used in successful expressions of what users themselves wanted to do. This metric can give us useful insights about the intended versus the perceived value of technology, rather than about the difficulty versus the ease of performing a fixed range of tasks with it, and the time it takes to learn it.

One of the potential results of emphasizing epistemological aspects in design, and of viewing design products as epistemological products themselves, is that users will know more about designers. Interestingly, all the user-centered mantras in HCI have repeated the need to know the users. This is undeniably a fundamental requirement for designing good products. But we have never seen a suggestion that users should know designers. The dominant metaphor that software artifacts are like concrete artifacts (like mechanical tools, electric appliances, pieces of furniture) has promoted the view that we don't need to know about who designed them and for what. But, as I have tried to show in this book, software artifacts have an intellectual nature. All about them is a representation, a selected expression of selected meanings for selected purposes. And users must share such representations with designers in order to express what they want to do, even if what they want to do does not coincide with what designers thought they would want to do. Isolating users from the origin and motivation of representations they have to use while interacting with software is a major constraint, since it creates the need for representations to be *self-evident*, which is precisely what we have the greatest difficulty achieving in any sort of communication. If designers assume that their representations are self-evident to users, and users fail to understand them and use them productively, very negative feelings may arise. Designers may be frustrated by their incapacity to produce a self-evident artifact, and users may be frustrated by their incapacity to understand a self-evident artifact. But once the myth of self-evidence is brought to light and we begin to see software artifacts as just another type of communication, nonevident meanings naturally become the topic of clarification dialogs, and users and designers are not trapped in a situation where every doubt, mistake, and deviation is a reason for blame and frustration. Perhaps by viewing software in this new communicative light, we can identify the epistemic value of information technology and make more intrepid explorations of where all of this can lead us.

7.4 Signs on the Road Ahead

John Carroll (2003) has said that the scientific fragmentation in the field of HCI is one of the important barriers to be transposed if we want to make progress. Because there are too many approaches, too many techniques, too many technologies, too many theories, seeing the big picture is extremely difficult. As a consequence, when building interactive software artifacts we are not always sure of (and maybe not even aware of) where and why old or new knowledge applies. This situation decreases our ability to make appropriate and justifiable choices in HCI design, and increases the feeling expressed by some—that scientific theories can't help us build quality artifacts any better than sheer individual talent and professional practice. It also jeopardizes the value of crucially important scientific findings in HCI, because of equivocal expectations about the scope of their account.

Scientific fragmentation can be improved by an appropriate epistemology. But to date, because of its interdisciplinary character, the epistemology of HCI—if explicitly addressed at all—has itself been a patchwork of epistemological borrowings from psychology, computer science, anthropological disciplines, engineering, and design. The result of this patchworked epistemology is that sorting scientific issues from nonscientific ones, distinguishing between essence and circumstance, and even identifying the permanent goals of the discipline have been extremely difficult. Implemented systems are at times taken for sufficient representation of the disciplinary knowledge they claim to contain. Fundamental research questions are abandoned because technological evolution has replaced the infrastructure where they were being investigated. Premature implementations of incomplete and imprecise knowledge are marketed and stir economic resources to accelerate progress based on assumptions that are not clearly understood by researchers themselves.

Our motivation to work on semiotic engineering has always been the elasticity of the theory in accommodating within the same ontological perspective bits and pieces of HCI knowledge that can't be handled satisfactorily by any other single theory. Previous attempts to use a single theoretical framework to bridge phenomena in the human and the computer domain, like the human information processor (Card, Moran, and Newell 1983), have been the result of carrying a model that works for one into the domains of the other, where it originally does not belong. They have been metaphorical accounts. The semiotic base of the theory presented in this book, however, extends over human and computer domains without having to resort to metaphors. Computers do not have to be viewed as humans, or humans as computers, for the ontology or methodology of the theory to be consistent. Humans and computers are native citizens in the domain of semiotics, and hence of semiotic engineering. And this is a peculiar and advantageous situation held by this theory in comparison to many others in this field. It means, for example, that the epistemology of semiotics is in principle amenable to supporting a very wide range of scientific investigations in HCI, and it carries the promise of fighting the battle of fragmentation, so sharply expressed by Carroll (2003).

But this theory may also be felt as a threat. First and foremost, it embraces the view that human meanings cannot be fully known, and consequently not be completely (or adequately) encoded in computer systems. This is threatening because it shakes the foundations of many design and evaluation methods and practices, where the ultimate match between system meaning and user meaning determines the goal of design and the quality of software. If the user's meaning is an evolving unlimited process of interpretation, halted and resumed for contingent reasons, and shaped by unpredictable factors that emerge during the process itself, the aura of rationality that HCI has so strongly struggled to preserve seems to vanish in the air. In defense of semiotic engineering, I can invoke two main arguments. One is that taking users' meanings to be fixed and ultimate targets that can be captured in computer systems doesn't change the reality of what users do. And this reality is often disconcerting for any one who takes time to sit and watch what happens when users interact with software. The other is that humans are all perfectly equipped to handle unlimited semiosis. We do this all the time. So, maybe the trouble with computers is not really that they can't capture and account for all that we mean while we interact with software, but rather that this is not what they should be doing in the first place. Maybe computer systems are more like storytellers than looking glasses. Every story has an author, and listeners naturally know this. They may identify themselves with one or more characters, or perhaps with none of them, and still think that the story is a great one. The same is true of systems. Even if users don't recognize "themselves" as the model user in the system, they may step into the model user's shoes and enjoy the plot just as much.

Another reason why semiotic engineering may be felt as a threat is that it may be wrongly interpreted as a denial of all technological developments achieved in recent years, a regression into verbose and tutorial styles of interface. Talking about the designer's deputy's discourse and communicating design rationale to users sounds like a case for pervasive AI and verbal communication as the exclusive alternative in HCI. But, although verbal communication allows for fine types of expression, not easily achieved by other alternatives, there are numerous kinds of signification systems that can be encoded in the computer medium. They can be explored by semiotic theories and combined with one another in order to maximize the efficiency of communicative processes involved in HCI. Abundant verbal communication is neither a requirement nor a necessarily good alternative for interaction. The challenge is to spot the best opportunities for efficient nonverbal communication, when nonverbal signs are powerful enough to communicate more clearly and better the designer's understanding and intent, and to provide access to verbal communication whenever we spot the opportunity (or need) to negotiate potentially incongruous meanings. In other words, verbal communication should be an available resource, not the only possibility for interaction.

Semiotic engineering may also be mistaken as a self-defeating theoretical alternative, because it rests on the assumption that users are interested in knowing more about the artifacts that they use. Since people don't usually care to read online documentation and prefer trial and error to using help resources that come with applications, seeking to let them know more about the system they interact with may seem like an illogical choice. The immediate and superficial argument in favor of the theory is that, if we look at human communicative behavior, the economy of conversation in goal-oriented situations suggests that interlocutors do go into very sophisticated meaning-negotiating processes under certain basic conditions. For example, they may do so when they believe that getting the right meaning is needed for the achievement of their goals; they believe that the negotiation will not cost them much; and they believe that the benefits of negotiation outweigh the risks of misunderstandings. Trial and error suppresses meaning-negotiation processes and replaces it with repeated attempts at guessing rather then asking. But this strategy may turn into a problem when guesses fail one after the other, or when guesses don't reach far enough (e.g., when only part of the meaning is understood, and the part that is not understood leads to other communicative breakdowns in situations that are not perceived to be related). For this reason semiotic engineering uses communicative breakdowns during HCI as an opportunity to convey useful elements of the design vision and intent. This may substantially increase the impact of this kind of knowledge on the user's semiosis and raise the user's awareness about the ontological nature of software artifacts. But my deeper argument in favor of the theory is that semiotic engineering questions an implicit ethics in HCI, according to which users definitively don't need to know more about computers. They just need to be able to use them. The theory shows that, as a rule, designers and developers have been building computer artifacts that are not meant to be known. And thus it is not surprising that people are not inclined to, or not even capable of, knowing them. Users have had little ability to use the technology judiciously, and have instead been using it in good faith. From the moment we realize the arbitrariness of so many choices we make, we become ethically responsible for externalizing such choices, just like food manufacturers are ethically responsible for letting consumers know the ingredients they add to their products.

This book, like many others, asks more questions than it gives answers. Moreover, the spectrum of questions is very wide, and at times very deep. My purpose is not to immobilize research and professional practice with the amazing complexity of issues involved in designing interactive computer artifacts. The message of semiotic engineering is not that designers should not build these artifacts before they have the answer to all the questions that have been asked in this book. On the contrary, the message is that they might begin to create very different patterns of HCI right away if they explicitly present the computer systems they design as intellectual artifacts. By so doing, they will let users understand them, use them, relate to them, value them, and transform them, just as they do with other intellectual artifacts. The road ahead, however, is a very long one, for culture is not changed by individual speculation and will. There must be many more signs that semiotic engineering is in fact a useful theory of HCI. Some of the more immediate ones may come from exploring issues such as:

What does software intentionally produced as a metacommunication artifact look like?

Most software produced to date has been designed and evaluated with an emphasis on facilitating operation and control. It is very difficult to find interfaces designed to "tell" users about the various use strategies supported by the system, and when or why one strategy can be better than the other. As the Acrobat example has shown (see chapter 1), this kind of information is usually buried in online documentation and is really not designed to be communicated effectively to users. Exploring ways to communicate tactical and strategic aspects of software use, directly through the interface, should yield designs that are very different from what we now see.

How do users perceive this type of software, in comparison with software that is not so produced?

A whole range of comparative studies taking software that is traditionally designed in accordance with user-centeredness and usability guidelines, and software designed as a metacommunication artifact, can teach us many lessons. They are crucial to advancing knowledge in semiotic engineering and can contribute substantially to HCI in general. Such comparative studies have been difficult to carry out so far because there haven't been many different theories to support the elaboration of comparable hypotheses and methods in HCI design and evaluation.

How can the designers' intent be expressed during the design process? Which portions of it can make a difference in the users' experience if users are explicitly told about them? Which difference? Why?

Not all aspects of design intent are equally relevant for a user to know. Some are too technical, others are plainly commercial, and still others may not really make any positive difference in the quality of a user's experience. On the contrary, if designers begin to talk about such uninteresting issues, interaction may indeed get worse. So a key topic for research is to identify which aspects of the whole design vision can improve the user's experience. Capturing and conveying them appropriately can help us investigate the real effect of this type of knowledge on the user's experience and begin to formulate explanations about it.

In how many different ways can users be told about the designer's vision? How does this kind of communication impact the users' attitude toward computer technology? What may this impact mean for the software industry? What may it mean for individuals and society?

As this book has illustrated in numerous instances, communication is as varied as we can imagine. Thus, there are unlimited possibilities to convey the designer's message to users. Finding effective ways to do it will enable us to let users know more about computers and computing. In the long run, if we are successful with this sort of communication, we will probably begin to see changes in the users' attitude toward computer technology, and we can investigate the new kinds of intervention that technology can make in individual and collective life.

One of the most important signs of what semiotic engineering really means will come from how research itself is conducted. Because this is an integrative theory that gives us instruments not only to fight the scientific fragmentation identified by Carroll but also to position ourselves more actively and responsibly in view of how users experience software, perhaps it will inspire a greater number of epistemologically informed research projects. It will be interesting to see whether the new kinds of issues and results so achieved bring about new understanding in our field and give us, researchers and practitioners, a genuine sense of improvement.

Notes

1. In fact, designers may specify the encoding of meanings in an interactive application, but software developers program this specification into the actual computer system that users interact with. The passage from specification into programming may of course introduce mistakes and unspecified arbitrary programming decisions that directly affect the user's experience. This passage is itself a semiotic process, which can be analyzed with semiotic tools, but we will assume an ideal situation, where the designers' specification if faithfully translated into a computer program. However even in non-ideal situations where programming introduces novel or mistaken meanings into the application, compared to its specifications, the fact that designers and users are united under the same communicative process holds true.

2. Saying that "the designer's deputy *is* the system" is itself the result of collapsing the *medium* with the message.

3. The classical Turing machine model used as a formal characterization of all effective procedures presents some important features that can distinguish it from an adequate model of human activity based on meaning interpretation. The machine operates with a finite vocabulary (i.e., input tape symbols). Input symbols that do not belong to the machine's vocabulary and for which, consequently, there are no specified state transitions to be made, cause the computation to halt and fail. On the one hand, human *mental machinery* does not *halt* in this way in the presence of unknown vocabulary items. For example, if one doesn't not know what "metalinguistic" means in a sentence like "The use of metalinguistic resources helps users find what interface signs may mean," one can try to infer this meaning from context and find a reasonable solution (e.g., "metalinguistic" means "something related to the explanation or definition of what signs mean"). This is an effect of ongoing semiosic processes and abductive reasoning that characterize human meaning interpretation. On the other hand, when communicating ideas, one can *invent* new words, on demand, to fill an instant expressive need. By definition, these new words are not part of the interlocutors' vocabulary but are expected to be interpreted appropriately by force of contextual, etymological, grammatical, or other factors. For instance, if one says something like "This device is so tiny that it would be more appropriate to refer to it as a 'fingertop' rather than a 'palmtop,'" the non-English word *fingertop* typically poses no difficulty for one's interlocutor in communication. A classical Turing machine would not produce such inventive output unless there were rules to generate it (but then what would be the invention?). Moreover, unlike the human speaker, who can explain what he means by "fingertop" and why he used

this invented word, the machine cannot say why it uses any word. The reasons and explanations for a given machine's behavior can only be given by a higher-order machine. This constraint is associated to the halting problem in computation. Turing machines can take other Turing machines as input. But if they take *themselves* as input there may be input symbols for which the machine will never stop transitioning among its internal states, producing from zero to an infinity of results.

Although an infinite production of results might tempt us to say that such machines are appropriate models of unlimited semiosis, they are not. Unlike what happens in human unlimited semiosis, the machine cannot decide that it is satisfied with what an input symbol means. Some higher-order machine must provide it with the criteria for satisfaction and give it a command (input) to proceed with computation later, if there is the need, the opportunity, the resources—in short, *the reason why* it should continue.

4. The Turing machine model for computer programs indicates that some programs can *compute forever*, producing from zero to an infinite number of output symbols (all the same, all different from one another, with periodic repetitions, with random repetitions—all these are possibilities). Human unlimited semiosis is different from computation that produces an infinite sequence of symbols because, as mentioned in section 4.4, human unlimited semiosis is halted and resumed because the human interpreter *decides* to do it. Computer programs, however, cannot *make decisions* about their *own* computation. They can only *execute* them. Decisions about their execution have to be made by another program that contains the metalanguage of the program being executed.

Bibliographic References

Ackerman, M. 2000. The intellectual challenge of CSCW: The gap between social requirements and technical feasibility. *Human-Computer Interaction* 15(2): 181–203.

Alexander, C. 1977. *A Pattern Language*. New York: Oxford University Press.

Andersen, P. B. 1997. *A Theory of Computer Semiotics*, 2nd ed. Cambridge: Cambridge University Press.

Andersen, P. B. 2001. What semiotics can and cannot do for HCI. *Knowledge-Based Systems* 14(8): 419–424.

Andersen, P. B., B. Holmqvist, and J. F. Jensen. 1993. *The Computer as Medium*. Cambridge: Cambridge University Press.

Aristotle. 1980. *Aristotle's Categories and Propositions (De interpretatione)*. Trans. with commentaries and glossary by Hippocrates G. Apostle. Categoriae. Grinnell, IA: Peripatetic Press.

Aristotle. 1984. *The Rhetoric and the Poetics of Aristotle*. New York: The Modern Library College Edition.

Austin, J. L. 1962. *How to Do Things with Words*. Cambridge, MA: Harvard University Press.

Barbosa, C. M. A. 2002. MetaCom-G*: Especificação da comunicação entre membros de um grupo. M.Sc. diss. Departamento de Informática, PUC-Rio, Rio de Janeiro.

Barbosa, S. D. J. 1999. Programação via interfaces. Ph.D. thesis, Departamento de Informática, PUC-Rio, Rio de Janeiro.

Barbosa, S. D. J., and M. G. de Paula. 2003. Designing and evaluating interaction as conversation: A modeling language based on semiotic engineering. In *10th International Workshop on Design, Specification and Verification of Interactive Systems, DSV-IS'03*, 13–27. Funchal, Ilha da Madeira.

Barbosa, S. D. J., and C. S. de Souza. 2000. Expanding software through metaphors and metonymies. In *International Conference on Intelligent User Interfaces IUI2000*, 13–20. New York: ACM Press.

Barbosa, S. D. J., and C. S. de Souza. 2001. Extending software through metaphors and metonymies. *Knowledge-Based Systems* 14(1–2): 15–27.

Barnard, P., J. May, D. Duke, and D. Duce. 2000. Systems, interactions, and macrotheory. *ACM Transactions on Computer-Human Interaction* 7(2): 222–262.

Bastien, J. M. C., D. L. Scapin, and C. Leulier, 1999. The ergonomic criteria and the ISO/DIS 9241-10 dialogue principles: A pilot comparison in an evaluation task. *Interacting with Computers* 11(2): 299–322.

Bellotti, V., S. Buckingham Shum, A. MacLean, and N. Hammond. 1995. Multidisciplinary modelling in HCI design . . . in theory and in practice. In *Proceedings of ACM CHI '95: Human Factors in Computing Systems*, 146–153. New York: ACM Press.

Bødker, S. 1989. A human activity approach to user interfaces. *Human-Computer Interaction* 4(1): 171–195.

Bowers, J., and J. Churcher. 1988. Local and global structuring of computer mediated communication: Developing linguistic perspectives on CSCW in Cosmos. In *Proceedings of the 1988 ACM Conference on Computer-Supported Cooperative Work*, 125–139. New York: ACM Press.

Braa, K., and R. Vidgen. 1997. An information systems research framework for the organizational laboratory. In *Computers and Design in Context*, ed. M. Kyng and L. Mathiassen, 381–400. Cambridge, MA: The MIT Press.

Broadbent, G. 1980. Architectural objects and their design as a subject for semiotic studies. *Design Studies* 1(4): 207–216.

Brown, G. 1995. *Speakers, Listeners, and Communication*. Cambridge: Cambridge University Press.

Brown, J. S., and P. Duguid. 1992. Enacting design for the workplace. In *Usability: Turning Technologies into Tools*, ed. P. S. Adler, and T. A. Winograd, 164–197. Oxford: Oxford University Press.

Card, S. K., T. P. Moran, and A. Newell. 1983. *The Psychology of Human-Computer Interaction*. Hillsdale, NJ: Lawrence Erlbaum.

Carroll, J. M. 1998. *Minimalism beyond the Nurnberg Funnel*. Cambridge, MA: The MIT Press.

Carroll, J. M. 2003. *HCI Models, Theories, and Frameworks*. San Francisco: Morgan Kaufmann.

Carroll, J. M., and M. B. Rosson. 1987. The paradox of the active user. In *Interfacing Thought: Cognitive Aspects of Human-Computer Interaction*, ed. J. M. Carroll, 26–28. Cambridge, MA: The MIT Press.

Cawsey, A. J. 1993. *Explanation and Interaction: The Computer Generation of Explanatory Dialogues*. Cambridge, MA: The MIT Press.

Chandler, D. 2002. *Semiotics: The Basics*. New York: Routledge.

Clark, H. H. 1996. *Using Language*. Cambridge: Cambridge University Press.

Cunha, C. K. V. 2001. Um modelo semiótico dos processos de comunicação relacionados à atividade de extensão à aplicação por usuários finais. Ph.D. thesis, Departamento de Informática, PUC-Rio, Rio de Janeiro.

Cypher, A. 1993. *Watch What I Do*. Cambridge, MA: The MIT Press.

Cypher, A., and D. Canfield-Smith. 1995. KidSim: End user programming of simulations. In *Proceedings of ACM CHI '95: Human Factors in Computing Systems,* 27–34. New York: ACM Press.

da Silva, S. R. P. 2001. Um modelo semiótico para programação por usuários finais. Ph.D. thesis, Departamento de Informática, PUC-Rio, Rio de Janeiro.

da Silva, E. J., C. S. de Souza, R. O. Prates, and A. M. Nicolaci-da-Costa. 2003. What they want and what they get: A study of light-weight technologies for online communities. In *Proceedings of the Latin American Conference on Human-Computer Interaction*, 135–146. Rio de Janeiro: PUC-Rio.

Danesi, M., and P. Perron. 1999. *Analyzing Cultures*. Bloomington: Indiana University Press.

de Paula, M. G. 2003. Projeto da interação humano-computador baseado em modelos fundamentados na engenharia semiótica. M.Sc. diss., Departamento de Informática, PUC-Rio, Rio de Janeiro.

de Saussure, F. 1972. *Cours de Linguistique Générale*. Paris: Payot.

de Souza, C. S. 1993. The semiotic engineering of user interface languages. *International Journal of Man-Machine Studies* 39(4): 753–773.

de Souza, C. S., and J. Preece. 2004. A framework for analyzing and understanding online communities. *Interacting with Computers* 16(3): 579–610.

de Souza, C. S., and K. Sedig. 2001. Semiotic considerations on direct concept manipulation as a distinct interface style for Learnware. In *Anais do IHC2001-IV Workshop sobre Fatores Humanos em Sistemas Computacionais*, 229–241. Porto Alegre, RS: SBC.

de Souza, C. S., S. D. J. Barbosa, and S. R. P. da Silva. 2001. Semiotic engineering principles for evaluating end-user programming environments. *Interacting with Computers* 13(4): 467–495.

de Souza, C. S., R. O. Prates, and S. D. J. Barbosa. 2003. Adopting information technology as a first step in design: Lessons learned from working with Brazilian social volunteers. *Interactions* 10(2): 72–79.

de Souza, C. S., R. O. Prates, and T. Carey. 2000. Missing and declining affordances: Are these appropriate concepts? *Journal of the Brazilian Computer Society* 1(7): 26–34.

Delio, M. 2001. Eudora retards flames. *Wired News*. Available at http://www.wired.com/news/technology/0,1282,38723,00.html. Accessed Sept. 12, 2000.

DiGiano, C., and M. Eisenberg. 1995. Self-disclosing design tools: A gentle introduction to end-user programming. In *Proceedings of DIS95*, 189–197. New York: ACM Press.

Dourish, P. 1997. Accounting for system behavior: Representation, reflection, and resourceful action. In *Computers and Design in Context*, ed. M. Kyng and L. Mathiassen, 145–170. Cambridge, MA. The MIT Press.

Dourish, P. 2001. *Where the Action Is*. Cambridge, MA: The MIT Press.

Dourish, P., J. Holmes, A. MacLean, P. Marqvardsen, and A. Zbyslaw. 1996. Freeflow: Mediating between representation and action in workflow systems. In *Proceedings of the 1996 ACM Conference on Computer-Supported Cooperative Work*, 190–198. New York: ACM Press.

Eco, U. 1976. *A Theory of Semiotics*. Bloomington: Indiana University Press.

Eco, U. 1984. *Semiotics and the Philosophy of Language*. Bloomington: Indiana University Press.

Eco, U. 1987. *Travels in Hyperreality*. London: Picador.

Eco, U. 1988. On truth: A fiction. In *Meaning and Mental Representations*, ed. U. Eco, M. Santambrogio, and P. Violi, 41–59. Bloomington: Indiana University Press.

Eco, U., M. Santambrogio, and P. Violi. 1988. *Meaning and Mental Representations*. Bloomington, IN: Indiana University Press.

Ellis, C., S. Gibbs, and G. Rein. 1991. Groupware: Some issues and experiences. *Communications of the ACM* 34(1): 39–58.

Farkas, D. K. 1998. Layering as a safety net for minimalist documentation. In *Minimalism beyond the Nurnberg Funnel*, ed. J. M. Carroll, 247–274. Cambridge, MA: The MIT Press.

Fetzer, J. H. 1988. Program verification: The very idea. *Communications of the ACM* 31(9): 1049–1063.

Fischer, G. 1998. Beyond "Couch potatoes": From consumers to designers. In *Proceedings of the 3rd Asia Pacific Computer Human Interaction Conference*, 2–9. Piscataway, NJ: IEEE Computer Society.

Fitt, P. M. 1954. The information capacity of the human motor system in controlling amplitude of movement. *Journal of Experimental Psychology* 47: 381–391.

Flores, F., M. Graves, B. Hartfield, and T. Winograd. 1988. Computer systems and the design of organizational interaction. *ACM Transactions on Information Systems* 6(2): 153–172.

Garcia, A. C. B., and C. S. de Souza. 1997. ADD+: Including rhetorical structures in active documents. *AIEDAM—Artificial Intelligence for Engineering, Design and Manufacturing* 11(2): 109–124.

Gelernter, J., and S. Jagganathan. 1990. *Programming Linguistics*. Cambridge, MA: The MIT Press.

Gibson, J. J. 1979. *The Ecological Approach to Visual Perception*. Boston: Houghton Mifflin.

Golightly, D., and D. Gilmore. 1997. Breaking the rules of direct manipulation. In *IFIP TC13 International Conference on Human-Computer Interaction*, ed. S. Howard, J. Hammond, and G. Lindgard, 156–163. London: Chapman Hall.

Grice, H. P. 1975. Logic and conversation. In *Syntax and Semantics, Speech Acts*, vol. 3, ed. P. Cole and J. L. Morgan, 41–58. New York: Academic Press.

Gruber, T. R. 1993. Toward principles for the design of ontologies used for knowledge sharing. *International Journal of Human-Computer Studies* 43(5–6): 907–928.

Gugerty, L. 1993. The use of analytical models in human-computer interaction. *International Journal of Man-Machine Studies* 38(4): 625–660.

Halasz, F. G., and T. P. Moran. 1982. Analogy considered harmful. In *Proceedings of the Conference on Human Factors in Computing Systems*, 383–386. New York: ACM Press.

Hayakawa, S. I. 1972. *Language in Thought and Action*. Orlando, FL: Harcourt.

Hollan, J., E. Hutchins, and D. Kirsh. 2000. Distributed cognition: Toward a new foundation for human-computer interaction research. *ACM Transactions on Computer-Human Interaction* 7(2): 174–196.

Holst, S. J. 1996. Directing learner attention with manipulation styles. In *Proceedings of CHI '96: Conference Companion*, 43–44. New York: ACM Press.

Hopcroft, J. E., and J. D. Ullman. 1979. *Introduction to Automata Theory, Languages and Computation*. Reading, MA: Addison-Wesley.

Hutchins, E. L., J. D. Hollan, and D. A. Norman. 1986. Direct manipulation interfaces. In *User-Centered System Design*, ed. D. A. Norman and S. W. Draper, 87–124. Hillsdale, NJ: Laurence Erlbaum.

Jakobson, R. 1960. Linguistics and poetics. In *Style in Language*, ed. T. A. Sebeok, 350–377. Cambridge, MA: The MIT Press.

Johnson, D. G. 2001. *Computer Ethics*, 3rd ed. Upper Saddle River, NJ: Prentice Hall.

Jørgensen, H. D. 2001. Interaction as a framework for flexible workflow modelling. In *Proceedings of the 2001 International ACM SIGGROUP Conference on Supporting Group Work*, 32–41. New York: ACM Press.

Josephson, J. R., and S. G. Josephson. 1994. *Abductive Inference. Computation, Philosophy, Technology*. New York: Cambridge University Press.

Kammersgaard, J. 1988. Four different perspectives on human-computer interaction. *International Journal of Man-Machine Studies* 28(4): 343–362.

Kaptelinin, V. 1996. Activity theory: Implications for human-computer interaction. In *Context and Consciousness*, ed. B. A. Nardi, 103–116. Cambridge, MA: The MIT Press.

Kaptelinin, V., B. A. Nardi, and C. Macaulay. 1999. The activity checklist: A tool for representing the "space" of context. *Interactions* 6(4): 27–39.

Kirsh, D., and P. Maglio. 1995. On distinguishing epistemic from pragmatic action. *Cognitive Science* 18: 513–549.

Lakoff, G. 1987. *Women, Fire, and Dangerous Things*. Chicago: University of Chicago Press.

Lakoff, G. 1988. Cognitive semantics. In *Meaning and Mental Representations*, ed. U. Eco, M. Santambrogio, and P. Violi, 119–154. Bloomington: Indiana University Press.

Lakoff, G., and M. Johnson. 1981. *Metaphors We Live By*. Chicago: University of Chicago University Press.

Landauer, T. 1991. Let's get real: A position paper on the role of cognitive psychology in the design of humanly useful and usable systems. In *Designing Interaction: Psychology at the Human-Computer Interface*, ed. J. M. Carroll, 60–73. New York: Cambridge University Press.

Leech, G. 1983. *The Principles of Pragmatics*. London: Longman.

Leite, J. C. 1998. Modelos e formalismos para a engenharia semiótica de interfaces de usuário. Ph.D. thesis, Departamento de Informática, PUC-Rio, Rio de Janeiro.

Lewis, C., and D. A. Norman. 1986. Designing for error. In *User-Centered System Design*, ed. D. A. Norman and S. W. Draper, 411–432. Hillsdale, NJ: Laurence Erlbaum.

Lieberman, H., F. Paternò, and V. Wulf. Forthcoming. *End User Development: Empowering People to Flexibly Employ Advanced Information and Communication Technology*. Dordrecht: Kluwer Academic Publishers.

Marcus, A. 1992. *Design for Electronic Documents and User Interfaces*. New York: Addison-Wesley.

Marx, G. T. 1994. New telecommunications technologies require new manners. *Telecommunications Policy* 18(7): 538–551.

McLuhan, M. [1964] 2002. *Understanding Media*, 2d ed. Cambridge, MA: The MIT Press.

Medway, P., and B. Clark. 2003. Imagining the building: Architectural design as semiotic construction. *Design Studies* 24(3): 255–273.

Moore, J. 1995. *Participating in Explanatory Dialogues*. Cambridge, MA: The MIT Press.

Morris, C. 1938. *Foundations of a Theory of Signs*. Chicago: University of Chicago Press.

Mullet, K., and D. Sano. 1995. *Designing Visual Interfaces*. Mountain View, CA: SunSoft Press.

Nadin, M. 1988. Interface design and evaluation. In *Advances in Human-Computer Interaction*, vol. 2, ed. R. Hartson and D. Hix, 45–100. Norwood, NJ: Ablex Publishing Corp.

Nadin, M. 1997. Signs and systems. A semiotic introduction to systems design. Available at http://www.code.uni-wuppertal.de/uk/all_pdf_files/sign+sys.pdf. Accessed January 2004.

Nake, F., and S. Grabowski. 2001. Human-computer interaction viewed as pseudo-communication. *Knowledge-Based Systems* 14(8): 441–447.

Nardi, B. A. 1993. *A Small Matter of Programming*. Cambridge, MA: The MIT Press.

Nardi, B. A. 1996. *Context and Consciousness*. Cambridge, MA: The MIT Press.

Newton, S. 2004. Designing as disclosure. *Design Studies* 25(1): 93–109.

Nielsen, J. 1994. Heuristic evaluation. In *Usability Inspection Methods*, ed. J. Nielsen and R. L. Mack, 25–62. New York: John Wiley & Sons.

Nielsen, J. 2001. Ten usability heuristics. Available at http://www.useit.com/papers/heuristic/heuristic_list.html.

Norman, D. A. 1986. Cognitive engineering. In *User-Centered System Design*, ed. D. A. Norman and S. W. Draper, 31–61. Hillsdale, NJ: Laurence Erlbaum.

Norman, D. A. 1988. *The Design of Everyday Things*. New York: Basic Books.

Norman, D. A. 1999. Affordance, convention and design. *Interactions* 6(3): 38–42.

Norman, D. A., and S. W. Draper. 1986. *User-Centered System Design*. Hillsdale, NJ: Laurence Erlbaum.

Ogden, C. K., and I. A. Richards. 1946. *The Meaning of Meaning*, 8th ed. New York: Harcourt, Brace & World.

Paternò, F. 2000. Model-based design and evaluation of interactive applications. London: Springer-Verlag.

Peirce, C. S. 1931–1958. *Collected Papers of Charles Sanders Peirce*, vols. 1–8, ed. C. Hartshorne and P. Weiss. Cambridge, MA: Harvard University Press.

Prates, R. O. 1998. A engenharia semiótica de linguagens de interfaces multi-usuário. Ph.D. thesis, Departamento de Informática, PUC-Rio, Rio de Janeiro.

Prates, R. O., and C. S. de Souza. 1998. On the rationale of interface semiotics for multi-user applications. In *Proceedings of the Joint Conference on the Science and Technology of Intelligent Systems ISIC/CIRA/ISAS'98*. Gaithersburg, MD: IEEE Press.

Prates, R. O., S. D. J. Barbosa, and C. S. de Souza. 2000. A case study for evaluating interface design through communicability. In *International Conference on Designing Interactive Systems DIS2000*, 308–317. New York: ACM Press.

Prates, R. O., C. S. de Souza, and S. D. J. Barbosa. 2000. A method for evaluating the communicability of user interfaces. *ACM Interactions* 7(1): 31–38.

Preece, J., Y. Rogers, and H. Sharp. 2002. *Interaction Design*. London: John Wiley and Sons.

Preece, J., Y. Rogers, H. Sharp, D. Benyon, S. Holland, and T. Carey. 1994. *Human-Computer Interaction*. Reading, MA: Addison-Wesley.

Puerta, A., and J. Eisenstein. 1999. Towards a general computational framework for model-based interface development systems. In *International Conference on Intelligent User Interfaces IUI99*, 171–178. New York: ACM Press.

Puerta, A. R. 1996. The MECANO Project: Comprehensive and integrated support for model-based interface development. In *Computer-Aided Design of User Interfaces*, ed. Jean Vanderdonckt, 19–25. Namur, Belgium: Presses Universitaires de Namur.

Rappin, N., M. Guzdial, M. Realff, and P. Ludovice. 1997. Balancing usability and learning in an interface. In *Proceedings of CHI '97*, 479–486. New York: ACM Press.

Reeves, B., and C. Nass. 1996. *The Media Equation*. Cambridge: Cambridge University Press.

Reppening, A., and T. Sumner. 1995. Agentsheets: A medium for creating domain-oriented visual languages. *Computer* 28(3): 17–25.

Rogers, Y., L. Bannon, and G. Button. 1994. Rethinking theoretical frameworks for HCI: A review. *SIGCHI Bulletin* 26 (1): 28–30.

Schank, R. 1975. *Conceptual Information Processing*. Amsterdam: North-Holland.

Schön, D. A. 1983. *The Reflective Practitioner*. New York: Basic Books.

Schön, D. A., and J. Bennett. 1996. Reflective conversation with materials. In *Bringing Design to Software*, ed. T. Winograd, 171–184. New York: Addison-Wesley.

Searle, J. R. 1969. *Speech Acts*. Cambridge: Cambridge University Press.

Searle, J. R. 1979. *Expression and Meaning*. Cambridge: Cambridge University Press.

Sedig, K. 1998. Interface style, flow, and reflective cognition: Issues in designing interactive multimedia mathematics learning environments for children. Unpublished Ph.D. diss., Department of Computer Science, The University of British Columbia, Vancouver, Canada.

Sedig, K., M. Klawe, and M. Westrom. 2001. Role of interface manipulation style and scaffolding on cognition and concept learning in learnware. *ACM Transactions on Computer-Human Interaction* 8(1): 34–59.

Sellen, A., and A. Nicol. 1990. Building user-centered online help. In *The Art of Human-Computer Interface Design*, ed. B. Laurel, 144–154. Reading, MA: Addison-Wesley.

Shankland, S. 2000. New email software can help you bite your tongue. *CNET News.com*. Available at http://news.com.com/2100-1040-245790.html?legacy=cnet. Accessed Sept. 15, 2000.

Shannon, C. E., and W. Weaver. 1949. *The Mathematical Theory of Communication*. Urbana: University of Illinois Press.

Shneiderman, B. 1983. Direct manipulation: a step beyond programming languages. *IEEE Computer* 16(8): 57–69.

Shneiderman, B. 1998. *Designing for the User Interface*, 3rd ed. Reading, MA: Addison-Wesley.

Shneiderman, B., S. Card, D. A. Norman, M. Tremaine, and M. M. Waldrop. 2002. CHI@20: Fighting our way from marginality to power. In *CHI '02 Extended Abstracts on Human Factors in Computer Systems*, 688–691. New York: ACM Press.

Silveira, M. S. 2002. Metacomunicação designer-usuário na interação humano-computador. Ph.D. thesis, Departamento de Informática, PUC-Rio, Rio de Janeiro.

Silveira, M. S., C. S. de Souza, and S. D. J. Barbosa. 2001a. Augmenting the affordance of online help content. In *Interactions without Frontiers, Proceedings of the Joint AFIHM-BCS Conference on Human-Computer Interaction IHM-HCI '01*, vol. 1, 279–296. London: Springer-Verlag.

Silveira, M. S., C. S. de Souza, and S. D. J. Barbosa. 2001b. Semiotic engineering contributions for designing online help systems. In *Proceedings of the 19th Annual International Conference on Computer Documentation*, 31–38. New York: ACM Press.

Silveira, M. S., C. S. de Souza, and S. D. J. Barbosa. 2003. Um método da engenharia semiótica para a construção de sistemas de ajuda online. In *Proceedings of the Latin American Conference on Human-Computer Interaction*, 167–177. Rio de Janeiro: PUC-Rio.

Simon, H. 1981. *The Sciences of the Artificial*, 2nd ed. Cambridge, Mass.: The MIT Press.

Suchman, A. 1987. *Plans and Situated Actions*. New York: Cambridge University Press.

Sundar, S. S., and C. Nass. 2000. Source orientation in human-computer interaction. *Communication Research* 27(6): 683–703.

Sutcliffe, A. 2000. On the effective use and reuse of HCI knowledge. *ACM Transactions on Computer-Human Interaction* 7(2): 197–221.

Wegner, P. 1995. Interaction as a basis for empirical computer science. *ACM Computing Surveys* 27(1): 45–48.

Wharton, C., J. Rieman, C. Lewis, and P. Polson. 1994. The cognitive walkthrough method: A practitioner's guide. In *Usability Inspection Methods*, ed. J. Nielsen and R. L. Mack, 105–140. New York: John Wiley and Sons.

Winograd, T. 1987. A language-action perspective on the design of cooperative work. *Human-Computer Interaction* 3(1): 3–30.

Winograd, T., and F. Flores. 1986. *Understanding Computers and Cognition*. Reading, MA: Addison-Wesley.

Software and Online Databases and Services

Active Worlds®. Activeworlds Incorporated.

Acrobat® 5.0.5. Adobe Systems Incorporated.

Amazon.com, Inc. Available online at http://www.amazon.com.

Arachnophilia© 3.9. © 1996–1998, Paul Lutus.

DOS®. Microsoft Corporation.

Eudora® 3.6 Light, Eudora® 5.0.2. Qualcomm Incorporated.

HCI Bibilography: Human-Computer Interaction Resources. Available online at http://www.hcibib.org/. Accessed December 2003.

Lotus® 1-2-3® (9). Lotus Development Corporation. © 1988–1998

Lotus® Freelance® Graphics (9). Lotus Development Corporation. © 1988–1998

Lotus® SmartSuite® (9). Lotus Development Corporation. © 1988–1998

Lotus® WordPro® (9). Lotus Development Corporation. © 1988–1998

Mac OS® Finder. Microsoft® Apple Computer, Inc.

Microsoft® Windows® 98 and Windows® 2000. Microsoft Corporation.

Microsoft® Excel 2002. Microsoft Corporation.

Microsoft® Office 2002. Microsoft Corporation.

Microsoft® Outlook 2002. Microsoft Corporation.

Microsoft® PowerPoint 2002®. Microsoft Corporation.

Microsoft Word 2002. Microsoft Corporation.

MSN Messenger® 5.0. Microsoft Corporation.

Opera© 7.11. Opera Software ASA.

Pine 4.58—a Program for Internet News & Email. Computing & Communications at the University of Washington.

PhoneWorks® 2002. RingCentral, Incorporated.

SmartFTP© v1.0.979. SmartFTP. Available online at http://www.smartftp.com. Accessed December 2003.

StageCast™ Creator 1.0. StageCast Software, Inc.

StuffIt Expander. Alladin Systems, Inc.

Super Tangrams. E-GEMS and University of British Columbia.

SWI Prolog© 5.2.6. 1990–2003 University of Amsterdam. Available online at http://www.swi-prolog.org/. Accessed December 2003.

The Coordinator. Action Technologies, Inc.

The Peirce Edition Project | EP 1. Introduction. Indiana University—Purdue University Indianapolis. Available online at http://www.inpui.edu/~peirce/. Accessed December 2003.

Treemap© 3.2. HCIL. University of Maryland College Park. Available online at http://www.cs.umd.edu/hcil/Treemap/. Accessed December 2003.

Unix 4.1. The Open Group.

Visual Basic for Applications 6.3. Microsoft Corporation.

Windows® 98 CD Player. Microsoft Corporation.

Windows® Media Player 9. Microsoft Corporation.

Windows® NetMeeting 3.0. Microsoft Corporation.

WinVi© 2.71. © Raphael Molle 1994–1999. Available online at http://www.winvi.de/en/. Accessed December 2003.

WinZip® 8.1. WinZip Computing, Inc.

Author Index

Subject Index

Software Index